THE WORD
ON THE STREET

THE NEW PUBLIC SCHOLARSHIP

SERIES EDITORS

Lonnie Bunch, *Director, National Museum of African-American History and Culture*

Julie Ellison, *Professor of American Culture, University of Michigan*

Robert Weisbuch, *President, Drew University*

The New Public Scholarship encourages alliances between scholars and communities by publishing writing that emerges from publicly engaged and intellectually consequential cultural work. The series is designed to attract serious readers who are invested in both creating and thinking about public culture and public life. Under the rubric of "public scholar," we embrace campus-based artists, humanists, cultural critics, and engaged artists working in the public, nonprofit, or private sector. The editors seek useful work growing out of engaged practices in cultural and educational arenas. We are also interested in books that offer new paradigms for doing and theorizing public scholarship itself. Indeed, validating public scholarship through an evolving set of concepts and arguments is central to **The New Public Scholarship**.

The universe of potential contributors and readers is growing rapidly. We are teaching a generation of students for whom civic education and community service learning are quite normative. The civic turn in art and design has affected educational and cultural institutions of many kinds. In light of these developments, we feel that **The New Public Scholarship** offers a timely innovation in serious publishing.

Civic Engagement in the Wake of Katrina, edited by Amy Koritz and George J. Sanchez

Is William Martinez Not Our Brother?: Twenty Years of the Prison Creative Arts Project, Buzz Alexander

The Word on the Street: Linking the Academy and the Common Reader, Harvey Teres

THE WORD ON THE STREET

Linking the
Academy and the
Common Reader

HARVEY TERES

THE UNIVERSITY OF MICHIGAN PRESS   ANN ARBOR

lo/750901H

Published in the United States of America by
The University of Michigan Press
Manufactured in the United States of America
⊚ Printed on acid-free paper

2014   2013   2012   2011   4   3   2   1

A CIP catalog record for this book is available from the British Library.

Library of Congress Cataloging-in-Publication Data

Teres, Harvey M., 1950–
    The word on the street : linking the academy and the common reader
/ Harvey Teres.
        p.   cm. — (The new public scholarship series)
    Includes bibliographical references and index.
    ISBN 978-0-472-07136-4 (cloth : alk. paper) — ISBN 978-0-472-
05136-6 (pbk. : alk. paper)
        1. Literature—Study and teaching—United States.   2. Literature—
Appreciation—United States.   3. Literature—History and criticism—
Theory, etc.   4. Books and reading—Philosophy.   5. Literacy—Philosophy.
6. Literature and society.   7. Politics and literature.   I. Title.
    PN70.T38   2011
    807.1073—dc22   2010024624

For Xueyi

The task is to restore continuity between the refined and intensified forms of experience that are works of art and the everyday events, doings, and sufferings that are universally recognized to constitute experience. Mountain peaks do not float unsupported; they do not even just rest upon the earth. They *are* the earth in one of its manifest operations.

—JOHN DEWEY, *Art as Experience*

Acknowledgments

It has been a long haul, perhaps too long, but not because I lacked generous and timely assistance from many quarters. The following colleagues provided important information, vital conversation, or comments on portions of the book manuscript: Steven Cohan, Paul Elitzik, Constantine Evans, Ken Frieden, Michael Goode, Carl Kaestle, Richard Kroll, Elizabeth Lasch-Quinn, Sanford Sternlicht, Michael Szalay, and David Yaffe. Syracuse University's Bird Library has a terrific staff, and the following librarians were immensely helpful during the early stages of my research: Randall Bond, Wendy Bousfield, Nancy Pitre, and Carole Vidali. Over the course of four years, I served alongside many committed colleagues on the Academic Affairs Committee of the Syracuse University Senate, where, after four years of hard work, we developed a new tenure and promotion policy rewarding publicly engaged scholarship. I owe a debt to all of them, especially the estimable chairs Louise Phelps and Larry Elin and the following members in particular: Bruce Abbey, Kal Alston, Janine Bernard, Hub Brown, Pat Burak, Peter Castro, Pat Cihon, Steven Cohan, Natasha Cooper, Tim Eatman, Gerry Greenberg, Esther Gray, Diane Grimes, Mark Heller, Carol Lipson, Eric Spina, Scott Strickland, and Mel Stith. The task of revising the tenure and promotion policy at Syracuse would very likely not have occurred without the extraordinary leadership of associate provost Kal Alston, vice chancellor and provost Eric Spina, and chancellor Nancy Cantor. All three continue to work wisely and energetically to propel Syracuse to the forefront of innovation in American higher education, and it has been my very good fortune to have found myself, past the midpoint of my career, in a position to be able to work with them and contribute to their vision of public scholarship.

I would also like to acknowledge the contributions of the many fellow community members I have had the pleasure of working with on the CNY Reads campaigns of the past few years. Among them I would like to single out Dianne Emmick, Liz Loftus, and Phil Memmer. Jan Cohen-Cruz, Tim Eatman, Julie Ellison, and David Scobey, my colleagues at Imagining America, have helped me to better understand the key issues faced by advocates of publicly engaged scholarship. In addition, I wish to thank my many students over the years who have helped me learn about the subjects I take up in this book, especially those students in my undergraduate courses The Culture Wars and Twentieth-Century American Poetry and my graduate students in Aesthetics, Politics, and American Public Life; The New Aesthetics; The Public Voice of Twentieth-Century American Poetry; and Going Public. Special thanks to those students who took a chance and involved themselves in public projects: Steven Deutsch, Carina Engleberg, Josh Frackleton, Marty Gottlieb-Hollis, Gina Keicher, David Medeiros, Lindsay Morgan, Kate Overholt, Lara Rolo, Dan Vallejo, and Tim Woolworth.

Although I have not received any outside funding to help me complete this book project, I was the recipient of two vital research sabbaticals and some additional research funding provided through the good offices of Cathryn Newton, former dean of the College of Arts and Sciences at Syracuse University.

Finally, I am most grateful to my wife for her steady encouragement and support. I have been the very fortunate and not-always-deserving recipient of her clarity of mind, kindness, and astonishingly sweet disposition.

Portions of chapter 1 have appeared as "The Critical Climate" in *A History of the Book in America* (Chapel Hill: University of North Carolina Press, 2009), portions of chapter 4 have appeared as "The Journey Resumed?" in the *Valve,* September 3, 2008 (http://www.thevalve.org), and portions of chapter 6 have appeared in *Intellectual History Newsletter* 19 (1997). I thank Harcourt, Inc. for permission to quote the entirety of Charles Simic's poem "Factory" from his *Sixty Poems* (New York: Harcourt, 2007).

Contents

Introduction

A labor organizer credits opera for the spiritual equilibrium he needs to do his job well. A young Vietnamese waitress finds beauty in the proper presentation of food. A body shop owner pores over dozens of magazines for design ideas before restoring a '39 coupe. A woman forsakes her career as a lawyer to open an art gallery in a poor black community.

Some time ago, a colleague of mine in the Syracuse University English Department declared that her job had nothing whatsoever to do with teaching students to appreciate or to be inspired by literature. Indeed, beauty has been banished from literary and cultural studies for some thirty years, where it continues to be viewed as little more than the preferences of the elite and powerful—in other words, as primped-up ideology. For my part, I have long worked for social change, yet none of my political commitments or my twenty-five years of teaching has ever caused me to disparage the pleasures of admiring accomplished writing or skillfully crafted art in general. But regrettably, within the academy, literature and art have become politicized in a way that has often viewed aesthetics as just another domain plagued by the pernicious effects of power and authority, while the possible relation between aesthetic experience and democracy is widely neglected. Though concerned with politics, today's English departments can resemble monasteries in their aloofness from everyday life (including actual political issues, organizations, and constituencies) and in their disregard for the pleasures of reading experienced by students, professors themselves, and the common reader. How many of us, after all, take the time in the classroom to register our responses to the artistry of the texts we read and to encourage considered judgments as to the quality of the writing we encounter? Literary theory has contributed enormously to the range of questions we ask about literature and culture, but because of institutional and professional constraints, it has neither established meaningful contact with the broader public and the very constituencies whose interests it often claims to represent nor provided much perspective on how we might contribute to the public conversation about the arts and the quality of the cultures and discourses we share. The time is ripe to test the insights of literary theory by expanding our purview not just conceptually but practically. This requires critics who are read by the average citizen, but the migration of so many critics and intellectuals from the public to the academy over the past generations has meant fewer efforts to make contact with common readers who do not happen to take their courses or read their books. Indeed, by "common reader" I do not mean "mediocre" reader or some essentialist notion of a homogeneous group, but rather the millions of diverse, ordinary readers who do not make their living as literary scholars, critics, writers, or publishers. By drawing attention to this very broad constituency I have it in mind to continue, however modestly, in the distinguished tradition begun by Richard Altick in *The English Common Reader* and developed by scholars like Raymond Williams, Janice Radway, Jonathan Rose, and the many others who focus on readers in the emerging field of the history of the book.

The Word on the Street dissects the problem of a literary academy that has been too reluctant to engage with the public outside the classroom, offers examples of alternatives from the past, and opens a road to a future of publicly engaged scholarship that collaborates with the common reader and his or her pleasures, thereby helping to realize both Emerson's hope that our "delegated intellects" might become "Man Thinking" and also Dewey's vision of a cultural democracy. This book provides timely critical insights into a growing initiative in higher education today, called "the new public scholarship," "civic engagement," "public humanities," or "publicly engaged scholarship." This initiative has grown rapidly over the past several years as a response to what some consider a national crisis of legitimacy for the humanities, evidenced by questions about their relevance in the current economic downturn and an increasingly technology- and corporate-driven economy, shrinking endowments, recalcitrant legislatures, and diminishing budgets and student enrollments. I believe these problems are real and may indeed require the kinds of solution I recommend in this book. But my main argument is that we need publicly engaged scholarship for reasons that are internal to the humanities and literary studies in particular. These reasons have to do with restoring a dynamic research agenda to a profession that in some respects has lost its way and can find itself by building new, reciprocal, and sustained relationships with a wider public that needs and in some cases desires some of the very skills and insights that generations of professionals have patiently and proudly developed.

Chapter 1, "Public Culture and Academic Culture," assesses the changing cultural environment in the United States from the end of World War II to the present, especially in light of the absorption of American intellectuals into the academy and their retreat from regular engagement with public issues and audiences. Chapter 2, "Revitalizing Literary Studies," provides an agenda for transforming the English department through publicly engaged scholarship. Such scholarship is meant not to replace traditional scholarship but, rather, to accompany it and, in fact, bring to the public sphere the skills of rigorous, disinterested scholarly protocols that have long been a hallmark of what we do. Instead of talking about a post-theoretical moment, I advocate applied theory and appeal to my colleagues to end the neglect of liberal theorists like Robert Dahl, Ronald Dworkin, Amitai Etzioni, Martha Nussbaum, John Rawls, Michael Sandel, and Amartya Sen, who, I argue, offer more specific and relevant possibilities for action in our flawed capitalist democracy than have many of the theorists more familiar to literary scholars. I show how publicly engaged scholarship can make academic literary studies more responsive to the world off campus and thereby more robust and better positioned to meet its own needs and the needs of a twenty-first-century democratic society. Chapter 2 presents historical background for an understanding of the causes and consequences of the academy's century-long retreat from civic engagement. Drawing on the scholarship of Thomas Bender, Burton Bledstein, and Gerald Graff, I narrate a story of the gradual incorporation of academic culture into the center of American life, accompanied by a progressive impoverishment of the public sphere. As Graff and others show, public, amateur literary culture thrived in the United States until the early decades of the twentieth century. At least part of its demise was because the process of professionalizing the humanities seemed to require that as sharp a distinction as possible be drawn between the emerging academic literary culture and the merely amateur culture of civic society. I argue that this stark division was not necessary when it arose, has done significant damage ever since, and must be bridged through a reorientation of the academic humanities today. The latter is already taking place in higher education today through initiatives encouraged by Ernest Boyer's influential *Scholarship Reconsidered* (1990) and Imagining America, a consortium of nearly ninety colleges and universities founded in the late 1990s devoted to publicly engaged scholarship. In the last part of chapter 2, I draw on my experiences as a leader of the successful effort at Syracuse University to change its tenure policy so that publicly engaged scholarship is officially counted, properly evaluated, and duly rewarded.

Chapter 3, "Post-9/11: Why the Public Needs Literary Critics," closely examines an influential literary piece that ran in the *New York Times* less than two weeks after 9/11, luridly titled "Novelists Gaze into Terror's Dark Soul," in which novels by Fyodor Dostoevsky, Henry James, and Joseph Conrad were quite badly misinterpreted, and thus their dim view of law enforcement and counterterrorists was completely ignored. I argue that the *Times* article was symptomatic of the American press's dereliction of duty when it came to critically examining the Bush administration's so-called war on terrorism. A more vigilant, civic-minded professoriat would perhaps have slowed the sprint to war with Iraq by contributing to a more honest and thoughtful public conversation.

Chapter 4, "Lionel Trilling as Public Intellectual," seeks a model for renewed civic engagement in Trilling's concern for an active communion between intellectuals and what he called "one's own people." I offer a rejoinder to Trilling's critics, who have emphasized his alleged remoteness, his mandarinism, or, in the words of Ann Douglas, his "omnivorously elegiac prose." In fact, Trilling's response was very nearly Whitmanesque in its appeal for communion, or adhesiveness, among citizens who care about culture and democracy. "There comes a moment," he trenchantly observed, "when the faces, the gait, the tone, the manner and manners of one's own people become just what one needs, and the whole look and style of one's culture seems appropriate, seems perhaps not good but intensely *possible*." To demonstrate Trilling's commitment to the common reader, the chapter contains the first description and assessment of more than two dozen book reviews Trilling wrote for the *New York Evening Post* in the late 1920s that have heretofore remained unexamined by scholars. I also discuss the recent publication by Columbia University Press of Trilling's unfinished novel *The Journey Abandoned*.

Part 2, "Whence Beauty?" explains why theorists throughout the academy came to be paralyzed by beauty, scorning any notion of art's inspirational or palliative value, preferring instead the pleasures of "unmasking" art, thereby allowing *Vogue* and Christian Dior to define beauty for us. How have we come to such a state of affairs? What kinds of critic and what sorts of sensibility have been discarded—temporarily, I hope—in the process? What has become of what F. R. Leavis termed in *Education and the University* "a training of intelligence that is at the same time a training of sensibility"? Instead of learning alertness to the subtle forms and devices that distinguish a work of art from a social document, a generation of students and citizens has dispensed with aesthetic experience in favor of the hunt for a text's ideological propositions, conflicts, contradictions, and deficiencies. They have chosen this rather than submit to the pleasures and insights that arise when literal reality is suspended in favor of an imaginative virtual reality that paradoxically illuminates it.

"What we fear," observes the literary critic Denis Donoghue in "The Practice of Reading," "is that our students are losing the ability to read, or giving up that ability in favor of an easier one, the capacity of being spontaneously righteous, indignant, or otherwise exasperated." Too often, the goal of reading has become "interrogating" the text rather than being challenged by it, mastering it through superior political awareness rather than surrendering temporarily to the author's world.

Today, many of us find ourselves experiencing our literary preferences as secret and guilty pleasures—pleasures whose revelation, we fear, would expose our privileged social positions more readily than would records of our credit card transactions. Among modern American writers, Mary McCarthy and Susan Sontag most insistently encouraged us to abandon our guilt and our fear and to openly declare what we consider beautiful and why. Chapter 5, "Mary McCarthy's Beauty," examines a critic whose attraction to beautiful things never compromised her politics and even enhanced them. Mary McCarthy obligates us to "fess up" precisely in order to arm ourselves against what the critic Barbara Herrnstein Smith calls "the power and inertia of social and cultural elites." The thing that gave coherence to McCarthy's life and works was her love of beauty, not as an indulgence or compensation, but, to borrow a phrase from Kenneth Burke, as "equipment for living." I illustrate the importance of McCarthy's love of beauty and attendant aesthetic judgments in *Memories of a Catholic Girlhood* and *Vietnam* and see them as antidotes to the cynical materialism that passes for radical criticism today.

Chapter 6, "The Decline of Aesthetic Literacy and the New Aesthetics," explains the absence of aesthetics in academic literary studies today. By the term *aesthetics*, I mean simply the appreciation of beauty, but there is, of course, nothing "simple" about aesthetics. Is *taste* not just another word for the preferences of elites with particular values that lead to the pursuit of valu*ables*? These are the suspicious questions that have led theory and criticism since the 1960s to provide answers that presume to discredit notions of beauty, judgment, and taste and to diminish the importance of aesthetic experience. A detailed examination of two representative and influential books that espouse or assume these views—respectively Barbara Herrnstein Smith's *Contingencies of Value* (1988) and Michael Denning's *The Cultural Front* (1996)—reveals problems with this line of thinking, not least of which is its neglect of the actual aesthetic experiences of real people.

Chapter 7, "When Everyone Misreads the Same Book," looks at the proliferating "One City, One Book" campaigns around the country, which have promoted reading, dialogue, and multiculturalism and have no doubt imparted valuable civics lessons to lots of people. But what have such campaigns done for "aesthetic literacy," or the ability to recognize and respond to artistic forms and strategies that make literature something other than social document? My time in the field investigating the local CNY Reads campaign for *The Grapes of Wrath* in central New York revealed a troubling absence of concern for the pleasures of the text or, indeed, for any of the key issues that have engaged discerning readers of Steinbeck's novel since its publication in 1939. Wherever I went—a gala kickoff ceremony, a high school class, a lecture on censorship, a performance by a Steinbeck impersonator—I was struck by the uniform consideration of the novel's dissident and progressive outlook regarding class, gender, power, and social justice and by an equally uniform neglect of fundamental matters pertaining to craft and aesthetic experience. These matters, not surprisingly, have concerned some of our best critics since the novel's publication—Lionel Trilling, Alfred Kazin, Irving Howe, Harold Bloom—and I consider what is lost when common readers are not exposed to the judgments of critics so that they in turn may weigh in and thereby participate in conversations that are vital to the maintenance of discerning, critical citizens.

Chapter 8, "Reading Simic in Syracuse," is a sequel to "When Everyone Misreads the Same Book." In 2008–9, the Syracuse community took the bold and unprecedented step of choosing *Sixty Poems* by the outgoing poet laureate Charles Simic for its reading campaign. Among the hundreds of "One City, One Book" campaigns that have arisen since the movement began in Seattle over a decade ago, none has ever chosen a poet. Along with some of my students, I was actively involved in the programming for this campaign. In January, we held a Poetry Palooza event at the local indoor mall, at which we read Charles Simic poems all day and conducted a poetry writing contest that invited members of the public to compose poems on refrigerators (supplied by Best Buy) using magnetic letters. We received over eighty submissions and gave out $175 worth of prizes. In chapter 8, I also describe an ambitious project in which I prepared a dozen of my students to join me in bringing Charles Simic's poetry to several high school classes in the Syracuse area.

In chapters 9, 10, and 11, I focus attention where it belongs: on the people who make, buy, and respond to art—the people, in other words, whose voices have only rarely been heard in the academy. If there are political and ideological effects of art (or, indeed, other effects), it makes sense to hear what those who experience art and beauty themselves have to say. My subjects are a dozen members of the Syracuse area: they include a labor organizer, a ballet teacher, an auto restorer, a waitress, an exotic dancer, a director of a community choir, and several store owners.

I raise perennial aesthetic issues with my subjects. Plato would have banned the poets from his ideal state, Aristotle replied that art made for better citizens, Hume argued for standards in taste, and Kant claimed that pure art lacked practical consequence. Why should we not include ordinary Americans in the conversation? Plenty of consumer surveys seek their opinions; otherwise, they stay locked out of aesthetic conversations. I indicate how their lives with beautiful things are more complex and interesting than deciding on air fresheners. As John Dewey reminded us long ago in his neglected classic *Art as Experience,* "In order to *understand* the aesthetic in its ultimate and approved forms, one must begin with it in the raw; in the events and scenes that hold the attentive eye and ear of man." Only here, in the daily experiences of average people, can we begin to grasp the real meaning of art, artistry, and beauty within the larger social realm and thereby create a continuum between the professors and critics, on the one hand, and the broader population, on the other. One of the great ironies, of course, is that the skepticism of beauty among elites has often arisen in the name of equality and inclusion, as if artistic discrimination and racial or political discrimination share some sort of kinship. They do not. To the contrary, the more reasonable hypothesis is that living with beautiful things and making aesthetic judgments about them are enabling experiences for citizens in a democracy. If politics is, after all, the art of making social choices and changes in order to secure a better quality of life, surely the ability to determine quality is enhanced when exercised on aesthetic objects. My exchanges with political progressives also reveal that art can play a vital political role by providing much-needed rest, restoration, and equilibrium during otherwise tumultuous, taxing activities. In other conversations, my subjects speak of the vital importance of cultivating taste, judging artistic quality in their work and others', and aspiring to improve their craft and critical skills. Much of this goes against the grain of a flawed academic egalitarianism that, as Elaine Scarry argues in *On Beauty and Being Just,* confuses distinction with hierarchy, appreciation with exclusion. Finally, I discuss my subjects' aesthetic experience as spiritual experience, a comparison several of them explicitly make, which presents a serious challenge to a literary academy that, for a half century, has consciously eschewed nearly everything that smacks of religion in the name of materialism or antimetaphysics.

The Word on the Street is a book about the vital importance of publicly engaged scholarship in the humanities. It aspires to present examples of what such scholarship might be like, especially where aesthetics is concerned. In doing so, it encourages the profession to break with a century of academic literary and cultural study that rarely engages with the surrounding world even as it tries to understand it. The final section of this book is meant to encourage my colleagues to consider the possibilities of adding literary anthropology and other forms of empirical research to the traditional modes of analysis that have long predominated inside the literary academy.

PART 1

The Academy and the Public

CHAPTER 1

Public Culture and Academic Culture

Despite significant changes since midcentury in American critical culture (the culture that flows from the serious review of books, ideas, and the arts), it continues to attract only a small minority of Americans, a circumstance widely considered inevitable and thus acceptable. However productive this culture has been, American society has not made significant progress toward realizing either Emerson's hope, expressed in "The American Scholar," that its "delegated intellects" might become "Man Thinking" or John Dewey's goal of an American cultural democracy. In both visions, critical culture becomes part of the processes of everyday life, and the average citizen, by cultivating imaginative and critical skills, takes an active part in discussions of ideas and the arts.

Literacy rates indicate that the United States continues to fall short of this ideal. Based on a series of studies done during the 1970s and 1980s, Stedman and Kaestle estimate that approximately 20 percent of the population, some 35 million people, have "serious difficulty" performing common reading tasks, and an additional 10 percent "are probably marginal in their functional-literacy skills."[1] These figures show no significant divergence from others accumulated since the 1940s. During this period, illiteracy has discouraged a large portion of the population from engaging in the public discussion of arts and ideas, despite their other competencies. According to the 2002 National Endowment for the Arts *Reading at Risk* report, nearly half of Americans eighteen years of age or older, 43.4 percent in 2002 (up from 39.1 percent in 1992), did not choose to read books of any kind. Of those who read books, the survey showed that the percentage of adult Americans reading literature dropped sharply since 1982. In that year, 56.9 percent read literature, compared to 46.7 percent in 2002, a decline that represented a loss of some 20 million potential readers. The survey established that the rate of decline in literary reading was accelerating, that women read more literature than men, and that literary reading by both groups was sharply declining, as was the rate of literary reading among all educational levels, age-groups, whites, African Americans, and Hispanics. The steepest decline in literary reading was among the youngest age-groups. The rate of decline for the youngest adults (18–24) was 55 percent greater than that of the total adult population (–28 percent vs. –18 percent); thus, "over the past twenty years young adults (18–34) have declined from being those mostly likely to read literature to those least likely (with the exception of those age 65 and above)." As NEA chairman Dana Gioia observed, the survey "presents a detailed assessment for the decline of reading's role in the nation's culture."[2] This decline seems to have been confirmed by the National Assessment of Adult Literacy, given in 2003 by the Department of Education, which found that only 31 percent of college graduates scored at a proficient level when asked to read lengthy, complex English texts and draw complicated inferences. More recent studies by the NEA—*To Read or Not To Read* (2007) and *Reading on the Rise* (2009)—offer a slightly more optimistic picture. Neither study suggests a sea change in the reading (or lack of reading) habits of Americans, but both studies show that the rate of decline has ebbed in some areas and even turned into gains in other areas. In particular, rates of reading among whites, African Americans, and Hispanics increased, and, most important, reading rates among eighteen- to twenty-four-year-olds improved dramatically from a 20 percent decline in 2002 to a 21 percent increase in 2009. In his accompanying summary report, Gioia attributes at least some of this improvement to the aggressive high school literary initiatives led by his agency. As yet, it is too early to tell whether the increasing sales of electronic book readers, such as Amazon's Kindle, Sony's Reader, or Barnes & Noble's Nook, will boost the reading rates of the general population.

Circulation figures for selected reviews and magazines of literary and political opinion underscore the relatively small number of highly literate readers from 1950 to 2005, notwithstanding minimal gains in the proportion of this readership to a total population that nearly doubled from 151 million to nearly 300 million. During that time span, circulation for the *Atlantic Monthly* went from 176,068 to 395,620; for *Commentary,* from 19,553 to 35,000; for *Esquire,* from 784,665 to 708,774; for *Harper's,* from 159,357 to 226,425; for the *Nation,* from 35,106 to 188,982; for the *New Republic,* from 32,680 to 65,115 combined; for the *New York Times Book Review,* from 1,116,944 to 1,682,208; for the *New Yorker,* from 332,324 to 1,051,919; and for *Poetry,* from 4,000 to 10,000.[3] The demise of several important periodicals, considered alongside others founded since 1950, reinforced this overall pattern. Lost were the *New York Herald Tribune Book Review* (675,105 in 1950), the *Saturday Review* (100,823 in 1950), and an avant-garde literary culture that had thrived through the teens and twenties and continued into midcentury in the pages of little magazines such as the *Kenyon Review,* the *Southern Review,* the *Sewanee Review, Poetry,* and *Evergreen*

Review. Most of these little magazines survive and have been joined by numerous literary reviews since the 1960s that have insured a steady stream of excellent, culturally resonant writing whose effects have nonetheless been less dramatic than those of their modernist predecessors. This said, it is noteworthy that the past several years have witnessed the demise of four distinguished publications: *Grand Street, Lingua Franca, Partisan Review,* and the *Public Interest.* Current literary reviews include the *American Poetry Review* (13,500 combined), *Granta* (96,000—including Britain and the United States), the *Hudson Review* (4,700), the *Paris Review* (10,000), *Ploughshares* (6,000), and the *Threepenny Review* (10,000 combined). Several dozen strictly academic journals and a host of other publications founded after 1950, especially online sites, have added new readers and vitality to critical culture. A selected list includes the *Baffler* (30,000), *Boston Review* (10,000 combined), *Dissent* (7,400), *First Things* (32,000), the *London Review of Books* (42,721—including Britain and the United States), *Monthly Review* (5,321), *Mother Jones* (240,764), *National Review* (160,896), the *New Criterion* (8,000 combined), the *New York Review of Books* (128,432), *Raritan* (3500 combined), *Reason* (40,550), *Salmagundi* (5100), *Tikkun* (20,000 combined), the *Times Literary Supplement* (35,204—including Britain and the United States), *Utne Reader* (225,540), *Vanity Fair* (1,208,644), the *Village Voice* (253,961 combined), and the *Weekly Standard* (80,395). In 2000, however, only *Vanity Fair* was among the top hundred by circulation in the United States, where total magazine circulation numbered nearly 250 million. Today, the vast majority of literate Americans continue to read other things, although, as mentioned, numerous new online sites, such as *Slate, Salon, ALDaily,* and *n+1,* have attracted large numbers of readers and browsers who may not have otherwise become as deeply involved with ideas and the arts.

As for book readers, the increasing dominance of the market by best sellers and best-selling authors—between 1986 and 1996, sixty-three of the one hundred best-selling titles were written by only six writers[4]—suggests that reading has embraced a narrowing range of books despite a doubling of per capita books purchased in 2005 (ten) compared to 1955.[5] A study published in 1949 directed by the Social Science Research Council revealed that these patterns established themselves as early as the immediate post–World War II era. Among the twenty top best-selling authors in fiction in 1947, for example, nineteen had been on a previous list. With the exception of Sinclair Lewis and John Steinbeck, all of the authors were producing undistinguished, popular fare for a broad audience.[6] This trend has no doubt been encouraged by the diminishing amount of fiction published by mass circulation magazines; recently, for instance, the *Atlantic Monthly, GQ,* and *Esquire* have scaled back. Also diminished has been the number of books under review by competent critics writing for a general educated audience. At a time when struggling American newspapers are slashing coverage of the arts in general—according to a study conducted by the National Arts Journalism Project at Columbia University, from 1998 to 2003 the space given to cultural coverage in major American papers dropped roughly 25 percent[7]—newspapers continue to cut back on book reviewing in order to cut costs. The *New York Times Book Review,* for instance, averages thirty-four reviews per issue today compared to fifty per issue in 1950.[8] The *Boston Globe,* continuing a national trend, reduced the size of its book review section, and in 2008, the Sunday *Los Angeles Times Book Review* folded. Although online Web sites have compensated for some of these losses, readers are finding fewer and fewer reviews that resist what Emerson in his notebooks called the "mush of concession" with sharp and eccentric discriminations between the achieved and the mediocre.[9] Another indication that a smaller proportion of readers have access to critically acclaimed books is the steady decline of book clubs, which once provided good books to a large general readership. At its peak before the dominance of the chain stores, the Book-of-the-Month Club sold eleven million books a year, and a major selection could attract upwards of a million readers.[10] Slightly smaller was the Literary Guild, followed by many more specialized clubs. These clubs provided books to vast numbers of readers without access to bookstores; moreover, committees of critics made the club selections with an eye toward quality as well as profitability. Today, Oprah's Book Club offers guidance and suggestions to readers beleaguered by a marketplace that presents them with a bewildering array of books through publicity and advertising machines that make it difficult to know what is really good. Oprah provides a service that others have not provided for some time, and thus she attempts to fill a void left by the decline of the older clubs and the blunting of critical conversation as a whole.

Perhaps the most dramatic change in the critical culture of the United States since midcentury has been that many critics no longer assume that such a culture exists, with some claiming that it never did. A plausible case can be made that until fifty years ago, educated citizens could turn to certain publications, intellectuals, and institutions and find there a public discussion of arts and ideas (albeit limited, in ways I will enumerate), but the consensus today is that, for better or worse, no such broad-based elevated and respected discourse exists. Because of diversification and segmentation, a smaller proportion of the overall public reads the same publications and critics and thus participates in a common dialogue. The very notion of a "general public" served by a coherent critical culture has been described as "the silhouette of a phantom" by the critic Jacques Derrida, an allusion to Walter Lippmann's famous characterization in *The Phantom Public* (1925).[11] Historians and critics attempting to explain the dispersal and decline of critical culture generally cite as reasons the rise of the academy, changes in the culture at large, and changes in the market.

The Rise of the Academy

In a memorable phrase from "A Critic's Job of Work," the redoubtable mid-century critic R. P. Blackmur once referred to criticism as "the formal discourse of an amateur." For many readers today, such a description will seem quaint, for we are separated from Blackmur by seventy-five years during which many critics and much of the critical discourse they produced were absorbed into the academy, where the process of professionalization and specialization has taken place nearly unabated. According to the National Center for Educational Statistics, between the years 1960 and 1990, the number of colleges and universities increased from 2,000 to 3,595, enrollment went from 3.5 million to 15 million, the number of doctoral degrees granted increased from 10,000 to over 38,000, and faculty numbers jumped from approximately 281,000 to more than 987,000.[12] These decades also saw a dramatic increase in the number of scholarly journals and books published by academic presses. In part motivated by efforts to close a perceived "technology gap" after the Soviet Union shocked the United States with the successful Sputnik flight in 1958, Congress passed the National Defense Education Act, which greatly increased government involvement in higher education. Between 1960 and 1990, federal aid to students rose from $5.1 to $11.2 billion, and research and development funds increased from $2 billion to $12 billion. The demographics of American college students also changed considerably between the years 1960 and 1990, as the proportion of women increased from 37 percent to 51 percent and that of minorities from 12 to 28 percent.[13] The greatest growth occurred in the new system of community colleges, which enrolled 400,000 students in 1960 compared to 6.5 million in 1990.[14] Today, nearly half of all Americans have had at least some higher education, and nearly a quarter hold a degree. According to the Department of Education, the rate of college enrollment immediately after high school completion increased from 49 percent in 1972 to 67 percent by 1997 but has since fluctuated between 62 and 69 percent. According to education secretary Arne

Duncan, the United States now ranks tenth in the world in the rate of college completion for twenty-five- to thirty-four-year-olds. "A generation ago," he asserts, "we were first in the world, but we're falling behind. The global achievement gap is growing."[15]

These developments have had several direct effects on critics and criticism. Beginning in the 1950s, when many leading critics took academic posts, the primary site from which critical culture emanated shifted from an urban and broadly public one, often connected to communities of writers and artists, to an institutional environment with particular affiliations, practices, and protocols. For academic critics coming of age in the 1950s and 1960s, the model was no longer the public one of Emerson, Fuller, DuBois, or Dewey; the cosmopolitan, engaged criticism of the "Young Americans" Randolph Bourne, Van Wyck Brooks, Waldo Frank, or Lewis Mumford; or that of the New York Intellectuals, who so powerfully shaped the public discussion of literature, culture, and politics from the 1940s through the 1960s. Instead, the ideal became theoretically informed criticism produced by professionals, many of whom were politically committed yet relatively detached from ongoing political movements, parties, or public debates. To be sure, much of this criticism was shaped, to varying degrees, by the transformative social movements of the period of the civil rights movement, the racial and ethnic nationalist and internationalist movements, the antiwar movement, the women's movement, the environmental movement, and the gay rights movement. But the tendency was to retreat from the broader audience of educated readers that had previously sustained a semiacademic (and sometimes antiacademic) public critical culture. These developments changed the language of criticism, which on the whole became more self-reflexive, specialized, and obscure. Freed from the pressures of immediate political exigency, critics developed complex, sophisticated techniques for investigating the often tacit relationship between literature and power, language and ideology—offering new perspectives on what Lionel Trilling in *The Liberal Imagination* once famously called "the dark and bloody crossroads where literature and politics meet." Within the academy, criticism entered an exhilarating period during which the New Criticism, which had dominated during the 1950s and 1960s, gave way in the 1970s to various theories of interpretation that vied for supremacy: structuralism, deconstruction, reader-response criticism, Marxism, feminism, psychoanalysis, New Historicism, queer theory, postcolonial studies, and cultural studies. Similar influences arose within the other humanities disciplines, particularly history and art history.

The results have changed critical culture in several ways. First, the literary and cultural traditions of previously neglected groups were given unprecedented attention, so that literary and artistic canons were expanded to include works by women, gays and lesbians, members of ethnic and racial minorities, and the working class. Anthologies, textbooks, and the range of books published all reflected this dramatic new interest in previously excluded authors and experiences. Second, the notion that literature and art should be free from political considerations was uniformly challenged. They were understood instead to have a close but complex relation to ideology and networks of social power. Third, questions of artistry, craft, taste, and value either gave way to inquiries into ideology or, in some cases, were considered to be essentially the preferences of elites and thus mechanisms of power and hierarchy. Instead of cultivating sensibilities and making value judgments, academic critics were intent on challenging the priority of mainstream over marginal cultural traditions, canonical over noncanonical texts, and highbrow over popular culture. Produced within an ideological ethos of multiculturalism, egalitarianism, anticapitalism, feminism, and a general skepticism of authority, academic critics replaced the New York Intellectuals' mandarinism of the streets, as it were, with the populism of the pedagogue. Gone was the widespread midcentury disdain for what many intellectuals had termed "mass culture" or what the Frankfurt critics Max Horkheimer and Theodor Adorno called the "culture industry." Beginning in the 1960s, academic critics greatly expanded what counted as literature and culture worth taking seriously. Thus, a democratization of outlook accompanied the academic critics' narrowing conception of their audience.

However one weighs the consequences of criticism's specialized and ideological turn, changes in higher education by the early twenty-first century had undermined whatever promise of far-reaching influence academic affiliation had earlier held. Ironically, even though specialization made literary studies look more like the natural and social sciences and despite the critics' embrace of popular culture, the humanities (and the liberal arts generally) have continued to lose ground, and both undergraduate and graduate students. Currently, the most popular undergraduate major is business, which accounts for 20 percent of all degrees granted.[16] Louis Menand has noted that "there are almost twice as many undergraduate degrees conferred every year in a field known as 'protective services'—largely concerned with training social workers—as there are in all foreign languages and literatures combined."[17] Between 1966 and 1993, the percentage of bachelor's degrees granted in the humanities shrank

from 20.7 to 12.7, the proportion of doctoral degrees from 13.8 to 9.1.[18] A concomitant decline in English majors has long caused concern in that discipline,
with a fall from 7.6 percent of all college majors in 1970 to 4.2 percent in 1997,
a drop in absolute numbers from 64,342 to 49,345.[19] The latter development is
one of the reasons for the shrinking market for literary scholars and for the diminished importance of literature for a generation reared on other media and
trained in other skills.

No doubt, students' anxiety about job prospects in an economy increasingly ambivalent about the value of a humanities education has contributed
mightily to this trend. For some critics, the shrinking popularity and authority
of the humanities is to be attributed at least in part to the rise of theory and
specialization in the academy, which discourages the development of reading
skills necessary to a vital critical culture. What has been lost is what F. R. Leavis
termed "a training of intelligence that is at the same time a training of sensibility. . . . I mean the training of perception, judgment and analytic skill."[20] Instead of learning alertness to the subtle forms and devices that distinguish a
work of art from a social document, a generation of students and citizens has
dispensed with aesthetic experience in favor of the hunt for a text's ideological
propositions, conflicts, contradictions, and deficiencies. The goal has become
"interrogating" the text rather than being challenged by it, mastering it
through superior political awareness rather than surrendering temporarily to
the author's world. The poet Billy Collins, for instance, writes of his students
that "all they want to do / is tie the poem to a chair with rope / and torture a
confession out of it. / They begin beating it with a hose / to find out what it really means."[21] They do this rather than submit to the pleasures and insights
that arise when literal reality is suspended in favor of an imaginative virtual reality that paradoxically illuminates it. "What we fear," observes the literary
critic Denis Donoghue, "is that our students are losing the ability to read, or
giving up that ability in favor of an easier one, the capacity of being spontaneously righteous, indignant, or otherwise exasperated."[22]

Although indifference to the insights and pleasures of verbal culture undeniably limits the scope of firsthand perception and thus limits critical culture
in general, it is difficult to determine just how extensive the damage has been,
especially if we consider that increased ideological sensitivity, regardless of
how unimaginative or unliterary, has contributed to students' and thus to the
public's awareness of the cultures and experiences of formerly neglected
groups. Advocates of an ideological approach to literature and the arts argue
that imaginative identification with the "other" is precisely what is required of

readers and audiences and that, without developed critical awareness of the social dynamics that both surround and inhere in art, the most cultivated sensibility will fail to contribute to the needs of an egalitarian society. Furthermore, the multiplicity and decentralization characteristic of American higher education have meant that a university-centered literary scene has permitted a greater geographic diffusion of literary culture than was the case when "intellectual" was synonymous with "New York."

This debate extends to the question of the appropriate modality of cultural authority, for there are those who believe that the public is best served by the intellectual who consistently addresses his or her writing to a broad, educated audience, while others believe that the public is best served by the academic whose expertise is manifested within a narrower (though nonetheless public), professional and institutional setting. If democracy is fully realized, as Dewey believed, "when free social inquiry is indissolubly wedded to the art of full and moving [public] communication,"[23] the public will need both public intellectuals and specialists. During the first half of the twentieth century, the American public benefited from a large and impressive corps of the former. Until the 1960s, leading critics and public intellectuals rarely held PhDs, were usually unaffiliated or intermittently affiliated with the university, and published in the commercial press. These figures included James Baldwin, Daniel Bell, Louis Brandeis, Randolph Bourne, William Buckley, Rachel Carson, Malcolm Cowley, Herbert Croly, Max Eastman, T. S. Eliot, Ralph Ellison, Waldo Frank, Betty Friedan, Paul Goodman, Clement Greenberg, Elizabeth Hardwick, Michael Harrington, Oliver Wendell Holmes, Irving Howe, Jane Jacobs, C. L. R. James, Randall Jarrell, Alfred Kazin, Irving Kristol, Dwight Macdonald, Mary McCarthy, H. L. Mencken, Lewis Mumford, Ralph Nader, William Phillips, Norman Podhoretz, Philip Rahv, Ayn Rand, Harold Rosenberg, Gilbert Seldes, Susan Sontag, Edmund Wilson, and Tom Wolfe. Even those with doctorates and professorships often appealed to a nonacademic audience through the commercial press, including Hannah Arendt, John Dewey, W. E. B. DuBois, Felix Frankfurter, John Kenneth Galbraith, Richard Hofstadter, William James, C. Wright Mills, David Riesman, Meyer Schapiro, Arthur Schlesinger Jr., Lionel Trilling, and Thorstein Veblen, to name a few. Since the 1960s, some nonacademics gained prominence as public intellectuals, but there have been fewer of them, suggesting that the freelance or journalist public intellectual is on the wane. A selective list of these figures includes Renata Adler, William Bennett, David Brooks, Gregg Easterbrook, David Halberstam, Christopher Hitchens, Pauline Kael, Hilton Kramer, Anthony Lewis, Charles

Murray, Katha Pollitt, Andrew Sullivan, Gore Vidal, Leon Wieseltier, and George Will. A considerable number of academically trained and affiliated intellectuals have attempted to reach a wider public through books and articles with a commercial appeal. A partial list includes Robert Alter, Saul Bellow, Allan Bloom, Harold Bloom, Robert Bork, Noam Chomsky, Frederick Crews, Morris Dickstein, E. L. Doctorow, Ronald Dworkin, Thomas Frank, Milton Friedman, Henry Louis Gates Jr., Doris Kearns Goodwin, Gertrude Himmelfarb, June Jordan, Henry Kissinger, Christopher Lasch, Louis Menand, Toni Morrison, Daniel Patrick Moynihan, Martha Nussbaum, Cynthia Ozick, Camille Paglia, Richard Posner, Richard Rorty, Edward Said, Elaine Showalter, George Steiner, Cornel West, Patricia Williams, Garry Wills, and James Wood.

Despite their significant contributions, these public intellectuals have not comprised a corps of independent intellectuals engaged in mutual public conversation. Ironically, the egalitarian and often subversive intent of much of the literary and cultural criticism that has emanated from the universities since the 1960s has been largely contained within academic culture. Despite admirable forays into broader sectors of the public sphere, and despite frequent appeals to transgress boundaries in general, most academics continue to be strongly encouraged by their circumstances to remain ensconced within their institutional networks. When academics are invited by the media to address a wider public, their time is severely curtailed, and the nature of their discourse is altered to enhance its entertainment value. When an academic addresses the public today, he or she usually does so as a "rent-an-intellectual." The rates are daily, and they are low. By and large, the public conversation is dominated by ubiquitous media and political "pundits," whose range of opinion and depth of thought are not sufficient to sustain a vital critical culture. The so-called culture wars of the 1980s and the post-9/11 public dialogue are cases in point.

The Larger Public Culture

The rise of the academy was not the only factor refashioning American critical culture in the middle and late twentieth century. Suburbanization, shifts in cultural values, technological change, alternative leisure activities, and increased corporate cultural prowess have all contributed substantially to what Michael Kammen has usefully termed "the decline of cultural authority and the rise of cultural power."[24]

Suburbanization was not only a centrifugal geographical force from the 1950s onward; along with academicization, it also led to intellectual decentralization. Abandoned urban neighborhoods meant bereft cultural communities as big-city newspapers declined, theaters and cultural organizations went under, and independent bookstores began closing their doors. Despite the rise of New Age, left-wing, feminist, and children's bookstores beginning in the late 1960s, cities eventually saw many of their established independent bookstores disappear. The typical independent bookstore owner either owned his own building or paid low rent to keep down the overhead; moreover, easy access was rarely a problem, because in the city, stores did not have to rely on street traffic and a prominent location. Suburbanization, with its concentration of retail stores in the shopping mall, changed all that. Mall rents were prohibitively high, and this made it nearly impossible for independent bookstores to sustain a viable inventory. Thus, in the 1990s alone, the number of independent bookstores declined from 5,400 to 3,200.[25] Beginning in the 1970s, the first wave of chain stores—Waldenbooks and B. Dalton—took over the suburban bookselling market, only to be supplanted in the 1990s by the superstore chains Barnes & Noble and Borders, which until recently accounted for over 50 percent of all retail books sold. Despite the efforts of these stores to bring together readers and authors, as well as readers with one another, they have not been able to reproduce some important elements of the critical culture of former times—the sense of community, the shared readerly passions, and the bookseller's expertise.

It is no coincidence that Sal Paradise, the narrator of the signature Beat novel *On the Road* (1957), left town at the same time and on the same road as the white American middle class. Paradise just kept driving. The Beats and their progeny within the counterculture represented a serious challenge to the established critical culture of the 1950s and to the idea of a homogeneous public sphere. This critical culture had been shaped by an array of dissident, independent intellectuals, many of whom were part of the New York intellectual milieu, who in the 1930s and 1940s had stood for a union of radical politics and avant-garde art (namely, literary modernism and abstract expressionism), but who were seen by many within the younger generation as having traded in their dissidence for influence, security, and accommodation. *Partisan Review's* famous 1952 symposium "Our Country and Our Culture" has often been cited as illustrative of this shift toward the political center—the "vital center," in the words of Arthur Schlesinger Jr.—for among the two dozen respondents to four queries about the role of the writer and intellectual in America, none highlighted the threats to democracy posed by McCarthyism, the abuses of global corporate or military power, or domestic race relations. Nearly all of the

respondents commented on the threats to serious culture posed by the proliferation of "mass" culture, either marketed straightforwardly as "kitsch," to use
the term made famous by Clement Greenberg, or dressed up in high-culture
disguise as "middlebrow." Only Irving Howe, Norman Mailer, C. Wright Mills,
and Philip Rahv warned of the waning of dissent among America's increasingly respectable intellectual elite. If there were any doubts about the new status of the New York public intellectuals, they were dispelled in 1956 when *Time*
magazine placed Jacques Barzun on its June 11 cover for a story entitled "Par-
nassus—Coast to Coast," in which it was observed that the "Man of Protest has
to some extent given way to the Man of Affirmation." Affirmation may be too
strong a word, but certainly the shift from noncooperation to participation
was palpable, in no small part because of the successful integration of avant-
garde art and literature into key portions of the culture at large. The New York
Intellectuals had developed a fruitful relationship with an important sector of
the public in which appreciation for craft, quality, and nuance prevailed (an
achievement not since duplicated), and they had helped open American culture to new forms, voices, and perspectives despite the fact that most Americans continued to be bewildered by much modern art and literature. But their
efforts were not sufficiently reflective of America's cultural variety, perhaps especially where the contributions of women and minorities were concerned,
and thus the New Yorkers were increasingly seen as lacking the popular, multicultural, and international scope demanded by the new generation.

With their rejection of the authority of the New York critical world, the
Beats and then the counterculture ushered in a new cultural era—first dubbed
"postmodern" by the New York Intellectuals—in which established (and newly
established) hierarchies, styles, and priorities of cultural criticism gave way to
skepticism toward highbrow culture, redemptive modernism, established
standards of taste, and, in many cases, taste itself. By doing away with distinctions between high and low, avant-garde and conventional, and artistic and
commercial, both artists and critics encouraged vital new cultural hybrids. Pop
artists and celebrities brought the visual arts down from the rarified heights of
abstract expressionism by making elements of mass and popular culture
central to their art. In the visual arts, Jasper Johns, Andy Warhol, Robert
Rauschenberg, and Roy Lichtenstein led the way. Authors such as Kathy Acker,
John Barth, Donald Barthelme, Richard Brautigan, and Robert Coover deliberately rejected what they regarded as somber, portentous modernism, in favor
of the interplay of signs and texts that derived from all levels and walks of life,
including fairy tales, advertisements, TV shows, comics, and the movies. In

dance, ballet—itself transformed by George Balanchine, Jerome Robbins, and Agnes de Mille—gave ground to modern and jazz through the contributions of extraordinary choreographers such as Martha Graham, Paul Taylor, Alvin Ailey, Twyla Tharp, and Merce Cunningham. Popular music experienced an era of unprecedented creativity and range, as previously marginalized musical traditions such as the blues, rock and roll, folk, bluegrass, and country, now in the hands of dozens of highly talented artists and producers, took over the radio waves and utterly transformed the musical tastes of millions. The Hollywood film industry refashioned itself by giving new power to independent directors, including Robert Altman, Peter Bogdanovitch, Stanley Kubrick, and the so-called movie brats Francis Ford Coppola, George Lucas, Martin Scorcese, and Steven Spielberg. Even television responded to the changing culture, with controversial new programming like *All in the Family.* In each of these arts, a corps of critics helped to fend off the inevitable uniformity and standardization, perennial problems in mass culture, and contributed to change by encouraging audiences to appreciate innovation and to demand and expect more of it.

What was unique about these changes in the cultural climate was that they were tied to dramatic technological developments that brought immediate access and more choices (within a limited range) to the vast majority of Americans. Television, of course, led the way. By the 1970s, the average amount of viewing time per day had reached four and a half hours, a number that has remained constant ever since.[26] The options made available by television—and thus its appeal—further increased with the widespread use of convenient remote control devices, cable, satellite transmission, the VCR, video games, and, more recently, the DVD. MTV forever changed the look and sound of the small screen. Changes in film technology were less dramatic but certainly consequential, including sophisticated sound systems and extraordinary advances in computer-generated special effects. Multiplex theater complexes replaced single-screen venues, providing a larger portion of the population with easier access to more films, although, again, within a range that excluded a large number of innovative, experimental, and foreign films. Technological change in recorded music, from the LP to the cassette to the CD, significantly improved sound quality and durability. Finally, the computer and Internet have led to an array of new cultural practices that involve some older ones (creating hypertext; screening films; downloading music, newspapers, magazines, and books) and some new ones (e-mailing, online chat rooms, blogging, texting, twittering, and so on).

These technological changes have generated much debate. So far as their effects on critical culture, they have been both large and small, depending on one's perspective. Although a Harris poll conducted as recently as 1998 identified reading as the single most popular leisure activity among Americans,[27] reading has nonetheless lost ground to its many alternatives in terms of frequency and importance in the lives of ordinary Americans.[28] It is unclear, though, whether this has had an adverse effect on the quality of critical culture, which has never relied on widespread participation in order to achieve high levels of accomplishment. Recent history has shown that to sustain a culture that produces, publishes, and discusses the very best fiction, poetry, and criticism, a community of ten to twenty thousand knowledgeable, critically discerning readers is sufficient. Despite the fears of post–World War II critics like Dwight Macdonald and Clement Greenberg, the scope and popularity of mass culture alone have not diminished the creative output that is the foundation of a critical culture.

The degree to which ordinary Americans practice critical understanding and judgment is another question. It is quite clear that since the 1960s, any clearly discernible intellectual elite with significant taste-making authority has since given way to something else. Whether that something else has been increasing standardization and a more vulgar, controlled, and passive public has been a matter of dispute, although those advocating this view no longer prevail. Most scholars of popular and mass culture—the field now has a name, *cultural studies*—argue that consumers of mass culture enjoy a significant degree of choice and, beyond that, participate in shaping their experiences and the very forms, styles, and content of the cultural products they consume. Many of the same critics acknowledge the erosion of popular culture (culture generated by ordinary people) in the face of the ubiquity of mass culture (culture produced for vast numbers by anonymous but responsive corporate entities), but they stress that forms of popular culture still manage to play an important role in shaping mass culture. Indeed, many critics maintain that the critical culture has come to play a similar role, for its initially unpopular innovations and insights have been gradually absorbed into the wider culture and have given rise to changes in what Wallace Stevens in "A Postcard from the Volcano" termed "the look of things." In this view, critical culture has not so much been destroyed or diminished as refashioned and redistributed; that is, mass culture has exposed vast numbers to an array of cultural art forms and practices and, in so doing, has empowered and equipped ordinary people to make their own choices about what to experience and how to respond to those experiences. The critic William Phillips, echoing Alexis de Tocqueville, observed some seventy years ago in *Horizon* that "culturally what we have is a democratic free-for-all in which every individual, being as good as every other one, has the right to question any form of intellectual authority." Michael Kammen adds, "For many Americans, that 'free-market' attitude toward cultural authority would persist right down to the present."[29]

After World War II, European and American artists and intellectuals alike were appalled at the vulgarity and conformity of American culture, with its Spam, bubble gum, Disneyland, Tupperware, and literature and arts that were less than world-class. By the 1980s, however, American culture had greatly expanded its appeal, in part by raising its standards and incorporating elements of style and technique from numerous and diverse sources, including high culture itself. Some discerning critics, such as James Agee, Leslie Fiedler, David Riesman, Gilbert Seldes, and Robert Warshow, noted these trends even earlier. For example, in his classic study of American society, *The Lonely Crowd*, Riesman observed, "The speed with which the gradient of taste is being climbed has escaped many critics of the popular arts who fail to observe not only how good American movies, popular novels, and magazines frequently are but also how energetic and understanding are some of the comments of the amateur taste-exchangers who seem at first glance to be part of a very passive, uncreative audience."[30] Riesman went on to cite the critical competence of aficionados of jazz, movies, and comic strips. Since the 1960s, similar claims have been made regarding a host of audience sectors, including informed, passionate, and opinionated enthusiasts of jazz, blues, alternative rock, spectator sports, wine, gardening, antique cars, film, and so on. In this view, the practices of critical culture have been widely distributed to encompass larger populations and their cultural interests. Critical culture, it might be said, has multiplied and now manifests itself as the more discriminating element within a range of American subcultures.

Some critics argue that this interaction of "high" and "low," of "high" and "middlebrow," or of popular and mass culture represents a process of leveling and amalgamation that renders the former categorical distinctions among taste levels unworkable. Whereas a movement like abstract expressionism was at one time thought to embody the purest, most sublime forms of high modernism, critics today are more apt to explore connections to mass culture, as, for instance, Robert Hughes does in his discussion of Marilyn Monroe and Willem de Kooning's fondness for cigarette ads. The process of using styling to create and enhance desire among the masses intensified during the 1950s and has proliferated ever since. What Robert Hughes aptly termed the "cataract of styling" that began in the 1950s, "fridges, toasters, Formica countertops, juicers, microwaves—gaudy, lush, avocado-colored and hot pink, chrome everything, and big,"[31] continues to grow exponentially as dynamic retail, design, and packaging industries produce Michael Graves tea kettles for Target, modernist furniture for Ikea, and haute couture for the masses. This has had the effect of both equalizing and raising taste levels across the board. Advertising has contributed enormously to this process: today, the Gap cites Jack Kerouac in its ads, Levi's cites Walt Whitman, and Microsoft cites Gandhi. We see a similar development if we look at the changing role of the museum in American society. Once the repository of traditional art for the elite, museums have opened their doors to hoi polloi since the 1960s with blockbuster exhibitions. Equally important, since the 1960s, they have actively transformed the market for art, buying up contemporary art objects at an extraordinary rate, thereby institutionalizing the avant-garde or, at least, significant sectors of it and perhaps suffocating it with its sometimes awkward embrace. What had once been art's signature values of aloofness and defiance can now have the look of gratuitous, self-dramatizing posturing.

The mainstreaming of erstwhile controversial, countercultural values and styles has not gone unrecognized. Several recent popular sociological studies have stressed the humanizing and democratizing effects of this process. With titles like *Nobrow: The Culture of Marketing, the Marketing of Culture* and *Bobos in Paradise* ("bobos" are *bo*urgeois *bo*hemians), these books witness America's cultural egalitarianism and widespread improvements in quality and taste. However, there is reason to be wary of such Panglossian diagnoses. It is one thing to argue that members of a new elite, empowered by education and high test scores and shaped by the values of the 1960s, have swept away the WASP establishment, with its rigid, puritanical culture, thereby bringing to American popular culture a new diversity, spontaneity, and engaging informality. This may indeed constitute a significant achievement. But it is not the equivalent of giving priority to the best that writers, artists, crafters, and critics produce for both the "high" and the popular arts. Nor is it the same as devoting significant social resources to creating a public eager for the best because they have valued it since childhood, when they attended schools that fueled an expectation of excellence. If some of the passion and appreciation for the exceptional in sports, let us say, were to be found elsewhere in our culture, we would perhaps have more cause for self-congratulation.

Market Forces

Indeed, the cultural improvements previously described bring with them serious problems. A half-dozen multinational corporations—whose size and influence have grown substantially during a decade of government-sanctioned mergers and acquisitions—now wield the power to produce, distribute, and promote culture in the United States. The entertainment sector in general is dominated by General Electric, parent company of the vast NBC radio, TV, and cable network; Disney, whose holdings include ABC and major interests in film, theme parks, magazines, music, newspapers, and sports; Westinghouse, owner of CBS and telephone, wireless, and satellite communications systems; and, largest of all, Time Warner, which controls AOL, the Turner Broadcasting System (CNN, TBS, TNT, and much more), large holdings in book and magazine publishing, home video, TV programming, and an array of music and motion picture and cable companies, not to mention its influence over the home computer through AOL. The situation is the same in publishing. Despite total book sales in 1998 of more than $28 billion, the numbers go from large to small when we look at who controls the industry. Aside from the university presses, a dwindling number of independents, and an increasing number of struggling minor presses, trade publishing in America is controlled by seven media conglomerates. The largest is Time Warner ($43 billion in sales),[32] owner of the Book-of-the-Month Club and Time-Life Books. The second largest is Disney ($32 billion), which owns Hyperion Books. Next is Rupert Murdoch's News Corporation ($24 billion), which owns Basic Books, Harper-Collins, and William Morrow. The German Bertelsmann ($23 billion) owns Random House, which includes Ballantine (Del Rey, Fawcett, and Ivy), the Bantam Dell Group, Crown, Doubleday, the Knopf Group (Anchor, Everyman's Library, Pantheon, Schocken, Vintage), the Modern Library, Villard, and the Literary Guild. The CBS Corporation ($14 billion; until recently, part of Viacom) owns Simon & Schuster, Scribner, the Free Press, and Pocket Books, among many others. The British Pearson PLC ($7 billion) is owner of Dutton, Macmillan, Mentor, Penguin, Perigee, Plume, Prentice Hall, Putnam, Signet, and Viking. Finally, Holtzbrinck ($2.3 billion) controls Farrar, Straus and Giroux; St. Martin's Press; Hill & Wang; and Henry Holt and Company. Major independents include Wiley, Rodale, Tyndale, W. W. Norton ($100 million in 2001), Workman Publishing ($25 million), Grove/Atlantic ($13.5 million in 1999), Beacon ($4.5 million in 1999), New Left Books ($3.5 million in 1999), the

New Press ($3.5 million in 1999), and the nonprofit Library of America ($2 million in 1999). According to Andre Schiffrin, "Today the five largest conglomerates control approximately 80 percent of American book sales. In 1999 the top twenty publishers accounted for 93 percent of sales, and the ten largest had 75 percent of the revenues."[33]

Certainly, these conglomerates have produced stylish and engaging cultural products whose excellence has helped raise standards for consumers of mass culture. The view that the "culture industry" systematically suppresses innovation by selling the public recurrent and invariable forms or types and that its variety is merely "calculated mutation," in the words of Adorno and Horkheimer,[34] is no longer credible. Nonetheless, the limited degree of innovation and extent of experimentation and the high level of cautious control over the production, distribution, and consumption of cultural products all result from a highly competitive, market-driven cultural field in which the public's participation, taste, and critical involvement are often discouraged and curtailed, in part because they lead to unpredictable results. Corporations crave predictability; that is why they go to such great lengths to shape the desires and needs of the public. The larger the conglomerate is, the more opportunities there are to fashion the market. In 2001, for example, Time Warner marshaled its resources for the release of the film *Harry Potter and the Sorcerer's Stone*. Before the release, Harry Potter books had sold nearly $120 million worldwide. AOL users—who numbered approximately thirty-one million, half of all home Internet users—were led through numerous links to Harry Potter merchandise. Another Time Warner company, Moviefone, promoted and sold tickets. The company's phalanx of magazines—more than 160 titles, including *Time, People, Entertainment Weekly, Fortune,* and *Sports Illustrated*—featured cover stories, ads, and contests. Warner Bros. Studio advertised on Time Warner cable systems, which entered some 20 percent of wired American homes; and the Turner Broadcasting System, which included four of the top ten cable networks, aired promotions. Warner Music Group produced the soundtrack and sold CDs and cassettes. Advertising sold the worldwide rights to promote the film, along with its sequel, to Coca-Cola for $150 million. Online purchasers had their choice among Harry Potter toothbrushes, T-shirts, and much more.[35]

In the face of such corporate strategies, what power does Walter Lippmann's elusive "sovereign and omnicompetent citizen" of *The Phantom Public* have to actively shape his own culture? If market pressures, demands from investors, and capital-intensive, high-production cultural projects are shaping the cultural experiences and tastes of ordinary citizens, what room is left for a critical culture that might afford them greater insight and satisfaction? The seeming variety of consumer choices available obscures the fresher sources of cultural innovation associated with a critical culture that remains invisible and mysterious for a majority and elitist to many. Paradoxically, corporate intervention and academic indifference combine to leave the public sphere misshapen by corporate influence and imbued with a deep suspicion of educated classes, who seem to be guardians of a remote and exclusive culture and who seem to discourage popular cultural and political participation. The only major means at the public's disposal for "participating" in the cultural conversation are consumer choice, intermittent voting, and polls (as much a means of persuasion as a measure of opinion), all of which offer the public a subordinate and belated role in an often limited discourse.

Meanwhile, public opinion is formed by a privatized mass media whose news, analysis, and public service programming are shaped by operatives with an eye toward overall corporate profitability. Anxiety over ratings and concerns about alienating a public thought to require a daily dosage of affirmative news place limits on the broadest possible public conversation. That discourse is further constricted by the widespread acceptance of paradigms unduly shaped by the two major political parties, the corporate sector and its legion of influential lobbyists, government bureaucracies, the polling industry, and think tanks. The latter, as research centers that do not teach and are usually unaffiliated with the university, generally influence the critical culture indirectly. Only occasionally, in fact, do they directly address the public; their main audience, through which their considerable influence accrues, is made up of legislators, government bureaucrats, lobbyists, and other members of the political establishment. Think tanks tend to be conservative because they are usually funded by corporate sponsors seeking alternatives to universities that tend to be liberal and independent. With their disproportionate influence, think tanks provide expertise, specialization, and policy-making strategies to the elite; less frequently do their members contribute as public intellectuals to a broad and vital critical culture.

Finally, mergers and acquisitions within the publishing industry have, in some cases, threatened the critical culture. Although some determined publishers and their staffs have successfully struggled to maintain standards against bottom-line thinking, there is cause for concern that quality publishing, so vital to a thriving creative and critical culture, may be on the wane. Chains and online bookselling may have increased the number of excellent

books published, but these same chains have shortened the shelf life and life
expectancy that slow the turnover rate for all books. Indeed, the percentage of
books returned has steadily increased from 20 percent in the 1960s to over 40
percent in 2000.[36] Despite the unprecedented quantity of books sold in the
United States—over 2.5 billion are now sold yearly, far more than in any other
country—the number of per capita new books published each year, approximately seventy thousand, is small compared to many other countries. England, for example, with one-fifth the population, publishes the same number
of new books; and France, with one-quarter the population, issues twenty
thousand titles.[37] There are other effects as well. Increasing concentration on
best sellers and their authors means that beginning writers suffer when sales
do not meet expectations and that publishers are reluctant to plan future projects. Pay-for-display programs, which increasingly dictate which books receive
prominent placing in the chain bookstores, is yet another way that innovative,
risky writing is discouraged. Even more ominously, an increasing number of
articles have been pulled from magazines and books or withheld because they
are perceived by their corporate publishers to be unfavorable to themselves or
their advertisers.

If critical culture is in some ways threatened by these changes in commercial publishing, have the university presses provided refuge? Unfortunately,
this sector has been subject to increasing commercial pressure, and the results
have caused grave concern. Since 1990, for example, annual subsidies from
universities have in general decreased, libraries have diverted funds for book
and journal purchases to computer hardware and online services, chain stores
have demanded higher discounts that small presses can ill afford, and the cost
of publishing a monograph has increased disproportionately. Nearly all university presses have responded by scaling back operations; Oxford University
Press, for example, discontinued its publication of contemporary poetry, its
Clarendon imprint, and its Opus and Modern Masters series. Other university
presses have opted for more commercial titles or have stressed their regional
ties. In general, university presses have been forced to struggle to sustain the
level of scholarly, critical, and creative production of the past several decades.
Thus far they are barely staying afloat in the strong countervailing market currents. Many are turning to electronic publishing as a way of adapting to the
challenges and opportunities of a changing marketplace.

The same, in general, can be said for the traditional sources of critical culture: commercial publishing, the domain of journalistic and general criticism,

and the small nonacademic press. Beginning with the latter, American fiction and poetry continue to be well served by a handful of small distinguished literary houses like New Directions, Dalkey Archive, Archipelago, Coffee House, Copper Canyon, Four Walls Eight Windows, Graywolf, Milkweed, and Seven Stories. These intensely devoted presses continue to thrive, seemingly on little capital other than the quality of their editors' firsthand perception. Journalistic and general criticism, still a large and influential domain despite the erosion of its cultural authority, continues to supply small but essential sectors of the public with discerning considerations of books, ideas, and the arts. Despite the pressures of the academy, a talented corps of critics—some independent and some academically affiliated—has served the public and the arts well since 1950. These critics have encouraged artists and cultivated audiences for a growing range of cultural endeavors. They include literary critics and book reviewers like William Deresiewicz, Ralph Ellison, Elizabeth Hardwick, Michiko Kakutani, John Leonard, John Updike, and James Wood; drama critics like Claudia Cassidy, Brendan Gill, and Walter Kerr; film critics like Richard Corliss, Roger Ebert, Pauline Kael, Stanley Kaufman, Anthony Lane, and Richard Schickel; dance critics like Joan Acocella, Jack Anderson, Clive Barnes, Jennifer Dunning, Lawrence van Gelder, and Anna Kisselgoff; music critics like Robert Christgau, Gary Giddins, Albert Murray, John Pereles, Charles Rosen, Martin Williams, and David Yaffe; art critics like John Canady, Arthur Danto, Robert Hughes, Michael Kimmelman, Lucy Lippard, Peter Schjeldahl, and Sanford Schwartz; and critics of culture and politics like David Brooks, Joan Didion, E. J. Dionne, Todd Gitlin, Murray Kempton, and Frank Rich.

Any significant revitalization of critical culture through processes of cultural democratization will need to extend the critical work of these public intellectuals to encompass a greater portion of the general public they now serve well but incompletely. Key to this endeavor would be a general reorientation of the academic humanities so that a place is made for publicly engaged scholarship, by which I mean an active, reciprocal relationship with nonacademic constituencies that generates new knowledge. Such reorientation would of course accompany traditional outreach through inclusive programming, inviting community members onto campus, and so on. It would necessarily entail a change in academic culture so that professors interested in engaging with the public would actually be encouraged to do so by a revamped tenure and rewards system that recognizes the value of such work. Even were a small proportion of the humanities professoriat to choose such a path, it would mean many thousands of highly trained experts newly involved in shaping an improved, critical cultural conversation. This would be an enormous contribution to the public life of the nation.

Equally important, the critical culture will need to encompass a global perspective, especially in the wake of the 9/11 attacks and the subsequent intensification of American political and military involvement abroad. In the past, attention to foreign literatures and cultures has been uneven at best—a perennial problem for American culture. In recent history, it has been limited to a taste for the magic realist novelists of Latin America in the 1970s, a focus on the dissident cultures and writers of Eastern Europe during the 1980s, and an enthusiasm for Indian writers in English in the late 1990s. Clearly, increased efforts will need to be made to inform the public more comprehensively about global intellectual and artistic developments.

No doubt, such changes will need to be preceded by a serious national commitment to eradicating illiteracy, by educational reform that places due emphasis on reading good books, on finding ways to use the Internet creatively, on more sustained encounters with the arts, and on reciprocal partnerships between amateur and professional critics. Whether corporate America can afford such a renaissance remains to be seen. A thriving democracy can ill afford anything less.

CHAPTER 2

Revitalizing Literary Studies

Academic literary studies are in great need of renewal. In saying so, I am fully aware that I join a long line of predecessors who have largely failed to spark much change in an institutional world whose considerable inertia is immensely difficult to overcome.[1] Today, despite continuing to produce excellent scholarly books and effectively teaching tens of thousands of students, our profession finds itself, if not in a state of crisis (I hate the word *crisis*—it always calls to mind the quip about the left successfully predicting ten of the last two crises), at least in a state of high uncertainty about its future. Today's English department lacks vivacity, to the point that stagnation and demoralization do not seem altogether inappropriate terms in describing the current malaise. For those of us who have been around for awhile, the current atmosphere is a far cry from the excitement of previous decades when, along with colleagues from many other disciplines, we rushed to read the latest work of literary theory by any of one or two dozen scholars. Those days are long gone, but what have the heady days of theory given way to? It is difficult to say: certainly, the many mediocre and the few superb literary and cultural studies of our day do not seem to engender much enthusiasm or accrue much momentum toward any large intellectual projects. The "literary theory and criticism" shelves in the bookstores gather dust in the far corners. Graduate students of English, their numbers dwindling, as are the number of our undergraduate majors, often seem to flounder due to lack of inspiring direction from the profession and emulate their faculty mentors by latching onto theories a quarter-to half-century old that too often result in unnecessarily derivative work. When they complete that work, they are faced with what has been a steady underemployment or unemployment rate that has hovered around 50 percent for many years.[2] As I documented in the last chapter, the decline of English and the humanities has been palpable, and calls like the recent one in the *New York Times* article "In Tough Times the Humanities Must Justify Their Worth" just seem to multiply.[3] Clearly, both internal and external consideration must be borne in mind when assessing the reasons for our increasingly unsatisfactory state and in any consideration of alternatives. But I want to be clear about one thing before proceeding: I do not offer the following recommendations because I consider my profession hopelessly hermetic, scandalously overspecialized, ridiculously irrelevant, or full of disgruntled, alienated academics yearning to be free. The problems I have identified are real, but they do not amount to a catastrophe, and they are not without significant exceptions. I categorically reject the narrative of failure deployed by some of my colleagues who advocate as I do the need for publicly engaged scholarship. We need not build on the embers of a collapsed structure: that structure will do quite nicely as a home, thank you, though it ever so badly needs paint, perhaps an addition or two, and a bit of landscaping. It is time for us to fix up the place and become better neighbors in the process.

I am suggesting, as a major initiative within the profession, a more ready embrace of the public and its problems. I recommend we achieve this, first of all, by developing innovative research projects that bring literature and criticism to bear on the lives of those outside our academic community. In much of the rest of this book, I offer my own modest and frankly incipient examples of what these projects might look like. They are intended to raise possibilities rather than to present finished pieces of work, and they take their place alongside similar kinds of projects now being developed by colleagues who have associated themselves with a growing academic initiative (I hesitate to call it a "movement," as some advocates do) that encourages publicly engaged scholarship, in some cases under the auspices of Imagining America, a consortium of nearly ninety colleges and universities interested in promoting civic engagement within the academic humanities, arts, and design. This organization promotes projects that involve direct interaction with particular communities and constituencies. I advocate such work, but I also advocate a significant expansion of public intellectual work in the form of reviews and articles in refereed commercial publications and on Web sites intended for an audience of common readers. *Neither of these initiatives should replace traditional scholarship; rather, they should supplement it.* In the unlikely event that publicly engaged scholarship should ever encroach on the production of traditional scholarship to the point that more than a modest minority of scholars are doing it, I believe adjustments would need to be made to restore the predominance of traditional scholarship.

The research agenda I have in mind would involve scholars in a sustained and reciprocal interaction with nonacademic constituencies in order for us to better understand American literary culture in all its ramifications. As a profession, we have now devoted several decades to the analysis of the political and ideological causes and effects of particular literary texts, but we have done so without any broad effort to consult with actual readers other than our students and ourselves. Even reader-response theory has contented itself with examining the responses of "ideal" readers who are invariably the theorists themselves. It little credits our profession that a century of inquiry has yielded so few studies by scholars willing to spend significant time in the presence of nonacademic readers or that a recent fascinating study of the public presence of American poetry, entitled *Songs of Ourselves: The Uses of Poetry in America,* was written by a historian, Joan Rubin, and not a literary scholar. Janice Radway, who ventured out beyond the campus to write her classic *Reading the Romance,* remains one of our exemplary scholars in this regard, and certainly the study of the history of the book, fan culture, and film spectatorship have yielded other examples. With books such as these as models, we as a profession ought to go forth and, where possible, place the many interesting historical claims of the past decades regarding literature's political and ideological effects on readers under the added crucible of rigorous empirical research.

To return for a moment to Imagining America, founded in 1999 by humanists from inside and outside the academy whose mission has been to "strengthen the public role and democratic purposes of the humanities" through support of publicly engaged academic work and the structural changes in higher education that such work requires, a "major task is to constitute public scholarship as an important and legitimate enterprise" (www.imaginingamerica.org). To date, dozens of interesting projects are taking place at schools affiliated with Imagining America, such as Gregory Jay's Whiteness Studies initiative at University of Wisconsin, Milwaukee; the Kennesaw State University Keeping and Creating American Communities project's partnership with Georgia public schools; the University of Texas Living Newspaper project, Writing Austin's Lives, and Community Sabbaticals; the work of the Harward Center at Bates College; and Julie Ellison's Poetry in Everyday Life courses at the University of Michigan. Unaffiliated with Imagining America is the Changing Lives Through Literature reading program for prisoners, founded in 1991 by Robert Waxler, a professor of English at Dartmouth, now active in nine states. These are not simply service projects, nor are they essentially outreach efforts. They are partnerships that provide the ground for research that in turn leads to scholarship and to publication.

Another effort is to open up opportunities for scholars to publish for a wider public audience in the trade press, in magazines with mass circulation, in the dailies, and especially on the Internet. This need has been brought on

not only by the corporatization of the public domain, which would be challenged by strong works of literary and cultural criticism that appeal to a broad
educated audience, but by the severe problems that have enveloped the publishing industry and academic presses in particular. These difficulties have already placed the future of the monograph in some jeopardy, to the extent that
they compelled Stephen Greenblatt in 2002 to dispatch a "special letter" to
members of the Modern Language Association appealing to English departments to consider adjusting their publishing requirements for tenure so that
more emphasis is placed on articles and less on monographs. This will become
an increasingly necessary, if not altogether welcome, adjustment as academic
presses downsize and look to bring out work with a broad and sometimes
commercial appeal. Reaching a broader audience is desirable of course, but it
should not have to come at the expense of the monograph. In any event, professional organizations like the Modern Language Association, the Association
of Literary Scholars and Critics, the American Council of Learned Societies,
and Imagining America must make a major effort to work with the publishing
and journalism worlds to open up new opportunities that create greater access
for its members. To date, the Modern Language Association has moved
glacially when it comes to encouraging publicly engaged scholarship. But there
are hopeful signs. In the spring 2010 issue of the MLA Newsletter, the President
Sidonie Smith endorsed Kathleen Woodward's suggestion that we "conceptu-
alize our work as public goods (and not just professional scholarly products)."
In particular, academics must make an all-out effort to develop interactive
Web sites that attract both an academic and nonacademic audience. Wikipedia
and Google have become authoritative for much of the population; both offer
opportunities for scholars to improve the level of conversation through organized interventions. This entails creating subject matter and a language that
appeal to a range of constituencies. In the very near future, more people will
get their news electronically than via the print media. Electronic books themselves are rapidly joining research databases as fundamental sources for academics and the wider public, and Google's plan to make millions of volumes
available electronically will likely change the game entirely in the not-too-dis-
tant future. Old and new Web sites provide examples of where the profession
is already headed, with online journals proliferating and causing a widespread
reassessment of what constitutes a scholarly article. The Valve and World Literature Today are just a couple of examples of innovative Web sites. For too
long, the profession, with its high percentage of old-fashioned bibliophiles,
Luddites, and reluctant followers, has reacted to technological developments

rather than seize on them. This needs to change, and it will so long as young scholars are given the wherewithal to forge ahead to create electronic spaces for a nationwide literary culture that is interesting, rigorous, inclusive, and participatory.

I have indicated that the reorientation I seek for the profession is not meant to denigrate theoretical work; on the contrary, an apt description of the direction we need to go is not "post-theoretical" but, rather, "applied theoretical." In making theory more responsive to the actual experience of readers, not to mention the actual social and political realities of the day that illuminate our understanding of what we mean by the "public" and its problems (ongoing political movements, parties, policies, initiatives, etc.), we would do well to turn at least some of our attention to the body of theory that has been most influential outside literary studies: liberal theory. For twenty-odd years, political scientists, philosophers, and historians have wrestled with the work of John Rawls, Amitai Etzioni, Michael Walzer, Robert Dahl, Ronald Dworkin, Martha Nussbaum, Michael Sandel, Amartya Sen, Charles Taylor, and others. The work of these theorists has been at the center of much that has been vital within the social sciences and humanities, yet very few literary scholars are familiar with this body of work. Continental theory has brought us many insights, but we should not remain blind to the contributions of theoretical work expressly produced to deepen our understanding of capitalist democracies and American society (and Canadian society, for Charles Taylor). Indeed, by inquiring into the civic function and actual political effects of reading "good" books, Martha Nussbaum's *Poetic Justice: The Literary Imagination and Public Life,* following the work of Wayne Booth, offers new ways of reading within the broader context of active *citizenship,* as distinct from reactive *ideology.* Indeed, an immense amount of interesting work remains to be done around the place—and, in many cases, the absence—of culture, literature, and the arts in liberal theory.

We could do worse than to begin with the immensely influential work of John Rawls, who Thomas Nagel has called the most important political philosopher of the twentieth century. Some evidence supporting this claim would include the fact that his *A Theory of Justice* (1971) has sold more than two hundred thousand copies, has been translated into some two dozen languages, and has provoked over five thousand academic responses. Yet, as far I have been able to ascertain, the only detailed response to Rawls that has come from the literary academy has been a single journal article. It is an interesting one by Colene Bentley, titled "Rawls, Literary Form, and How to Read Politi-

cally," published in the *Dalhousie Review*. When we reflect on the reasons there
have been, by comparison, hundreds, if not thousands, of responses to Foucault, Althusser, and Lacan, we may very well attribute this grossly disproportionate emphasis to an unreasonable unwillingness to grapple with home-
grown liberal theories like Rawls's that have actually had a much greater
influence on American politics than any of the theories of the figures who have
bewitched so many American literary scholars. A second reason is no doubt
the pervasive bashing of liberalism, until very recently our profession's very
own designated "other," in which the careful consideration of liberal perspectives yields to smug caricature and mockery. Another reason for the lack of interest in Rawls is his conspicuous neglect of literature, art, and culture
throughout his work—Bentley calls him "probably the least literary of political theorists"[4]—but such an explanation lacks interpretive suppleness and
imagination. The fact that *Justice as Fairness: A Restatement* (2001), Rawls's revised and compressed version of *A Theory of Justice*, is literally wrapped up in
a reproduction of John Marin's striking modernist watercolor *Deer Isle, Islets,
Maine* (1922) that graces its cover is itself an invitation to think about the relationship between Rawls's theory and art.

That relationship is closer than has been thought. One could even say that
the very basis of Rawls's theory of justice resembles literary experience insofar
as it arises out of the imaginary act of projecting a just social arrangement out
of the temporary fiction of thinking all agents involved are unaware of anyone's wealth, intelligence, physical well-being, gender, ethnicity, or race. Rawls
calls this the "veil of ignorance," a key feature of his "original position," but in
his schema, of course, the "not knowing" is a deliberate act of self-limitation
that leads to agreement on broad principles that constitute the "fair terms of
social cooperation." The metaphor of the "veil" is familiar to readers of
W. E. B. DuBois's *The Souls of Black Folk*, in which it serves as an important
emblem for the perspective of African Americans who, themselves hidden behind the veil, nonetheless possess the power to see outward and into the world
of their persecutors. In Rawls, the "veil" actually works as a shroud, or a cur-
tain that temporarily prevents seeing in or out. In DuBois, the veil serves to divide African American consciousness between seeing oneself as one really is
and seeing oneself as one's antagonists do, a debilitating but also a potentially
empowering perspective; in Rawls, the veil introduces a virtual or hypothetical
reality in which reasonable principles can be agreed on by rational citizens
precisely because they are risk-free—that is, they have no immediate and direct consequences for the real desires and interests of the individuals involved.

If this sounds familiar to literary scholars, it is because this is not an uncommon way of describing the aesthetic reading experience, in which literal reality, with all its contingencies, is momentarily suspended or bracketed as we enter a vicarious realm of freedom. Here, in this powerful world of "as if," experiments in thought and feeling "quicken, sharpen, and sweeten our being" and "help make us tolerant and mentally lithe," as Wendy Steiner nicely puts it in *The Scandal of Pleasure*.[5] Though Rawls is intent on tamping down pleasure (until the penultimate page of *Justice as Fairness*, where he observes that citizens of an effective democracy may justly take pleasure in their accomplishments), affect in general, and certainly scandal, his principles arise out of a process that is a kind of play: the unencumbered expression of reason that we call the free *play* of ideas. Rawls acknowledges that both the original position and the deliberative process that arises from it result in hypothetical, nonbinding agreements. He also acknowledges that the importance of the original position lies in the fact that it is "a device of representation."[6] Of all of this, we can say there is a kinship with what Thomas Mann has said of artists, "whose seriousness is of the absolute nature, it is 'dead-earnest playing.'"[7] To this extent, Rawls's project resembles an aesthetic one.

There is another aspect of Rawls's theory that is relevant to the possible direction literary studies may take, and it has to do with the uses to which his principles of justice are put. One of the more important of these is to provide publicly recognized and accepted "rules and procedures" that regulate the conduct of those participating in the political process. In a democracy, Rawls reminds us, these participants do not constitute a community, in which people share the same fundamental beliefs and values. What Rawls calls "reasonable pluralism"—the necessary existence of "profound and irreconcilable differences in citizens' reasonable comprehensive religious and philosophical conceptions of the world and their views of the moral and aesthetic values to be sought in human life"[8]—must always characterize a free society. One of the tests of principles of fairness is whether they serve to reconcile citizens who hold different basic beliefs and values. In other words, the principles must work to sustain the idea of society as "a fair system of cooperation over time,"[9] despite the acute difficulties of reaching political agreement among citizens whose basic beliefs and values may otherwise conflict. Establishing such a "stable overlapping consensus"[10] depends on repeated endorsement by all groups (regardless of the relative strength of their beliefs and values) of (a) the permanence of their basic rights and liberties; (b) the clarity and utility of the reasoning behind their shared understanding of justice as fairness; and (c) the open, free, and public exercise of reason. Only this can provide a sufficient bond of trust that will withstand the centrifugal force of radically disparate worldviews.

I would suggest that, properly understood, literature and aesthetic experience work in ways that parallel and reinforce efforts to create a "fair system of cooperation over time." They do so by affording their audiences shared participation in the individual and social conflicts depicted by authors and artists, but in a way that is always provisional. As teachers and authors, literary critics and scholars facilitate and improve the quality of this participation by imparting analytical, interpretive, and evaluative skills to others. Moreover, I would argue that the skillful and pleasurable manipulation of form these audiences encounter in the creative work they read renders an experience of appreciation and respect potent enough for them to want to extend those attitudes to others they are in dialogue with. This is precisely the arena of discourse many of us try to create in our classrooms. The public sphere needs it as well, and no one is better qualified to nurture it there than we are.

Although I myself have chosen to focus on the work of John Rawls, others are innovatively exploring literature's relation to other forms of liberalism, as well as the immediacies of political life in the United States, as an alternative to the often antistatist and apocalyptic politics that emerge from the disproportionate focus on Althusser, Deleuze, Foucault, Lacan, and others. Scholars like Amanda Anderson, Amanda Claybaugh, Sean McCann, Michael Szalay, and the aforementioned Colene Bentley are producing important work that turns our attention to the crossroads where literature and actual political figures, parties, elections, organizations, movements, and campaigns meet. Currently, a good deal of this work is concentrated within the fields of American and Victorian studies.[11] Closely related to these concerns is the question of aesthetics' relation to movements for political change. We need additional scholarly initiatives in the area of social movements and the role that literature and art have played within them. W. E. B. DuBois's extraordinary 1926 speech to the NAACP "Criteria of Negro Art," in which he argued vociferously for the central place of beauty within the movement for equality and civil rights, stands as the exemplary statement of what role aesthetics might play within reform and radical movements. DuBois challenged the expectations of his activist audience, whose habitual response to art and beauty was either impatient hostility or momentary, condescending tolerance. Since then, these attitudes have not changed on the left as much as we would like to think, for it is still the case that when most people align themselves with a political movement, their first impulse when it comes to writers and artists is to ask whether and how they show their solidarity. They are still a rather long way from asking the more pertinent question, which is whether and how the movement shows its solidarity with writers and artists. Countless research opportunities exist for critical examinations of the cultures and aesthetics of the myriad local, national, foreign, and global movements for social change of the past century and beyond—as a way of educating ourselves for more effective interventions of our own.

We need to make a place for ethnographic work in literary studies. The model here remains Janice Radway's *Reading the Romance* (1984), a study of fifty-odd midwestern women who read romance fiction. Radway is never content to infer political meanings from texts themselves. She is committed to understanding the act of reading as an *event,* with complex relations to the text's ideological predispositions and to a variety of personal, sociological, and ideological factors within the reader's world. This constellation makes up the reading experience for Radway, and her exemplary efforts to read women reading show us the way. This is true especially when the results are unsettling. Radway's readers, for example, typically rationalize rape scenes so long as the rapist/hero is unaware of the true identity of his victim/heroine and unaware of his unconscious love for her. In Kathleen Woodiwiss's *The Flame and the Flower,* the favorite romance novel of her informants, there are one attempted rape and four repeated rapes of the heroine by the hero in the first fifty pages. Yet Radway realizes that even here the response of the women is compensatory: the result of gender divisions in marriage in which wives and mothers reproduce others but no one "reproduces" them. But even Radway—having spent months with her subjects, hours interviewing them, pages surveying them—understands that more ambitious research projects are needed to understand the long-range effects of romance fiction on her subjects. Many other projects of this kind beckon.

Writing in the *Writer's Chronicle,* Ronald Goldfarb has referred to book clubs as "the ultimate form of civil intercourse among friends."[12] There are currently thousands of active book clubs operating in every state and among every demographic, including those in jails and prisons, and their members are the innumerable uncertified aestheticians that make up a significant part of our public. We should be more curious about this unexplored territory. We need an American version of Jonathan Rose's brilliant *The Intellectual Life of the British Working Classes.* The poet Kenneth Koch has left us the wonderful *Rose, Where Did You Get That Red?* about teaching poetry to children. Like Koch, many of our creative writing colleagues quite regularly venture outside of the academy. Perhaps we might join them and make their contacts with the reading public,

writing workshops, and the public schools subjects of our own work. We need
to collaborate with schools of education when possible, especially programs
that train English teachers, in order to better understand the role of literature
in K–12 education and enhance that role. Such projects present the opportunity
to involve ourselves with these readers and understand the "work" of art as
what books do with and in their experience. This sort of involvement would
contribute to re-creating a public sphere through the self-activation of citizens
who might in time expect more from public officials, the media, and the entertainment industry. In several of the following chapters, I offer a glimpse of
what this kind of publicly engaged scholarship might look like.

The pursuits I am advocating define a new type of scholar and a new type
of intellectual. Heretofore, the conversation regarding intellectuals and academic life has been shaped by a whole host of antitheses. Antonio Gramsci
gave us the "organic" versus the "traditional" intellectual; Michel Foucault, the
"specific" versus the "universal" intellectual; and Russell Jacoby, the "last"
(public) intellectual versus the academic. Other binaries have included the
critic versus the scholar, the generalist versus the specialist, the amateur or bel-
letrist versus the professional, the revolutionary versus the petty bourgeois intellectual, and the engaged versus the disinterested intellectual. Each of these
formulations is a response to the fundamental feature of intellectual life in the
twentieth century: its incorporation into the bureaucratic institutions of capitalist democracy, especially the academy. Thus, the social situation of intellectual life has seemed to divide the place of production, the modes of distribution, the audience, the purview, and the overall ecology of modern intellectual
life. It is my view, however, that the sites of intellectual work are no longer as
distinct as they once were, in large measure because the university has succeeded in legitimizing a considerably broad range of intellectual perspectives
and has so thoroughly encroached on the life of society in all its aspects as to
make the old divisions seem antiquated. As we survey these institutions of
higher learning, we see that academics in the sciences, the social sciences, the
professional schools, and the performing arts have regularly combined their
scholarly and intellectual work with ongoing public interaction. Ironically, it is
only in the traditional humanities, which often aspire to speak for social and
ideological awareness and the need for critical consciousness among the
masses, that actual connections to the public remain relatively rare. Surely,
were we to compile histories of individual English departments, we would encounter examples of individual forays into the public sphere: the nonspecial-
ized writing of a few public intellectuals, the occasional lecture at the local li-

brary, the op-ed piece in the local newspaper, the presentation to the local reading group, the writing workshops in local or regional jails and prisons led by our colleagues, and so on. But this sort of unheralded and unrewarded (but, for all that, hardly unreward*ing*) work is almost always done quietly by individual faculty members and is rarely recognized or encouraged by full departments. More often than not, it is work done by tenured faculty, for untenured faculty run the risk that these commitments of time and passion not only will not count for tenure but will reduce their chances of gaining it.

That these many admirable efforts have remained invisible to the profession as a whole is evidenced by their neglect in the single widely available history of the profession, Gerald Graff's recently revised *Professing Literature: An Institutional History,* an admirable chronicle of the *internal* developments and debates of our profession since the late nineteenth century. Save for passing glances at external social developments—the world wars, the affluent fifties, the explosive sixties—little in the book allows us to see the profession and its interrelationship with the wider culture and its challenges. Graff, of course, is well known for his call to "teach the conflicts," and in this book, he consequently moves from one academic debate to the next as his operating framework for presenting our history. But, again, these are almost exclusively *internal* conflicts: specialists against generalists around the turn of the twentieth century; scholars against critics in the early to mid-twentieth century; history against criticism from 1940 to 1960; and, most recently, traditionalists against theorists. How the profession has evolved in its changing relations to the larger culture, not to mention political and economic contingencies, largely escapes the book's purview—indeed, here is another vital area of interest that requires much more scholarly attention than it has received.

An exception is Graff's interesting and suggestive account of the origins of the profession during the latter three decades of the nineteenth century. He points out that before the emergence of the profession of literature, literary culture in America flourished within the college and the general community, anchored on campus by ubiquitous "debating societies, college debating clubs, student literary magazines, undergraduate prize competitions, and frequent public lectures and readings," all of which "constituted an informal literary education of impressive proportions."[13] To this we should add the Lyceum Movement; followed by Chautauqua, with its nationwide adult education networks buoyed by the Chautauqua Literary and Scientific Circle, which had enrolled some 180,000 people by 1891; and, finally, William Rainey Harper's ambitious program of organized reading groups under the auspices of the University of

Chicago Extension Department, which organized 2,700 groups and attracted fifty thousand members during its lifetime.[14] All of this provides the crucial context within which—or, rather, against which—literary studies arose as a distinct profession. Here is Graff's telling account of what was gained and what was lost with the birth of our profession: "The subsequent rise of litera-ture as a college subject with its own departments and programs coincided with the collapse of the communal literary culture and the corresponding es-trangement of literature from its earlier function in polite society, where it had been an essential instrument of socialization."[15]

In his indispensable *Intellect and Public Life: Essays on the Social History of Academic Intellectuals in the United States,* Thomas Bender makes a stronger and more thorough case than Graff. A key theme of his study is that, as he puts it, "the increasing incorporation of academic culture into the center of Amer-ican life, socially and intellectually, is accompanied and causally related to [*sic*] a progressive impoverishment of the public sphere."[16] The process of institu-tionalizing literary studies that opened the gulf between civic and academic spheres was too varied and complex for me to describe here—Bender's book, which ought to be required reading within the profession, examines this di-vergence in detail. Suffice it to say that the process entailed specialization within a system of disciplines, each of which developed its own conceptual framework as it became a distinct discursive and epistemic community funda-mentally separate from a shared public culture. It is noteworthy that Daniel Coit Gilman, who founded Johns Hopkins University as the first modern re-search institution in the United States after the German model, did not at first envision it as an alternative to the then-thriving public sphere of literary and scientific inquiry. As Bender reports, "For a decade after the founding of Johns Hopkins University in 1876, the tradition of civic culture was still strong. Daniel Coit Gilman was concerned about the relation of the university to it. One of his first acts as president . . . was a gesture to civic culture: the estab-lishment of a series of public lectures in Baltimore that would, he said, demon-strate 'the methods and principles on which we rely.' "[17]

A few years later, in 1879, Gilman responded favorably to a proposal that the American Social Science Association, one of many public organizations promoting serious inquiry and public education, merge with Hopkins. The vi-sion behind the proposal was a university giving direction to an intellectual enterprise with local, regional, and national impact that would connect the mutually beneficial activities of academic and nonacademic social inquirers. But the immense pressure to legitimize the new institution by emphasizing the differences between professional inquiry and amateur inquiry—or, in Max Weber's terms, the superiority of the "specialist" over the "cultivated man"[18]— was too difficult to resist, and so the profession of literature, along with others, arose out of the perceived need to sever the university's ties to the surrounding public and amateur culture. In Gilman's case, according to Bender, the plan to contribute to the tradition of civic culture was replaced by a plan to encourage professional associations, and so he lent his support to the Hopkins faculty members who formed the Modern Language Association in 1883, the American Historical Association in 1884, and the American Economic Association in 1885.[19] This, unfortunately, remains our most determinate legacy, despite the social role American higher education had played in the past and continues to play, exemplified by the direct civic engagement of the land grant movement, the Wisconsin Idea, and the many examples of individual academics who have insisted, sometimes at some risk to their careers, on transgressing the institutional boundaries whose origins Bender traces and which continue to shape our professional lives.

All the same, it is worth remembering that those of us who have chosen to address the multitudes and their problems beyond our campus borders were trained in universities whose rigorous modes of inquiry and relative autonomy made our expertise possible. Here, at the intersection of public need and specialized expertise, is where some of us might find ourselves. It is a confluence unaccounted for by the dichotomous frameworks for understanding the role of intellectuals that presume a fundamental irreconcilability between public engagement and specialized knowledge. Yet, as Clive James said with reference to fin de siècle Vienna, "the most accommodating and fruitful ground for the life of the mind can be something more broad than a university campus."[20] In a time when many of us despair of ever improving the quality of public communication—because critical reflection has given way to instrumental rationality or because "the new oracular figures" like popular psychologists, media celebrities, consultants, operatives, and public relations experts have taken over—the reasons for our reluctance are also the very reasons we need to intervene.[21] Morris Dickstein is right to assert that our main business ought to be to recapture the public sphere once occupied by men and women of letters and "treat criticism as a major form of public discourse."[22] What is needed are innovative efforts to bring the knowledge, expertise, and protocols of careful, critical thinking developed over generations within the academy to bear on the experiences and problems of our fellow citizens who make up the general public or, if you prefer, publics. If we grant that the American public

currently assumes a supine position in our flawed democracy—as elites repre-
senting traditional centers of economic, political, and military power make decisions in its behalf unencumbered by its participation—that is all the more
reason to build a participatory democracy that rests on, in Dewey's words,
"faith in the capacity of human beings for intelligent judgment and action if
proper conditions are furnished."[23] We are in a position to help create these
conditions through projects that bring us face-to-face with the nonacademic
public, enable us to share our analytical and evaluative skills with our fellow
citizens as we learn from the experiences and skills they bring to the relationship, and at once reduce credulity and passivity by raising the overall level of
public conversation when it comes to the arts, culture, and, indirectly, politics.
In a profession numbering tens of thousands, even a small fraction engaged in
this kind of scholarly work would contribute significantly to what Lewis Hyde
has envisioned as a "cultural commons"[24] and would lead to much-needed
change in American life. As Robert Westbrook suggests in discussing Dewey,
we must begin to make the transition from vesting full authority in our own
pronouncements to granting it to "the deliberations of ordinary men and
women skilled in the art of practical judgment."[25]

"'Scholarship in Action'—is that three words or two?" So goes the quip circu-
lated by my skeptical colleagues at Syracuse University who were initially opposed to a new initiative to encourage publicly engaged scholarship. In the
spring of 2009, Syracuse became one of the first American universities to revise its tenure policy so that faculty who do publicly engaged scholarship will
be rewarded for their contributions through the tenure and promotion
process, depending, of course, on the quality of that work. Since her arrival in
2005, Chancellor Nancy Cantor, one of the founding members of Imagining
America, has sought a closer, more reciprocal relationship between Syracuse
University and the surrounding community—and, beyond that, the wider
world. This is not mere outreach—inviting the public onto campus and spon-
soring community programs and events. It involves the kinds of initiatives I
describe in this book: developing scholarly projects with the vital needs of the
public in mind and generating research and new knowledge through interaction with the wider community.

I am of course aware that these changes are controversial. Within our own
discipline, Stanley Fish and others, defending the always-threatened autonomy
and professional expertise of the academy, have spoken out loudly against
"saving the world" during working hours. Outside the discipline, Jennifer

Washburn, in *University Inc.*, and Derek Bok, in *Universities in the Market-place*, offer accounts of university corruption and fear the encroachment of political power and the profit motive on critical scholarly inquiry. Related fears concern the diminishment of rigorous scholarly standards and the difficulties of assessing public scholarship. Still others, although they support public scholarship and even do it themselves as tenured faculty, despair of the prospects of changing an institution they consider nearly petrified, especially when tenure and promotion are concerned, which is crucial if public scholarship is ever to be given the chance to thrive.

One of the few advantages that accrues to the humanities due to its remoteness from the perceived needs of the corporate world and government agencies is that it has not had to protect itself from undue outside influence. Even during the culture wars of the 1990s, most humanists responded to the conservative onslaught on government funding of the arts by advocating continued support at established levels or even increased support. Only a very few responded by telling the National Endowment for the Arts to take a hike with its money stuffed in its backpack. But for some, the prospect of publicly engaged scholarship raises the specter of meddling, if not by the government, then by the political process and the private sector as well.

The changes at Syracuse were four years in the making, and during that time, each previously mentioned objection was debated at length. Indeed, the language of the policy itself reflects an acute awareness that the dangers of undue outside influence and inferior scholarship need to be avoided at all costs. What follows are key passages from the new policy passed by the University Senate, now part of the *Syracuse University Faculty Manual*.

Syracuse University is committed to longstanding traditions of scholarship as well as evolving perspectives on scholarship. Syracuse University recognizes that the role of academia is not static, and that methodologies, topics of interest, and boundaries within and between disciplines change over time. The University will continue to support scholars in all of these traditions, including faculty who choose to participate in publicly engaged scholarship. Publicly engaged scholarship may involve partnerships of university knowledge and resources with those of the public and private sectors to enrich scholarship, research, creative activity, and public knowledge; enhance curriculum, teaching and learning; prepare educated, engaged citizens; strengthen democratic values and civic responsibility; address and help solve critical social problems; and contribute to the public good.[26]

To allay fears that the policy would encourage inferior scholarship—perhaps in the form of political cant, corporate shilling, advocacy, or narrow pragmatics—the new language goes on to spell out criteria for judging the quality of all scholarship, including publicly engaged scholarship.

> All scholarship will meet common expectations in terms of 1) ways of doing the work (e.g., formulating problems, choosing topics of inquiry, framing questions, using systematic processes or methods, setting goals, making and carrying out plans, sustaining a scholarly agenda, observing ethical standards); 2) means of legitimating the work (e.g., providing theoretical foundations, making reasoned arguments, documenting the work, representing the work in various media, disseminating it to appropriate audiences and users, assessing outcomes or projects through review by appropriate evaluators); 3) connections to prior/current scholarship and to an intellectual community or communities (e.g., drawing on other scholars' work, contributing to current work, building on a scholar's previous work, placing work in an intellectual tradition); 4) qualities of the work (e.g., rigor, objectivity, caution, currency, originality, generativity, independence of thought, critical stance, commitment); and 5) significance (e.g., audiences addressed, importance of goals, relevance beyond immediate project, effect on field, contribution to the public good).[27]

These passages, along with several additional ones describing effective scholarship that were proposed by early opponents of the policy, eventually resulted in changes that gained the overwhelming support of the University Senate, whose majority are members of the faculty. Initial objections—based on the difficulty of distinguishing scholarship from service; of achieving effective assessment of public scholarship; of including some nonacademic evaluation in the process without relinquishing peer review; of "privileging" public over traditional scholarship; and of undermining the university's mission to produce disinterested, rigorous scholarship—were answered in lengthy conversations and e-mail exchanges that took place on a special blog specifically constructed to facilitate the conversation. The full discussion can be accessed at http://suse nate.wordpress.com, where readers who care to do so may inspect my responses to a range of articulate, understandable concerns voiced by esteemed colleagues.

In the remainder of this chapter, I compare my position to several of the more compelling alternatives circulating in the profession today. Among these are the more or less recent views of Stanley Fish, James Longenbach, Michael

Bérubé, and members of Imagining America who have a very particular—too particular in my view—notion of public engagement.

I am fully aware that any academic who wishes to alter the currents affecting the ship of state will have to deal with the big (Stanley) Fish, a gentle shark who patrols the waters and will do everything reasonably possible to bar your entrance. Ironically, when he is not on duty, he himself frolics in the very waters he declares off-limits to others, and there he makes his not insubstantial contribution to guiding that ship. It is a shame he insists on swimming solo and rebuffing all fish swimming in schools. I think it preferable for others to do as Fish has done: take the skills, conventions, protocols, and rigors of academic analysis and apply them to matters of public concern. In both *Professional Correctness: Literary Studies and Political Change* and *Save the World on Your Own Time,* Fish offers helpful distinctions between commitments to academic versus political values. Whereas I endorse his view that the proper place for espousing political views is not the classroom, where political views should be analyzed but not espoused, I cannot agree that the academy is the *only* place where teaching—or otherwise developing, applying, or transmitting the tools of analysis—can take place. Were Fish to grapple seriously with Rawls's idea of justice, with which he seems to be familiar, he would have to confront the compelling view that creating an effective public and democratic culture depends precisely on the extent to which the reasonable habits of mind Fish values are spread throughout society in order to offset the passions generated by conflicting comprehensive doctrines and beliefs. As I have already suggested, Fish's own career belies his conviction about the desirability of separate spheres. He attempts to wriggle out of the contradiction by claiming that he and the many other academics with access to the public serve merely as "rent-for-a-day" intellectuals. Yet he, like many others, has had a fairly regular public presence over the years. Fish has published several books that have attracted nonacademic readers, and his articles and essays in the nonacademic press and in commercial publications—he has been a frequent contributor to the *New York Times* and the *Wall Street Journal*—amount to more than the manifestations of a "rented" intellectual. By all appearances, he seems to enjoy the arrangement, and this is perfectly understandable. But he ought more readily to encourage company and competition. Indeed, it is true, as Fish claims (quoting Andrew Ross), that the academy is very much a part of the public sphere, involving millions of citizens—students, faculty, and staff alike. But this fact can just as easily support my claim that we need to reach wider sectors of the public with which we have fundamental interests in common as it supports Fish's claim that we need to respect the boundaries that distinguish us from the wider public. The disinterested pursuit of knowledge, the cultivation of the private imagination, and the marginality that these often require, even as preparation for performing more public roles, are immensely valuable and must be defended, but they are not inconsistent with greater involvement in public life. I hope my own off-campus experiences show that it is possible to espouse these very values—disinterested inquiry, cultivating sensibility and imagination, and temporary retreat from direct involvement in overly partisan politics—on a nonacademic but civic terrain among our more thoughtful fellow citizens.

Arguably, the past two decades have seen something of an example of what I am advocating in the public poetry movement. These efforts have not often resulted in publicly engaged *scholarship* per se, which requires that the scholar add to the body of knowledge shared by other scholars through oral or written analytical representations. But as public humanities projects, they offer models of the kinds of activities that might be the basis for engaged scholarship (see chapter 8). The public poetry movement includes, among other things, poetry (and, more recently, storytelling) slams; the Favorite Poem Project; poetry in the subways, in hotel rooms (in which inexpensive volumes of Whitman or Dickinson are placed alongside the Bible), and in the glove compartments of new Volkswagen Beetles; the phenomenal popularity of hip-hop; and the success of accessible poets like Billy Collins and Ted Kooser (with his syndicated poetry column). I would argue that the effort has been a valuable one: it has brought good poetry to tens of thousands of people who had not cared as much about good poetry before, and it has probably exposed many thousands to better poetry than they had encountered before. There are limitations to these public activities, of course. Clearly, they have not always or even often supported the best poets and poetry as judged by other poets and critics, and as James Longenbach persuasively argues in *The Resistance to Poetry,* perhaps something valuable has been threatened, if not lost, by these efforts: poetry's recalcitrance and resistance to the facile enjoyment that makes for too-easy consumption. As Longenbach writes, "It's difficult to complain about poetry's expanding audience, but it's more difficult to ask what a culture that wants poetry to be popular wants poetry to be. The audience has by and large been purchased at the cost of poetry's inwardness: its strangeness, its propensity to defeat its own expectations, its freedom to explore new (or old) linguistic avenues without necessarily needing to worry about economic success."[28] But must this be the inevitable result of a more public place for encountering poetry? I think not, and here I part company with Longenbach, whose concerns I share most profoundly but whose impatience with the possibilities of poetry in public I think is excessive. There are surely ways to carve out a place in the public experience and discussion of poetry that does not surrender to bombast, reductionism, or immediate accessibility but, rather, insists on making a space for the very features Longenbach rightly claims are essential to a great deal of poetry worth reading. Many of us struggle mightily to create just such a space in the classroom, and though it takes time, ingenuity, and patience, we manage. Choosing a more public venue for the presentation of serious poetry requires many of these same teaching skills and techniques, and once implemented, enough people will respond to them favorably to make the effort worthwhile. In my own public involvement, some of which I describe in later chapters, I have found that once made to feel sufficiently comfortable, many people relish the opportunity publicly to explore inward feelings and thoughts by poems (or any other art forms) that offer the same. I do not want to minimize the difficulties and distractions, but meaningful interactions can be achieved, and they can occur all the more frequently if the profession makes a serious commitment to encouraging them through fresh and creative public projects that involve teaching, scholarship, or both.

To some readers, it may seem as though I am advocating a wholesale move into cultural studies, perhaps along the lines advocated by Michael Bérubé in *Public Access: Literary Theory and American Cultural Politics* (London, 1994). Indeed, I share much of Bérubé's agenda, which calls for reconsidering higher education's proper place in American society, greater involvement in the broader public sphere, offering an alternative to the incendiary rhetoric and demagoguery that poisons our civil discourse, getting real about actual political circumstances as an alternative to the outsized and irrelevant (or outsized *because* irrelevant) political claims made within the profession, and rendering theoretical insights more accessible and sharing them with nonacademics. But I differ from Bérubé, at least in part, regarding the nature of publicly engaged scholarship. First, I do not equate it with cultural studies, a scholarly mode that, for all its various strands, has more or less rejected aesthetic experience and judgment as wholly inconsistent with the project it has taken on from its inception: exposing the dynamics of cultural and ideological power and the hierarchies it imposes. Consequently, there have been precious few cultural studies projects that have displayed much interest in aesthetic experience as something irreducible to politics or ideology, in the manner and mode of aesthetic judgment, in the standards applied therein, in the distinctions and discriminations so vital to ordinary citizens, in the spirituality often entailed in encounters with beautiful things, in the restorative powers of art, or in just about anything that does not lead directly to some encompassing effort of unmasking the political or ideological enemy. I think it fair to say that too many cultural studies projects have taken the path of advocacy, by which I mean that their agendas have been tailored to direct their readers to some preestablished political goal, as opposed to letting the chips fall where they may politically so long as the process of the inquiry and interaction produces understanding that may or may not directly endorse a particular political position or agenda. This said, I acknowledge my position to be political insofar as it posits a mild but nonetheless significant causal relationship between thoughtful, respectful dialogue among free citizens and the habits of mind that lead to liberal and progressive outcomes that I as a citizen support. But this is not to espouse advocacy under the name of scholarship, as Bérubé does by grounding his entire project in the partisan need to combat the spreading right-wing assault of the midnineties. By explicitly defining a renewed and more public cultural studies agenda as oppositional rather than as constitutive of broadly democratic values, he seems to erase the difference between scholarship and advocacy, though he admirably distances himself from the sometimes narrow leftism of the academy. All of this said, a revitalized cultural studies framework that values the experiences it has too often dismissed in the past would add immensely to new possibilities for the profession as a whole.

The same problem now confronts Imagining America, which must decide whether it wants to be a professional advocacy group or a professional group of public scholars. Apparently to keep peace within its ranks, it seems in no rush to decide: the issue is only informally discussed and debated among members and has not been directly addressed. A number of its leading members have involved themselves in local projects with fairly explicit political agendas, and they have indeed done interesting and effective work. But if Imagining America as an organization becomes associated with partisan public engagement, I do not think it will ever have the impact it must with regard to the academic humanities as a whole. It will cater to a relatively small constituency of committed activists, but without serious aspirations to transform the academy, it will founder and eventually die a slow and obscure death. Most of our colleagues in the humanities are skeptical of mixing scholarship and advocacy, and well they should be, because it is hard to maintain the high standards of the first when there are no restraints on the second. Imagining America needs to address the academic humanities as a whole with its legitimate concerns and carefully create a scholarly agenda that will appeal to a broad range of scholars everywhere. Thus far, some of the organization's otherwise very helpful publications spend a little too much time preaching to the converted rather than rigorously addressing the legitimate reservations of traditional scholars with persuasive historical and philosophical arguments. This said, the organization is to be commended for its ambitious agenda of visiting more and more campuses to work with sympathetic faculty and administrators in the effort to transform the academic humanities.[29] Its Tenure Team Initiative, in particular, is making significant progress toward strengthening public scholarship by encouraging colleges and universities to revise their tenure and promotion policies.

One obvious way to accomplish this would be to embrace and encourage the many academics that now serve at least in part in the capacity of public intellectual; that is, they address the common reader on issues of public concern through print or electronic media. Unfortunately, there are some within Imagining America who consider the vital contributions of public intellectuals past and present to be elitist in nature because, by talking *at* the public rather than *with* the public, they fail to create a sustained reciprocal relationship with their audience. This is a terribly provincial and self-limiting understanding of public intellectuals and what they have brought to the public conversation since Socrates. It has emphatically not been unidirectional communication (unless, of course, the state or some other entity shuts the conversation down) but has, to the contrary, been an invitation and at times a challenge to engage in further thought and dialogue, both public and private, without any particular terminal point. To characterize the role of public intellectuals as essentially unilateral is gravely to misunderstand the process by which ideas and judgments are distributed among readers and either accepted or rejected by them. Certainly, there have been differences in the degree of audience responsiveness and empowerment depending on historical circumstance and institutional arrangement, but awareness of these differences should not cause us to want to foreclose or otherwise diminish public intellectual work. If there have been public intellectuals who have lorded it over their audiences or who have defended or submitted to undeserving authority, the response must not be to retreat or somehow purify the politics of our public encounters; the response must be to add to the history of distinguished and independent intervention by public intellectuals whose contributions, regardless of immediate political outcome, improve the quality of discourse and thereby enhance the democratic features and functions of our civil society to better the chances of being human in a collective.

CHAPTER 3

Post-9/11: Why the Public Needs Literary Critics

After 9/11, I, like many of my colleagues, questioned the value of teaching novels in the midst of what seemed like apocalypse. Now, nearly a decade later, the thought of consulting literature for insight seems far less futile. Indeed, it seems crucial if we are to understand who we are as a people and how we have changed; how we have identified, understood, and fought our enemies; and whether the quality of our discussions and deliberations has been commensurate with our great need for knowledge and wisdom. This last consideration prompts the question whether the popular press and media, which, for better or worse, have profoundly shaped our conversations, have served us well. Many will agree they have not—that the national crisis of the past decade, instead of evincing fresh ideas and nuanced thinking about the baleful state of the world today, led to the diminution of serious ideas in the popular press and media.

In 2006, we marked the fifth anniversary of 9/11. It was also the second anniversary of an event hardly observed but, in its symbolic way, meaningful: the demise of the *New York Times* Arts & Ideas section (1997–2004). (Of course, today things have gotten even worse, as newsrooms shrink and entire newspapers are folding at an alarming rate.) The death of Arts & Ideas was not widely mourned; Lee Siegel no doubt spoke for many when he called the section "a weekly banana peel dropped in the path of human intelligence."[1] As an admirable but ultimately failed attempt by the *Times* to add some considered thinking to the prevailing welter of opinion and polemic, the project reminds us of how far we remain from what Ralph Ellison once called "the creation of conscious, articulate citizens . . . [as] an established goal of our democracy."[2]

The failure of the press to provide a critical counterpoint to the Bush administration's continuous mendacity has been much commented on, but it is part of a larger problem, the reluctance of the popular press and its owners to invest in the public's diminishing capacity—because of diminished opportunity—for serious thought. The popular press has rarely been the source of innovative, complex ideas, but we should expect at least its best portion to make challenging ideas available to its readers. Unfortunately, this was only rarely the case during the early years of the so-called war on terrorism. The press's willingness to confirm unexamined assumptions about ourselves and our enemies tarnished our democracy and made us less secure in the process. Susan Faludi has exhaustively probed some of the cultural roots of this disaster in *The Terror Dream: Myth and Misogyny in an Insecure America,* where she pillories the post-9/11 media chatter about "the death of irony and postmodernism" and the "cacophony of chanted verities" about the virtues of John Wayne and cowering "security moms" meant that America sought refuge in "centuries-deep reflexes" instead of honest confrontations with reality.

A representative instance of the problem—and one of particular concern to literary types like us—was an article published in the *New York Times* on September 22, 2001, only days after the attack on the World Trade Center towers and the Pentagon, with the lurid title "Novelists Gaze into Terror's Dark Soul." The piece dominated the front page of the now defunct Arts & Ideas section, and it included a color drawing of a ghostly figure lurking behind a short shelf of books, along with the teaser "A century ago, James, Conrad, and Dostoevsky warned their readers about violence." The article went on to offer misleading accounts of all three novelists. It exaggerated the degree to which they portrayed terrorists as purely evil, and it ignored their depiction of deeply flawed conventional societies poorly protected by inept law enforcement officials and ineffectual counterterrorist measures. The article reduced nuanced novelistic treatment to a vapid allegory of darkness and light, good and evil. With its motif of monomaniacal monsters bent on gratuitous violence, it strengthened fearful habits of mind exploited by an administration whose emerging policies would soon lead the nation on a reckless global search-and-destroy mission against poorly read, poorly understood threats. Of course, literary misreadings had nothing to do with Bush's war on terrorism, but the war on terrorism may have been a misreading of another—and far more destructive—kind. The *Times* thereby missed a crucial opportunity early in the aftermath of 9/11 to encourage sober and subtle thinking about highly volatile matters, certainly no easy task, but all the more wanted when New Yorkers could still smell the smoke. When emotions are raw and the rush of events is nearly overwhelming, journalists and intellectuals face the ultimate public challenge, a challenge literature is perhaps uniquely equipped to meet, when well understood.

The article's title was certainly evocative enough, and after lures about a suicide bomber and Tom Clancy, it reassured its readers that for all three novelists, "terrorism was a futile activity, its violence doomed to redound on the terrorists themselves. In their books, terrorists bungle jobs, blow themselves up, are murdered and commit suicide." Yet for each of these writers, terrorism was not the product simply of "dark souls," "pure evil," psychopathology, or incompetence, it was a broad social and moral problem whose roots were tangled within the very soil that gave rise to the whole society. Fyodor Dostoevsky, who wrote incisively about Russian nihilists in his 1871–72 novel *Demons* (known as *The Possessed* to readers who grew up on Constance Garnett), blamed Western materialism, atheism, and liberalism for causing such social disorder that portions of Russia's rootless intelligentsia embraced nihilist terror as a revolutionary strategy. Henry James, in *The Princess Casamassima*, placed a largely invisible conspiracy at the fringes of a Europe in such a state of rottenness as to suggest that a violent end may not have been wholly unwarranted. In *The Secret Agent*, Joseph Conrad's corrosive irony was largely directed at government officials who were supposed to protect the public from terrorists. The *Times* article's discussion of the novel was seriously flawed, in part because it misunderstood or misrepresented a basic plot element by suggesting that anarchists, rather than an operative at the Russian embassy, masterminded the plot to bomb the Royal Observatory in Greenwich.

For its authority, the article relied on scholars whose brief quotations seemed to lend legitimacy to its claims, but in at least some cases, their admirably discriminate scholarship, never explored in depth, actually belied the drift of the article and the very points their own decontextualized words were marshaled to support. Thus, the article quoted Edward Said, who two days earlier had observed in a piece for *Al-Ahram Weekly* that the anarchist leader in *The Secret Agent*, an American known as "the Professor," is "the portrait of the archetypal terrorist." But Said's essay was in fact an informed and passionate appeal for rhetorical restraint in the face of what he claimed were the already prevalent "Manichean symbols and apocalyptic scenarios" that saturated the American media.[3] Lionel Trilling was quoted to support the author's claim that the politics of the chief conspirator in *The Princess Casamassima*, Hoffendahl, are a "sham," because, in Trilling's words, "there is no organized mass movement; there is no disciplined party but only a strong conspiratorial center. There are no plans for taking over the state and almost no ideas about the society of the future." But Trilling in fact made no such claim in his much-admired 1948 essay "The Princess Casamassima." His description was meant only to distinguish the features of this earlier, anarchist movement from the later, communist one. Certainly, Trilling was not making invidious comparisons to the detriment of the former, for he was an implacable opponent of Stalinism.

The matter of authenticity was not at issue for Trilling: both movements were real enough as expressions of discontent and as powerful threats to disrupt civil society. In this sense, neither was a sham, and both had to be taken seriously as twisted manifestations of real social problems. They were fake only to the extent that they failed to live up to their stated ideals of opposing autocratic rule, fighting for the interests of the people, and empowering common citizens.

The expert most relied on by the article to provide scholarly ballast was Margaret Scanlan, whose *Plotting Terror: Novelists and Terrorists in Contemporary Fiction* is an admirable account of terror as a subject for writers. But not only does Professor Scanlon's book depart from the perspective of the article; its major goal is to debunk the sensationalized treatments of terrorism that have come to prevail within the mass media. The end of the cold war, she asserts, called for a new "'public enemy number one,' and terrorism stepped into that role. Now it is terrorists who lurk in every shadow, images of terrorist attacks that fill out television screens, and fears of new varieties—nuclear, biological, cyberterrorism—that drive calls for increased surveillance and larger defense budgets." She reminds us that "terrorists succeed when they seize headlines," and the terms of their representation and our understanding are thus often set by popular journalism and the electronic media.[4] Indeed, after the 9/11 attack, the three novels under consideration, suddenly seen as relevant to the times, were widely cited in the media. *The Secret Agent* in particular was referenced over a hundred times in the global media, having been discussed in the *Times* (London), *Time Out, Newsweek,* the *National Review,* the *Toronto Star,* the *Sydney Morning Herald,* the *Belfast News Letter,* the *Manchester Weekly Guardian* (UK), the *Ottawa Chronicle,* and the *Gazette* (Montreal).[5] Scanlon's book further challenges reductive thinking about terrorists by exploring the affinities writers on terrorism find between literary and terrorist plots and between literature and violence. Her perspective contradicts the article's representation of terrorism as an activity lacking any connection to civilized society and thus as wholly alien to conventionally held values and beliefs.

A brief look at these three novels and the public intellectuals who have written about them in the past reveals some very interesting possibilities for engaging the public in a discerning discussion of literature and politics. Reading Dostoevsky, James, and Conrad is more important than ever after 9/11, but only if we get them right.

Dostoevsky's *Demons* is set in a typical Russian town near St. Petersburg, where a group of rootless, cynical young intellectuals become sufficiently alienated from a decayed Russian society, with its self-absorbed and absurd chief denizens, to form a conspiratorial group devoted to terrorist tactics. They plot destruction and violence, and they eventually murder one of their own whom they suspect may reveal them to the authorities. Vladimir Nabokov had a low estimation of the novel—he called it "grand booming nonsense with flashes of genius illuminating the whole gloomy and mad farce."[6] Many critics have thought otherwise, including Irving Howe and Philip Rahv, who considered it to be one of the greatest political novels ever written. In *Politics and the Novel,* Howe acknowledged the pervasiveness of Dostoevsky's ridicule and the novel's "buffoonery" but argued that it nevertheless brilliantly portrays the vicissitudes beneath the order and predictability of ideology, the "great sickness of our times." "No other novelist," asserted Howe, "has dramatized so powerfully the values and dangers, the uses and corruption of systematized thought."[7] Howe went on to explain how, apart from Dostoevsky's own opinions, which often led to the novel's deeply satirical tone, the very process and form of dramatization in *Demons* yielded deep insight. What was unique about the novel, according to Howe, was its author's uncanny ability to distribute his prodigious "feelings of identification" to all his characters, thereby blessing them with full-voiced and unencumbered expression. No character, Howe observed, including the narrator, is given unchecked dominion over the novel.

It is precisely this aspect of Dostoevsky's novel that has attracted the attention of scholars over the past several decades and that is also most germane to the subject of terrorism. The critic most responsible for the attention has been Mikhail Bakhtin, the Russian polymath whose *Problems of Dostoevsky's Poetics* (1929) first examined that author's willingness to allow his characters the necessary autonomy to speak forcefully for themselves rather than have the author, often through an intermediary like the narrator or a major normative character, mitigate that force with explicit opinions and moral judgments meant to influence the reader. To describe Dostoevsky's novel, Bakhtin used the term *polyphonic,* which he came to understand meant achieving the quintessentially "dialogic" quality that defines the novel as a genre. Dostoevsky creates "not voiceless slaves . . . but *free* people, capable of standing *alongside* their creator, capable of not agreeing with him and even rebelling against him."[8] Although Dostoevsky's terrorists (and, I hasten to add, liberals) are indeed loathsome, they are also all-too-human in their self-contradiction, foolishness, and frailty; therefore, they are palpably interesting to us. Dostoevsky opens his characters to one another and, in so doing, opens them to us. Their fascination provokes our exploration into unknown personal landscapes with no center, no essence, "no final truth about people as long as they are alive."[9] We experience his terrorists as incomplete, and if the novel provides a lesson about how we might try to understand the terrorists that beset us today, we would do well to heed its rejection of condemnatory absolutes in favor of an open, "dialogic" disposition.

The *New York Times* article said of Henry James's *The Princess Casamassima* that, along with Conrad's *The Secret Agent,* it "suggests that terrorism represents a perversion of politics toward immoral ends." But this would not seem to distinguish terrorism from other methods of political manipulation and treachery, some of which we are all too familiar with. The novel tells the story of Hyacinth Robinson, an impoverished bookbinder who becomes entangled with a secret society of radicals working for a mysterious German terrorist named Hoffendahl. As a show of solidarity, Robinson agrees to accept an as-yet-unnamed assignment that will likely cost him his life, an assignment that later turns out to be the assassination of a powerful duke. But as Robinson develops a friendship with the Princess Casamassima and her aristocratic friends, who are sympathizers with radical causes but epicureans as well, he reconsiders his commitment to violence as his attraction deepens for what he calls "the monuments and treasures of art, the great palaces and properties, the conquests of learning and taste, the general fabric of civilization as we know it."[10] In the end, he decides that the only honorable solution is to turn his pistol on himself.

The *Times* article emphasized the fact that the conspiratorial group possesses no political agenda, which makes the novel seem "unnervingly up to date." Another analogy with current terrorist crimes is that the assassination of the duke is intended to frighten society rather than actually dismantle it. Both of these observations address the legitimate fear felt by many Americans at the time, but rather than encourage readers to consider the conditions of existence of our implacable new enemies, the article confirmed our prevailing emotions and, in so doing, implied that they were a sufficient response to the crisis. Had the article shown more interest in thwarting predictable tendencies toward intellectual shirking, it might have raised any number of other issues that arise from James's trenchant narrative. These include the dramatic inequities between the privileged and poor made immediate by James's richly evocative descriptions of misery and sumptuous living alike. Class oppression, certainly, must be counted as a chief contributor to the desperation felt by the erstwhile champions of the destitute who make the shabby Sun and Moon tavern a den of conspiratorial iniquity.

Had the *Times* article brought attention to this, readers might have been more apt to inquire into the role that global divisions of wealth and power play in the spread of terror as a weapon against what is perceived to be the impregnable fortress of the West. James was also interested in a subject *Times* readers needed to take seriously: the state of mind and spirit of the individual who commits the terrorist act. As the volunteer risking his life, Hyacinth Robinson undergoes a gradual conversion away from his early enthusiasms, and the causes of his change of heart are themselves instructive in terms of thinking about how to wean impressionable young zealots away from their impulsive commitments. Until very near the end, Robinson maintains that his changed beliefs would not compromise his promise to obey his mysterious leader Hoffendahl, and so, as is apparently the case with many suicide bombers today, the question of honor looms large even when belief may not. Finally, scholars have noted the ubiquity of surveillance and policing in James's London world and have linked these phenomena to the modern state's intervention into the private lives of its citizens.[11] Whether the scene takes place at the notorious Millbank Prison, the seedy Sun and Moon, or the princess's parlor, departures from the norm are observed and recorded with alacrity by all involved, especially those with power. Given what we now know about Abu Ghraib, Guantánamo, attempts to legitimize torture, "rendition" of prisoners to secret jails, warrantless domestic wiretapping, Patriot Act surveillance, and threats against the *New York Times* itself for reporting on the U.S. Treasury Department's monitoring of international banking transactions, is it too much to expect the article to have used the sterling opportunity made available by James's novel to have broached the matter of excessive and obsessive policing?

The *Times* article began its discussion of Conrad's *The Secret Agent* by describing the novel's chief nemesis, the Professor, who, not unlike the similar mysterious figures who now populate the news and haunt our thoughts, "paces the streets of London with a bomb strapped to his chest and is obsessed with creating the perfect detonator." The character is so sinister and obscene that when the *Times* article ambiguously identified the source of the bomb plot on the Royal Observatory, it allowed readers to think it likely that the Professor was the source: "When Verloc, a double agent, infiltrates the Professor's group, he is given the job of blowing up Greenwich Observatory, an assignment he passes along to his trusting half-witted brother-in-law, Stevie." Verloc of course, is not given his assignment by the Professor or anyone else in his group—it is not, in fact, assigned by any anarchist or terrorist. He receives the assignment from Vladimir at the Russian embassy, with the goal being to galvanize British law enforcement aggressively to pursue refugee Russian radicals, a key fact that remains obscure in the article despite mention that Verloc is a double agent.

Indeed, Conrad's anarchists are so indolent and inept that it is hard to imagine them carrying out acts of terror, another important fact neglected by the *Times* piece, which was likely rushed to print and saddled with the task of administering anaesthetics to its reeling readers. Ignored entirely was Conrad's withering representation of terror's sworn enemies, all of whom replace professional duties with personal and unethical motives: Mr. Vladimir, the First Secretary of the Russian embassy, who instigates the plot; Chief Inspector Heat, who pursues the wrong man; the assistant commissioner at the Special Crimes Department, who manipulates the investigation in deference to his wife's close friend the Lady Patroness; Sir Ethelred at the Ministry; and Verloc. Conrad's preoccupation with the corrupt abuses of law enforcement takes up more space in the novel than does his portrayal of the anarchists. Despite widespread belief that the novel is about the shadowy world of anarchists and terrorists, Conrad assaults with equal or greater vigor the unsavory world of counterterrorism. *The Secret Agent* was not the first novel ever written about anarchism and terror, but it was the first novel ever written about counterespionage.[12] Might not this chronicle of failure have had some relevance to what Americans faced in the aftermath of 9/11: an acute awareness that, in the words of Susan Faludi, "the events of that morning told us that we could not depend on our protectors: that the White House had not acted on warnings of an impending attack, that the Federal Aviation Administration had not made safe our airports and planes, that the military had not secured our skies, that the 9/11 dispatchers had not issued the necessary warnings, and that [New York City's] rescue workers, through no fault of their own, could not pluck their fellow citizens from danger—in short, that the entire edifice of American security had failed to provide a shield."[13]

In his 1920 Author's Note to the novel, Conrad sought to defend its accuracy by proudly telling his readers, "A visitor from America informed me that all sorts of revolutionary refugees in New York would have it that the book was written by someone who knew a lot about them."[14] Indeed, until 1919, revolutionaries had been operating rather effectively in the United States: not only had Wall Street and the attorney general's house been dynamited, but so had the homes of other officials and businessmen, and three dozen bombs had been found in the mail in packages addressed to prominent persons. The bomber of the house of attorney general A. Mitchell Palmer died in the explosion. These are the precursors of today's anthrax-laced letters and suicide bombers. But there was another side to the story. Just how many "revolutionary refugees" were left in New York in 1920 remains an open question, because in 1919, U.S. security forces assaulted radicals in the Palmer raids, named after the attorney general, part of the ubiquitous "red scare" of the immediate post–World War I period. Wartime sedition and espionage laws—including the 1917 Espionage Act, with which Rep. Peter King (R-NY) threatened to prosecute the *Times* several years ago—were used to rout anarchists and communists with unannounced raids against their homes and headquarters. On November 8, 1919, Communist offices in New York City were raided and literature was seized; many party members were arrested, and others went underground. As a result of raids undertaken on December 21, 1919, 249 foreign-born "undesirables" were herded onto the steamship *Buford* and deported to the Soviet Union (the ship was sardonically referred to by the conservative press as "the Soviet Ark"). Among the deportees were Emma Goldman and Alexander Berkman. On January 2, 1920, hundreds of agents raided over thirty Communist offices in twenty-three states and arrested or detained without warrant over six thousand people. Hundreds were prosecuted, though few actually served prison time. Despite criticism, even from some conservatives, regarding the scope of the raids and the poor conditions of detention, the attorney general emerged as "the nation's patriotic savior."[15] Given *The Secret Agent's* pointed exposure of official corruption and overzealousness, one appreciates Conrad's prophetic powers in light of this alarming record of repression across the Atlantic.

What examples have we from the past of academics with expertise in these matters serving as public intellectuals? The critic who has been read by the greatest number of Conrad readers has very likely been the forgotten Morton Dauwen Zabel, the original editor of and author of the introduction to Viking's and now Penguin's *The Portable Conrad*. This remains the all-time best-selling single volume of Conrad's work. Born and raised in Minnesota Lake, Minnesota, Zabel took his PhD from Chicago and, during the 1940s, associated himself with the New York intellectual circle, writing several of *Partisan Review*'s most important wartime pieces. In the crisis years of 1940 and 1941, Zabel wrote two key articles for *Partisan Review*. One was on Rimbaud; the other was a strategic, strongly worded, two-part assault on poet and newly appointed librarian of Congress Archibald MacLeish. Entitled "The Poet on Capital Hill," Zabel's essay excoriated the celebrated poet for his indictment of all writers and critics—MacLeish called them "the Irresponsibles"—who did not lend themselves or their work to the causes of democracy and antifascism. Pointing out that MacLeish's speeches were being printed and distributed by the U.S. Government Printing Office and thus represented a crude and particularly dangerous state-sponsored, semiofficial imposition on artistic and intellectual life, Zabel went on to defend the crucial importance of artistic independence and detachment as a necessary component of any truly democratic political culture. The alternative, he argued, was to be found in the Communist Party's Popular Front and in the slanders of Hitler and Goebbels, where art and ideas were made to conform to political necessity. Zabel's position reflected that of *Partisan Review*'s editors and the New York Intellectuals as a whole, who had conducted a bitter, increasingly successful, and heroic struggle against conformism to dominant points of view, as well as to totalitarian movements—what Orwell referred to generically as "those smelly little orthodoxies."

It was at this time—during the war and during intensive national and ideological debate—that Zabel wrote three essays on Conrad for the liberal *New Republic,* essays Zabel later combined for his introduction to *The Portable Conrad,* which first appeared in 1947 and has been in print ever since. Today, the introduction is likely to strike the average reader as insistently aesthetic in its concerns and therefore frustratingly resistant to the easy application to social issues that currently goes under the name of "relevance." Many academic readers will likely concur but will further consider Zabel's interest in form and technique—what Zabel refers to as Conrad's "honor in craftsmanship and purpose"—as rather quaint at best and ideologically dangerous at worst. It may be worth noting that Zabel began his fifty-page introduction by confronting a similar attitude he found pervasive at the time. "Today," he observed, "when the world in which [Conrad's] tales are set has receded to historic distance and become, with its standards of honor and fidelity, a dimming memory in men's minds, his work may appear to take on the quality of an elegiac memorial to a vanished and simpler order of life."[16] Zabel attributed this change of attitude toward Conrad to the violence and cynicism of the two decades between the wars.

As disruptive as those years were, however, they were but a prelude to the cataclysmic years in which Zabel published his three essays in the *New Republic,* 1940–42. The times seemed to call for a renewed appreciation for Conrad, because at precisely the same moment in time—June and October of 1941—Leavis published in *Scrutiny* the two essays on Conrad inaugurating the project that was to become *The Great Tradition.* Perusing the pages of the *New Republic* reveals just how deeply mired in crisis Zabel's essays were. "Conrad and

His Age," for instance, appeared in the issue of November 16, 1942, whose lead article was an editorial entitled "We Begin!" "This is it," the editors proclaimed, "the American Military offensive has finally been opened. . . . American and British air, land, and naval power are now working together in Africa. . . . We have proved our good faith, and we have taken the first step on the road to victory. The tide of the war has turned." The issue included articles on Hitler, Vichy France, the future of progressive politics in America, and the tasks of the Allied war effort in the developing world. Zabel's other *New Republic* essays competed for space with articles on the Soviet Union as an ally, isolationism, pacifism, antifascism, and Churchill.

Given this highly politicized and even militarized environment, it is tempting to conclude that Zabel's essays on Conrad were meant to provide readers with an aesthetic retreat from the nightmarish ordeal of the history they were living. But Zabel was no aesthete, and in his essays, he took up the formidable task of placing significant pressure on the manner and mode in which that history was being lived. This was *the* project, to be sure, of many in his generation, including his editors at *Partisan Review* and Leavis, who are dismissed by some revisionist literary historians as having been insufficiently politically aware.

What Zabel most valued in Conrad was the novelist's insistence on the centrality of what Montesquieu called *moeurs,* the range of values and beliefs, the habits of mind and the heart, that shape political behavior and institutions. Once we allow ourselves to reimagine the context that gave rise to this broadly political project, we may read the major concerns of Zabel's introduction as challenges to the political orthodoxies of the day—liberal and nonliberal alike. These concerns centered around Conrad's "brutally rigorous sincerity" in the face of "the easy rewards of sentimental provincialism and complacent nationalisms"; his suspicion of abstractions, philosophical and political alike, and his power to penetrate them to find their sources in action, emotion, and mind; his exploration of "the moral impotence and the nihilism of temperament" that remain when existence is suspended in sensation or idealism; his concern for the plight of the unmoored individual, without "the supports of friendship, social privilege, love" or the comforts of patriotic or dissident certitudes; and his "renovations of the form and craft of fiction" that make all of this possible.

Neither these particular understandings of Conrad's nor their application by Zabel to the political exigencies of wartime America have been of great interest to Conrad scholars these past several decades, nor were they of any interest to the author of the *Times* article. But as Mark Lilla observed, describing Raymond Aron's views in an essay entitled "The Lure of Syracuse" published in the *New York Review of Books* only days before the *Times* article, there is a great need for intellectuals to "bring whatever expertise they [have] to bear on liberal-democratic politics . . . —in short, to be independent spectators with a modest sense of their roles as opinion-makers and citizens."[17] Doing so would, on the one hand, provide alternatives to the varieties of hermetic, antistatist, and sometimes sectarian analytical modes that prevail in parts of the academy today; it would give us, in fact, the opportunity to test the findings of forty years of theoretical inquiry in the context of live political and ideological exigencies. On the other hand, bringing intellectual expertise to bear on politics in this way would provide alternatives to the often-empty pretenses of reading and analysis found in the popular media, in favor of genuine interpretive acts.[18]

If the popular media promotes Conrad in its ideological battles, others demote him in theirs. As I have suggested, for many, Conrad was too ambiguous in his judgments and too unpolitical in his metaphors. But these features illuminate his strengths, not his weaknesses. This is something we are perhaps better placed to understand now. As Tony Judt has pointed out, thanks to Primo Levi and Vaclav Havel, some have become familiar with the "gray zone." Some understand better that in conditions of extremity, there are rarely to be found comfortingly simple categories of good and evil, guilty and innocent. Some know more about the choices and compromises faced by men and women in hard times and are no longer so quick to judge those who accommodate themselves to impossible situations. Democratic societies, if they are to thrive, must attend to the quality of their discourse, measured by the degree to which they are capable of facing up to the actual moral and political complexities they encounter. The legacy of these three novelists—Dostoevsky, James, and Conrad—offers us a model of that quality and that complexity.

The pattern of avoiding the considerably complex and emotionally charged problems raised by these three novelists is not only to be found in the various rationales that were offered to support George W. Bush's foreign policy. Such a pattern also foreshadowed problems with the American press's subsequent coverage of the war on terrorism and the lead-up to the war in Iraq. Thanks partly to portions of the press corps that belatedly came out of hibernation and criticized their own behavior and partly, of course, to the Obama administration's change of policy, the American public is slowly coming around to believing that the Bush administration, in the name of fighting terrorism, waged one war of likely necessity and one war of choice for stated reasons that have been shown to be spurious and even illegal. In the commission

of these wars, it secured legislation that curtailed citizens' rights, and it engaged in law enforcement practices and legal maneuvering that many consider
unconstitutional. As Michael Massing amply demonstrated in *Now They Tell
Us* and as the *Times* and the *Washington Post* have themselves partially acknowledged, the press failed in its responsibility to keep the public informed
with independent, critical coverage of the Bush administration's policies. The
Times, the *Post*, and others relied far too much on sources sympathetic to the
Bush administration, while ignoring or diminishing dissenting views. The
Times virtually ignored the findings of both the International Atomic Energy
Agency, led by Hans Blix, and the United Nations Monitoring, Verification,
and Inspection Commission, led by Mohamed El Baradei. Nearly all, including
the *Times*, offered glowing accounts of Colin Powell's inferential and thus
flawed and compromised speech to the United Nations on February 5, 2003,
providing a rationale for war against Saddam Hussein. As Massing points out,
even after, on May 26, 2003, the *Times* published a lengthy self-criticism in
which its editor Howell Raines admitted that the prewar coverage "was not as
rigorous as it should have been," the paper was slow to respond to the seriousness of the Abu Ghraib prison abuses in May 2004.[19]

Massing reminds us that as American institutions, U.S. news organizations
covering an American occupation "invariably share certain premises and presumptions about the conflict." Thus, reporters "still tend to frame the conflict in
much the same way that U.S. officials do."[20] This is perhaps even truer when the
conflict appears to many as the global, apocalyptic one that officials call a "war
on terrorism." In the early days of the response to 9/11, some of the premises and
presumptions alluded to by Massing were formed and articulated. The treatment of Dostoevsky, James, and Conrad greatly simplified what these novelists
actually had to say about terrorism and terrorists and ignored what they had to
say about our erstwhile protectors in intelligence and law enforcement. Had
journalists and the public been more familiar with these writers or had the
Times been in the habit of publishing regular articles by literary critics and
scholars outside the book review section or the occasional essay in the *New York
Times Magazine* (as do many leading European newspapers), the paper would
have better equipped its readers to understand the troubling complexities we
faced as a nation. This is not to gainsay the fact that the *Times* gave space, usually on Sunday, to scholars and literary figures to contemplate literary and other
responses to 9/11. A day after the article in question, in fact, the magazine published an excellent essay by Richard Powers on the language of 9/11 reporting,
entitled "The Way We Live Now: 9-23-01: Close Reading: Elements of Tragedy;

The Simile." But these efforts were only intermittent and, moreover, functioned most often as metajournalistic correctives rather than as examples of normal journalism contributing regularly to the national conversation.

Obviously, daily newspapers operate quickly, and that is not going to change. Surely, 9/11 set the rhythms at a particularly frantic pace. The *Times* article and the many other journalistic treatments of literature dealing with terror suggest that if editors are not given the wherewithal to release their staff writers from other assignments in order to produce reliable literary journalism—if, in other words, under the circumstances, it proves impossible to give staff writers sufficient time to read novels carefully and familiarize themselves with relevant biographical, historical, and critical material—then newspapers ought to invite qualified critics and scholars to write these pieces. Certainly, when it comes to the three novels in question, scholars adept at writing for the educated public would be in a very good position to demonstrate how these narratives increase our understanding of our current dilemmas. They just have to be asked. Once asked, they need the support of institutions of higher learning that value and reward publicly engaged scholars.

CHAPTER 4

Lionel Trilling as Public Intellectual

Columbia University Press's recent decision to publish an early draft of an unfinished, untitled novel by Lionel Trilling is a welcome reminder that the critic and novelist who loomed so large in American culture until the 1970s continues to have a hold, at least on some of us. Although Trilling's influence is limited, he is admired by literary journalists and by those within the academy who address public issues and a public audience. But certainly for the vast majority of traditional academic scholars and their students, Trilling is a name from the past that connotes a moral and mandarin style of belles lettres that was swept aside by the theory revolution of the past half century. Of this I can testify with firsthand evidence. A few years ago, I had occasion to teach a graduate seminar on the New York Intellectuals; I assigned a dozen or so of Trilling's most influential essays and devoted a three-hour class to discussing them. After my students had completed the reading, but before the discussion began, I asked them each to write a paragraph on whether they thought Trilling would be an important critic for them in their future academic career. Here are several unedited samples of the responses I received.

> I think that Trilling's value lies in his ability to give compelling individual snapshots of ideas and literary works: his definition of "manners" is not only beautifully articulated, but has the ring of truth. Likewise, his intervention into debates on Dreiser and James in "Reality in America" is illuminating, particularly for the way he reminds us that style is not merely ornamental, but fundamentally generative of a writer's project. But I think that ultimately his concern with morality and literature is not a terribly useful approach to criticism—it seems a holdover from a cold war political mindset. Whether a book has significant "moral" qualities is not a question that leads us to understanding a text's place within cultural modes of production and political discourse. . . . Our work has shifted to cultural theorization and the understanding of systematic relations of the literary within and to a complex of social networks; the individual and isolated consideration of texts and authors practiced by Trilling doesn't seem immediately relevant.

I do think Trilling's use of nuances could be useful, and that his style could serve as a model for writing critical essays that are articulate and forceful. At the same time, most of his content does seem outdated, or at least dated. His interest in psychoanalysis is irrelevant today, and so is his insistence on an objective morality. He is fascinating as an historical figure and a historical intellectual, but the urgency of his writing then does not translate into urgency for me now.

I study Naturalist/Progressive Era writing. Trilling is dismissive of both. His unvarnished elitism discounts everything I love about late 19th–early 20th-century writing. Despite his contributions to the field as a whole, there is no reason to ever refer to him in my work.

I think it likely that my students would have written somewhat differently about Trilling had I asked them the same question *after* our seminar. I would hope that I succeeded at least in part in disabusing them of some of their notions regarding his understanding of morality, his elitism, and his irrelevance to students of late nineteenth-century and early twentieth-century writing. But although I probably corrected these several errors, I do not think I altered very dramatically their sense that Trilling could not reasonably be considered an important critic today. At seminar's close, I could not help but compare my students to the ones Trilling famously described in "On the Teaching of Modern Literature" who looked into the abyss depicted by modernist writers and casually assimilated the cataclysmic chaos they saw there. Whereas Trilling's students had responded to fierce moral, political, and artistic utterance with nonchalant acceptance, mine had responded with too-easy skepticism. As I considered my students' responses with growing distress, I was unsettled by the thought that I might rather have been teaching Trilling's students.

Anyone who has been teaching in the profession these past few decades will know why my students consider Trilling so alien. Upon his death in 1975, there was no living American literary critic whose standing both inside and outside the academy was higher, but this judgment soon changed dramatically, as continental modes of specialized and professionalized literary theory swept literary studies. Within a decade, Trilling's name had all but disappeared from the syllabus, and it was left to a platoon of prominent public critics—Louis Menand, Leon Weiseltier, David Bromwich, Lee Siegel, and David Remnick, to name a few—to continue in his line and keep his name alive within the public sphere. These have been decades that began in heady excitement but ended,

too often, in moribund scholasticism. What began as an apparent further exploration of the subjects Trilling and the New York Intellectuals dwelt on—the
intersection of literature and politics; the nature and role of popular culture;
the vicissitudes of ideology; and manners, morals, money, and class—what
Emerson called in "History" a "knot of roots whose flower and fruitage is the
world"—these concerns slowly devolved into increasingly hermetic considerations of texts and ideology with no discernible reference to constituencies,
movements, parties, or institutions outside the Byzantine world of disciplinary
politics.

I can recall reading Althusser on ideology and wondering what the com-
motion was, for Trilling had handled the issue of ideology in superior fashion
in "Manners, Morals, and the Novel." Althusser's formulation, "Ideology is a
'representation' of the imaginary relationship of individuals to their real conditions of existence,"[1] despite seeming to be a revelation to many, always struck
me as flawed by the same buried scientism, overly cognitive bias, and crude sociology characteristic of the doctrinaire notions of ideology it was meant to replace. Compare Trilling: ideology "is the habit or ritual of showing respect to
certain formulas ... [to which] we have very strong ties of whose meaning and
consequences in actuality we have no clear understanding."[2] Trilling preferred
to discuss "manners," or

> a culture's hum and buzz of implication. I mean the whole evanescent context
> in which its explicit statements are made. It is that part of a culture which is
> made up of half-uttered or unuttered or unutterable expressions of value. . . .
> They are hinted at by small actions, sometimes by the arts of dress or decora-
> tion, sometimes by tone, gesture, emphasis, or rhythm. . . .In this part of cul-
> ture assumption rules, which is often much stronger than reason.[3]

Trilling's idea makes it impossible to know the operations of manners, or ideology, without immersion in a given culture, and it rules out the condescending notion that all but the privileged few who are privy to the "real" conditions
of existence are the benighted bearers of false consciousness.

I recall also reading Gramsci appreciatively on hegemony and preferring
the Trilling of "The Fate of Pleasure," in which, as part of a limpid discussion
of Werner Sombart's *Luxury and Capitalism,* he commented on "the growing
tendency of power to express itself mediately, by signs or indices, rather than
directly, by the exercise of force."[4] Or, finally, I recall again reading Gramsci,
this time on "organic" versus "traditional" intellectuals, and sensing a greater

understanding in Trilling of the multiple possibilities available to intellectuals in the modern setting that a binary model such as Gramsci's could not accommodate. In "The Function of the Little Magazine" and in his response to the famous 1952 *Partisan Review* symposium "Our Country and Our Culture" (later expanded and published as an essay entitled "The Situation of the American Intellectual at the Present Time"), Trilling offered a cautious appreciation for the opportunities available to the critical intellectual who chose to address the world of experience available to most American citizens rather than posing against that world as an advocate of an alternative one.

Trilling's remarkable response to the *Partisan Review* symposium was a very un-Trillingesque statement, at least according to the way the adjective *Trillingesque* has been understood by critics who like to emphasize his remoteness, his mandarinism, and, in the words of Ann Douglas, his "omnivorously elegiac prose."[5] In point of fact, Trilling's response was very nearly Whitmanesque in its appeal for communion, or adhesiveness, between intellectuals and what he actually calls "one's own people."

> There comes a moment when the faces, the gait, the tone, the manner and manners of one's own people become just what one needs, and the whole look and style of one's culture seems appropriate, seems perhaps not good but intensely *possible*. What your compatriots are silently saying about the future, about life and death, may seem suddenly very accessible to you, and not wrong. You are at a gathering of people, or you are in a classroom, and, being the kind of unpleasant person you are, you know that you might take one individual after another and make yourself fully aware of his foolishness or awkwardness, and that you might say, "And this is my country! And this is my culture!" But instead of doing that, you let yourself become aware of something that is really in the room, some common intention of the spirit, which, although it may be checked and impeded, is not foolish or awkward but rather graceful, and not wrong. . . . Something of this sort of feeling is, I think, at work among American intellectuals at this time.[6]

Trilling wrote this as a momentous shift was taking place in America, for it was then that the chief agencies of American society—government, finance, industry, media, and the academy—availed themselves of a large new educated class of people with considerable training and intellectual skill. Trilling reminded his readers that although the use to which this immense pool of talent was put was rarely defensible, nonetheless the sociological fact that the place of intellect had changed could not be denied. "Intellect," he bluntly declared, "has associated itself with power, perhaps as never before in history."[7] For this reason alone—his awareness of the incorporation of intelligence in American society and his desire for some sort of adhesion to American actualities—Trilling ought to interest us. It is the reason I think his example has something to contribute to any current reconsideration of what role we might wish to have as academic humanists in the world beyond our campus borders.

These considerations bring me to the unfinished novel *The Journey Abandoned*, a text that portends what would likely have been a novel that beautifully addressed these all-important matters. Of course, we must be cautious when it comes to interpreting a text as partial as this; as Robert Warshow once wrote of Trilling's only complete novel, *The Middle of the Journey*, we should avoid the "tendency to place upon the material a greater weight of meaning than it can bear" (quoted by Geraldine Murphy in her useful introduction). This said, I want to focus on some of the important moral and social issues raised by the novel and to discuss their relevance to the matters I have previously broached. As Murphy observes, this is a novel that above all explores the class and institutional contingencies of intellectual life in midcentury America. It asks what it means to be an academic, what it means to be "a man of letters" (to use the old-fashioned term), and whether the two can be at all compatible. More dramatically, it asks whether the idea of moral integrity is consistent with success. Trilling certainly planned for a novel that would be consistent in this way. He clearly wanted to produce a morally complex novel, but he also wanted to appeal to a broad readership and thus to achieve commercial success. He states in his commentary on the novel that he wants to treat "the profession of the arts" in a matter-of-fact way in order "to make the ordinary reader more at home, less likely to think that he is engaged with a book that has a merely private—professional—reference."[8] To this end, Trilling sought to write what he termed a "less intellectualized, more open" novel than *The Middle of the Journey*.

The characters Trilling has depicted and the unfolding dilemmas they face (or, more accurately, will likely face) suggest a finished novel that would have confronted some morally complex matters with a great deal of subtlety and nuance and, moreover, that would likely have done so by manifesting a greater degree of negative capability than *The Middle of the Journey*, whose anti-Stalinist moral and political stance was unambiguous. Although Popular Front politics remains a concern of Trilling's in *The Journey Abandoned* and comes in for consistently ironic treatment, it does not seem the bête noire it once was.

Rather, the developing drama surrounding Jorris Buxton, the heroic figure modeled on the nineteenth-century poet and man of letters Walter Savage Landor, will inevitably provoke most of the characters, especially Buxton's young biographer Vincent Hammell, the novel's central character, whose shoulder Trilling looks over. Buxton's drama, like Landor's, is precipitated by a romantic relationship between the eighty-year-old humanist and scientist, a man of enormous scholarly distinction, and a teenage girl. It would seem that Buxton, following Landor, will publicly defend himself and the girl, who he believes has been used by a scheming and ambitious caretaker, Claudine Post. Trilling wrote in his preface that a modernized version of these events provided him with the opportunity to explore "what a really heroic person like [Landor] might be in modern America."[9] It is interesting that Trilling would be so taken with Nabokov's *Lolita* a decade or so after producing this partial draft of a novel. In the 1950s, he published the influential essay "The Last Lover," and, apropos the larger matter of public intellectual life, he appeared with Nabokov in a televised discussion of the novel. The fascinating conversation can be viewed on YouTube. Not to put too fine a point on it, Buxton's plight in *The Journey Abandoned* raises issues explored in Philip Roth's recent work, particularly *The Dying Animal.*

What Buxton might be to Vincent Hammell, his biographer, would undoubtedly matter most in the finished novel. Hammell's career parallels Trilling's early career in some important respects. Like Trilling, he is an outsider to academia—because of his midwestern background, his inferior class status, and what may indeed be his own repressed Jewish identity. In their early careers, both teach part time and lecture to nontraditional students from the community. Both write for local newspapers (Trilling wrote twenty-eight reviews for the *New York Evening Post* from December 1927 to September 1929, which I shall explore shortly). Both become involved with literary circles of mostly Jewish students partial to modernism, and both are deeply concerned with the roles of intellectuals. Hammell's chief publication is an essay entitled "The Sociology of the Written Word," described as an account of intellectual life *as* a profession. As Buxton's biographer, Hammell is strategically positioned to observe and meditate on a number of conflicts that illuminate the moral and institutional status of intellectual life in America. His response to Buxton's simmering scandal will force him to take full stock of the subject of his book and wrestle with the changing priorities of Buxton's unusual career, his troubled private life, his sense of honor, his courage, his innocence, and his recklessness. The wisdom of Hammell's own decision to write Buxton's biography will likely hang in the balance and perhaps, in the end, will provide the basis for a revised version of "The Sociology of the Written Word."

The other character who looms large in Trilling's exploration of the possibilities and confinements of intellectual life is Harold Outram, a brilliant scholar who, as Trilling describes it in his preface, has established himself by a "complication of professions." "It is at least a question," continues Trilling, "if he has not made his success by some compromise with his best talents."[10] Outram receives his doctorate in his early twenties, publishes a series of extraordinary essays and a well-received novel while still young, and then becomes the darling of the Left, "the pet of a hundred committees, clubs, leagues, and guilds."[11] He joins the proletarian literary movement but soon renounces the Communist Party and suffers a breakdown. Once recovered, he becomes a successful magazine writer and is then appointed director of the Peck Foundation, where he controls the dispensation of millions of dollars "for the advancement of American culture."[12] What I find most interesting about Trilling's handling of Outram is his apparent commitment to complicating his role. There are several strong clues that suggest Trilling will challenge the established binary behind the sentiment, so pervasive on the left in Trilling's day, that there's no failure like success. The first clue is that the most vehement critic of Outram, the man who most vociferously claims him to be a sellout, is his jealous erstwhile friend, the unsuccessful, unstable, and unreliable academic Teddy Kramer. Whereas Kramer sees Outram as a monster, Hammell's old friend Toss Dodge will not buy the guilty verdict assigned to Outram. By no means a normative character, Toss is nonetheless capable of insight, so his unwillingness to demonize the man who has lost his "integrity" (Trilling's scare quotes) raises real questions. It is impossible to know just who the cautionary figure of the novel will be, but I would argue that given the evidence at hand, Kramer is more likely to be that figure than is Outram.

The Journey Abandoned creates morally complex characters, unfolds dramas, and sounds themes that remind us of why its author should matter to us. Like all of Trilling's work—the fiction and the criticism both—this unfinished novel was meant to appeal to a broad educated audience without compromising taste or judgment. Democratizing culture and deepening liberal habits of mind to Trilling meant imparting a greater capacity to discriminate quality, not a greater tolerance for inferior work. I should add that it is not altogether clear that Trilling would have accomplished this with his novel. I suspect he abandoned the project because he came to realize its technique and style were simply not up to his standards.

Aside from *The Journey Abandoned* and the other work I have alluded to already, there is much else in Trilling's oeuvre with a similar perspective on the scholar or critic or novelist's public role. His famous essay "George Orwell and the Politics of Truth" is nothing if not a celebration of that writer's willingness to immerse himself in the lives of ordinary Englishmen because "he is not happy in the institutionalized life of intellectuality."[13] His "passion for the literal actuality of life," in Trilling's words, resembles that shown by the great nineteenth-century working-class leader William Cobbett in Cobbett's *Rural Rides*.[14] Among Orwell's books Trilling most admired were *Down and Out in Paris and London* and *The Road to Wigan Pier,* both of which describe the author's experiences living among working people. One is reminded that Trilling, as Thomas Bender has noted, did not publicly identify himself as an academic in *Partisan Review* until 1942, preferring the identities of "critic," "novelist," and "teacher," in that order.

There is the famous revisionary essay "William Dean Howells and the Roots of Modern Taste," which sought to revive a reputation scorned by those whose apocalyptic politics and taste for the tragic in literature caused them to condescend to a writer who had the unmitigated gall to direct his fellow writers to concern themselves with "the more smiling aspects" of American life. As Leon Wieseltier points out in his fine introduction to the selection of Trilling essays entitled *The Moral Obligation to Be Intelligent,* Trilling ardently praised Howells for devoting many chapters of a novel to its hero's hunt for an apartment. Earlier, of course, in one of his most influential essays, "Parrington, Mr. Smith, and Reality" (subsequently given the less polemical title "Reality in America"), Trilling had dealt a knockout blow to the reputation of Theodore Dreiser, but in doing so, he nonetheless praised Dreiser for having "the saving salt of the American mind, the lively sense of the practical, workaday world, of the welter of ordinary undistinguished things and, of the tangible, quirky, unrefined elements of life. He knew what so many literary historians do not know, that emotions and ideas are the sparks that fly when the mind meets difficulties."[15] Today, having come to terms with Dreiser but not with Trilling, we tend to forget that Trilling said such a thing. Last, there is Trilling's extraordinary biography of Matthew Arnold, still definitive, whose insistent engagement with issues of Trilling's own day—namely, anti-Semitism and fascism—continues to surprise and please.

I want to mention as well an important but overlooked project that Trilling undertook in 1951 in partnership with W. H. Auden and Jacques Barzun, the founding of the Readers' Subscription Book Club, which, after folding in 1963, was revived until, alas, in our own time, it succumbed, perhaps to return at a time more favorable to publishing and reading. The club's pitch, written by Auden, went as follows: "Poets and Professors and all those whose love of books exceeds their love of automobiles will welcome a chance to save in excess of 50 percent on their book purchases." As Jacques Barzun has reminded us, this was no grassroots affair. It started from the business end of things, and its primary purpose was to increase the sales of books. During the eleven years they wrote for the club, Auden, Barzun, and Trilling produced some 173 reviews and essays. I have not made a count of Trilling's contributions, but they number in the dozens. They cover novels, poetry, plays, history, art, and film, and they are written in an informal, relaxed, and sometimes quite personal manner, unlike his more vaunted essays. In "Remembering Lionel Trilling," Jacques Barzun recalls "taking in stride" Trilling's entreaty to "disseminate good books," for Trilling never regarded the general public with scorn. On the contrary, he directed his remonstrances at those of his fellow professors who lacked appreciation for the denizens and the dignities of ordinary life.

That these views were held by Trilling throughout his career is evidenced by over two dozen book reviews he wrote very early in it, from July 1927 to September 1929, for the *New York Evening Post,* compensation for which helped pay the rent while he was a graduate student, part-time teacher, and, as of June 12, 1929, husband to Diana Trilling. Much, of course, has been made of Trilling's concurrent contributions to the *Menorah Journal,* for here, many critics and literary historians have claimed, one can observe early evidence of Trilling's rejection of *Yiddishkeit* and, indeed, all forms of ethnic Jewish experience that discouraged, in Trilling's view, a genuinely cosmopolitan cultural perspective. But we may want to add to the interest in Trilling's relationship to Judaism a concomitant and apposite interest in his connections to the broader public, which of course included Jews; in this regard, these early reviews, so far as I know heretofore uncollected and unexamined, provide a rich resource for understanding the young critic's formative disposition regarding audience and his responsibilities as a critic.

The *New York Evening Post*—since 1993, Rupert Murdoch's *New York Post*—is the thirteenth oldest newspaper and the oldest continually published daily in the United States. It was established in 1801 by Alexander Hamilton and a group of Federalist Party investors, and for fifty years, beginning in 1829, it was edited by William Cullen Bryant, who made the paper a sanctuary of accomplished writing by featuring contributors such as Margaret Fuller in the 1840s and, later, Walt Whitman. Under the helm of E. L. Gotkin, the paper continued to support liberal causes and began the 1920s as a venerable liberal broadsheet. That tendency was temporarily interrupted in 1924, when the *Evening Post* was purchased by Cyrus Curtis, the conservative publisher of the *Ladies Home Journal*, who eventually, though only briefly, turned it into a sedate tabloid in 1933. J. David Stern then purchased the paper in 1934, changed its name to the *New York Post*, and restored its broadsheet size and liberal perspective. During the two years Trilling contributed to the paper, it continued its long-standing interest in the arts by including among its several cultural features a two- to three-page Literary Review section each Saturday, which included alongside Trilling reviewers such as Conrad Aiken, Clifton Fadiman, Kenneth Fearing, Muriel Rukeyser, Edwin Seaver, Tess Slesinger, and Herbert Solow.

What can we gather about Trilling's priorities as a young critic during these years? At the time, his main preoccupation was his graduate work in the Columbia University English Department, which eventually culminated in a doctoral dissertation on Matthew Arnold, published in 1939 as his first book. So it is no surprise that among his twenty-eight reviews for the *Evening Post*, he took on a disproportionate number of biographies and English writers, especially of the nineteenth century.[16] These included biographies of Thomas Lovell Beddoes, Aphra Behn, Robert Browning, Robert and Elizabeth Barrett Browning, Charles Dickens, Thomas Hardy, Samuel Richardson, Stendhal, Algernon Swinburne, and William Makepeace Thackeray. He reviewed seventeenth-century lyric poets; fiction by Philip Guedalla, H. H. Munro (Saki), Wyndham Lewis, and Virginia Woolf; and a critical study of English romanticism. Trilling devoted six reviews to European writers (Thomas Mann, Marcel Proust, Baruch Spinoza, Stendhal, and two to Comte de Gobineau), one review to several studies of aesthetics, and only five reviews to American writers (Joseph Auslander, Roger Burlingame, Clinch Calkins, Mathilde Eiker, and Glenway Wescott).

In *Intellect and Public Life*, which provided a critical context for my discussion in chapter 2, Thomas Bender devotes a chapter to Trilling, in which he claims that the critic no longer presents us with a model of compelling public intellectual work because he reached out exclusively to the middle class. Though Trilling spoke of variety and pluralism, "it was variety without real difference. Society was, for him, universally middle class."[17] Bender is not alone in registering his dissatisfaction with what he regards as Trilling's limited public audience—over the years, Joseph Frank, Cornel West, Ann Douglas, and others have leveled similar charges.[18] Such complaints are perplexing for a number of reasons. First, they do not present the alternatives available to Trilling at the time. Whom among America's literary and cultural critics *were* reaching a more diverse audience? It was surely not the critics who aspired to reach a working-class audience by associating themselves with the *New Masses* and the proletarian literary movement. Neither the *New Masses* nor any other "working-class" magazine at the time ever reached much of the working-class audience to which they aspired. Did critics of color? Richard Wright and, a bit later, Ralph Ellison and James Baldwin never gained a large working-class audience, and it is improbable that their reviews and essays reached an audience made of a significantly higher percentage of African Americans than did Trilling and other New York Intellectuals. Second, as for Trilling's characteristic preoccupations as a cultural critic, here his interests did indeed coincide with those of the great middle class as he understood it. Undoubtedly, these interests might have been broader. But as an academic, Trilling was exceptional in *having* extra-academic interests and, moreover, in granting to them the priority he did. This brings me to my third reason to question Trilling's critics: just how persuasive can academic critics be who carp about another critic's limited audience yet are themselves ensconced within their institutions and have no broad middle-class readership? I see no reason to be persuaded by scholars with *few* readers who begrudge Trilling his productive proximity to *many* readers because they were not *most* readers. It would seem to me to be more consistent and logical for advocates of public engagement to credit a critic such as Trilling for successfully crossing a barrier that has confined so many post–World War II academic critics and to direct their discussions of his limitations to the challenges we face in attempting to go beyond him. In 1929, the *Evening Post* was among the smallest of the New York City dailies, with a circulation of 107,678—by comparison, the circulation of the *Daily News* in that year was 1,224,243; the *Herald Tribune,* 419,488; the *Times,* 418,687; and the *Sun,* 307,707.[19] Nonetheless, Trilling's reviews reached a very substantial number of readers—far in excess of what all but a few of today's academics are able to reach. As Herbert Croly, founder and editor of the *New Republic,* observed, publics are made and unmade, and the job of the intellectual intent on encouraging civic discourse is to make a public rather than find one ready-made. In these reviews, the young Trilling set about the task that would consume him throughout his career.

When you read Trilling's reviews today, you encounter the occasional snooty passage that makes you worry about elitism and sexism. In his review of Mathilde Eiker's *Over the Boat-Side,* for example, he makes reference to "that dreariest of genres, the female literature of marriage," and his condescension is palpable when he remarks, "Miss Eiker attempts wit, and if her attempt is seldom successful, it seldom sinks much below smart geniality."[20] But in reading these reviews, you also marvel at the sophistication newspapers once allowed and the respect Trilling showed his readers. The reviews are replete with quotation, many rather extensive; the issues Trilling raises are complex, even scholarly, but they are always posed so that lay readers might understand the stakes involved; and the judgments of quality are frequent and refined, yet they come with the criteria made explicit. In "A Study of Terror-Romanticism," where Trilling is concerned to overturn the reigning "academic" understanding that the movement "was entirely a new thing," he refers to precedents in the porter scene in *Macbeth,* suspenseful door knocking in Chaucer, the night in *Agamemnon,* bats in John Webster, and haunted castles in *Hamlet* and *Beowulf.*[21] As indicated, biography, then as much a staple of the reading diet as it is today, preoccupied him as he sought to discourage and to avoid in his own work the excesses of faultfinding (he wrote of Vita Sackville-West's biography of Aphra Behn that "modern biography is determined to leave us no ideals at all—not even one of bawdiness") and overpraise ("Mr. Melville, having donned black cotton gloves and having scented himself with embalming fluid, heaps another shovelful of respect on Thackeray's grave").[22] Trilling's taste for Woolf's style in *Orlando* prompts him to list the ingredients: "It is feminine prose, and because it is not ashamed of being that, but proud of it, it is completely successful. It is prose that is conscious and artful (but not precious), very civilized, yet very personal and alive. It has almost entirely what Mrs. Woolf has called 'the most important part of style, the natural run of the voice in speaking.' It has wit and pleasant malice, but they are not sudden and apart from it, like set jewels, but are inherent in it, and do their work swiftly, casually, and unpressingly. It is at ease and yet alert."[23]

In all of this, the critic's commitments to art and artist are nicely balanced by solicitude toward his readers, who he variously refers to as "the intelligent reader," "the general reader," "the ordinary student," "the uninitiated student," and "the layman." With these epithets, Trilling registers awareness of a kind of diversity among his readers, pertaining to degrees of familiarity and acculturation rather than to race, ethnicity, or sexual orientation. I submit that this is a virtue of many good critics (not to mention teachers) and a necessity for journalistic critics, who encounter a broader range of both texts and readers than do critics writing for academic audiences and must adjust their tone and content accordingly. Morris Dickstein is wonderfully precise when he addresses the general requirements of successful reviewing and Trilling's particular achievement.

> In being obliged to meet the reader's immediate needs, the reviewer must create through his or her language what we often fear no longer exists: a community of shared literary values and social concerns. Good book reviewing is always relevant and contemporaneous, never merely antiquarian. Lionel Trilling was sometimes criticized for his use of the first-person plural; but at its frequent best his "we" spoke not for an in-group of the critic and his friends but for an acute sensibility attuned to the rhythms of the Zeitgeist and the nuances of the social mood.[24]

If academic literary and cultural studies are once again to experience the excitement and vitality of the 1970s, when theories and methodologies proliferated and the constricted agenda of the New Criticism was burst asunder, and if the humanities are to end the long hibernation by establishing vital links to the larger world, we could do worse than to look to the writing and practice of Lionel Trilling as a compelling, exemplary model for "elements that are wanted." Today, looking back on the heyday of the New Criticism, followed by its many alternative theoretical and methodological modes of analysis, we in the academy seem farther away than ever from the sort of interaction Trilling espoused. Despite widespread sentiment for and claims on behalf of the interests of marginalized constituencies, we find ourselves without mutually sustaining relations with nonacademic constituencies, movements, or organizations. Regarding our proximity to the broader public (or publics, as some prefer), I do not think our situation is markedly different from Trilling's own, which he described in his 1952 response. "The literary intellectual" (and here, we simply need substitute "the literary academic")

> is ignorant of the channels through which opinion flows. He does not, for example, know anything about the existence and the training and the influence of, say, high-school teachers, or ministers, or lawyers, or social workers, the people of the professions whose stock in trade is ideas of some kind. Nor does he have any real awareness of the ideas which pass current [sic] among these people, or the form in which they are found acceptable. He is likely to think of ideas, of "real" ideas, as being limited to the most highly developed, the most "advanced," the most esoteric ideas that he himself is capable of absorbing. . . . And when he tests society for the presence of the ideas to which he gives his at-

tention, he finds what he expects to find—no, they are not present, or they are not present in the form in which he knows them. But ideas of some kind, and by no means of a bad or retrograde kind, are indeed present.[25]

Trilling goes on to discuss his encounters with a group of high school teachers and a group of men concerned with revising the penal code. He reports that the seriousness of these people, their commitment to ideas, and their intellectual deliberateness were something that should not have been a revelation. They should not have been, according to Trilling, "for to the literary intellectual any profession other than that of literature condemns itself by the mere fact of its being a profession."[26]

Not all of what Trilling said about his colleagues still applies today. Academic literary and cultural studies are increasingly *inter*disciplinary, and our alertness to developments in other disciplines sometimes spreads to other professions as well. But otherwise, Trilling's assessment continues to be relevant. Rarely in our work do we encounter other professionals. Though our egalitarian sentiments, I think, have mitigated against the kind of pride of profession or disciplinary pride Trilling speaks of (except perhaps when it comes to the corporate world, to which we nearly uniformly condescend), we have in fact had as little occasion as Trilling's generation of scholars and intellectuals to interact with other professionals or, for that matter, to interact with nonprofessionals save for our students. Once enclosed by sectarian left-wing organizations and cultures or by bohemian communities, intellectuals inside the academy are now enclosed by the very institutions that sustain, protect, and enable their work.

PART 2

Whence Beauty?

CHAPTER 5

Mary McCarthy's Beauty

Beauty has been a very unpopular subject for a very long time now. On the dust jacket of Elaine Scarry's *On Beauty and Being Just*, one reads the following: "For two decades or more in the humanities, various political arguments have been put forward against beauty: that it distracts us from more important issues; that it is a handmaiden of privilege; and that it masks political interests." So, too, did John Guillory, in *Cultural Capital: The Problem of Literary Canon Formation*, present a closely argued revision of the then-prevailing attitudes about the canon and literary value. Observing that the current orthodoxy was to unmask the specificity of the aesthetic and reveal it as an illusory realm in which the preferences of elites become naturalized and operate hegemonically, Guillory claimed that, on the contrary, "the aesthetic is a privileged site for reimagining the relation between the cultural and the economic in social life."[1] One of the more characteristic and influential expressions of what remains the current orthodoxy is Barbara Herrnstein Smith's *Contingencies of Value*, in which she writes that "all [aesthetic] value is radically contingent, being neither a fixed attribute, an inherent quality, or an objective property of things but, rather, an effect of multiple continuously changing, and continuously interacting variables." More specifically, she continues, value is the "product of the dynamics of a system, specifically an economic system. . . . Canonical texts, therefore, become canonical not because of intrinsic worth, design, craft, or other poetic properties, but because the power and inertia of social and cultural elites have kept them in circulation."[2]

Such views have become familiar to us today, so much so, in fact, that many of us find ourselves experiencing our literary preferences as secret and guilty pleasures—pleasures whose revelation, we fear, would expose our privileged social positions. Mary McCarthy is one of the modern American writer-critics who most forcefully encourages us to abandon our guilt and our fear and to openly declare what we consider beautiful and why. I would argue that Mary McCarthy obligates us to "fess up" precisely in order to arm ourselves against what Smith calls "the power and inertia of social and cultural elites." We must remember that for McCarthy's generation, too, the idea that aesthetic judgment is fundamentally ideological was even more broadly pervasive among intellectuals than it is today. I refer, of course, to the doctrinaire Marxist mode of criticism and judgment, which in its own way detached aesthetic considerations from some otherwise interesting experiments in cultural literacy via the proletarian literary movement and, afterward, the Popular Front. The Marxist literary ethos with which Mary McCarthy contended as a young writer and critic was as deeply skeptical of aesthetics as are any of the more current and more subtle versions of mechanical materialism that police us today.

To regard Mary McCarthy as a combatant in the culture wars of her day is, of course, a commonplace. I need not retell that lurid story once again, in which she stars as the brilliant and beautiful knife-wielding writer-critic whose nearly every assertion is an assault and every judgment a prelude to armed struggle. How often have critics gasped or smiled at the bloodletting induced by this literary gladiator; how baffled when faced with the gentle, domestic, private Mary McCarthy. Carol Brightman, in her biography *Writing Dangerously,* did much to give the lie to this fractured portrait of McCarthy; I would contribute to the process of integration by suggesting that an element that gives a certain coherence to McCarthy's life and works has always been her love of beauty—not as an indulgence or compensation, but, to borrow a phrase from Kenneth Burke, as "equipment for living." I want briefly to illustrate the importance of McCarthy's love of beauty and attendant aesthetic judgments. One finds it everywhere in her work; it is the center of the design.

Discerning readers will realize very early that the preoccupation of the author of *Memories of a Catholic Girlhood* is neither accurate recollection nor religion. It is beauty. Above all, *Memories* is a *Künstlerroman*: certainly, within this extraordinary memoir, there is no subject or theme more important than the developing literacy and aesthetic sensibility of its writer. "What I recall best about myself as a child under six," writes McCarthy, "is a passionate love of beauty, which was almost a kind of violence."[3] Her recollection of the happy few years with her parents is rendered using such talismans as little diamond rings, an ermine muff and neck piece, a glorious May basket, beauty pins, a hyacinth plant, chocolate and cambric tea, red roses, and a little white mountain of sugar into which a peach is dipped. Later, to the orphaned and often abused young girl, beauty continues to be the measure of all things, though the attribute of fewer things. She reports that one of the "great shocks" connected with losing her parents was "an aesthetic one; even if my guardians had been nice, I should probably not have liked them because they were so unpleasing to look at and their grammar and accents were so lacking in correctness."[4] Of course, her guardians were not nice; they were cruel, and for several years they deprived Mary and her siblings of a decent upbringing. It is religion, we are told, that saved her, but not religion as conventionally understood—that is, as having something important to do with belief, faith, or ritualistic practice. The Roman Catholic Church, for McCarthy, was the repository of nothing more or less than beauty itself. "Our ugly church and parochial school," she famously recollects, "provided me with my only aesthetic outlet, in the words of the Mass and the litanies and the old Latin hymns, in the Easter lilies around the altar, rosaries, ornamented prayer books, votive lamps, holy cards stamped in gold and decorated with flower wreaths and a saint's picture. This side of Catholicism, much of it cheapened and debased by mass production, was for me, nevertheless, the equivalent of Gothic cathedrals and illuminated manuscripts and mystery plays. I threw myself into it with ardor, this sensuous life."[5] For McCarthy, deprivation did not exactly create her aesthetic sensibility, which was forged earlier. But deprivation provided a motive and myriad opportunities to *deploy* that sensibility, and thus, paradoxically, deprivation did not diminish but rather enhanced the role of beauty in her life. This deployment takes place continuously as McCarthy unleashes her barrage of lapidary sentences, each of which we read unavoidably as rebuke to the ugly sentence she was forced to serve in her youth. It is maybe the only possible strategy of someone who, having suffered injustice, "fell in love with justice"[6] and is also capable of crying happy tears when she sees an ablative absolute.

To continue for a moment on her design, the reason the italicized interchapters of *Memories* cast such a spell is not just that they are a unique structuring device; they constitute a continuous aesthetic commentary on the design of the memoir. Their pretext, of course, is the pursuit of accuracy: for example, McCarthy informs us, with alacrity and an earnestness that is sometimes suspect and amusing, that "there are several dubious points in the memoir" or that "there are some semi-fictional touches here"—as though confessing her venial sins to the priestly reader. But the wayward quest for verisimilitude is not, after all, what the interchapters are about. How could these warnings be taken with complete seriousness by thoroughly intoxicated readers? It is like a lover telling you after a verbally and physically arousing afternoon together, "By the way, there were some minor inaccuracies in my description of that moonlit beach scene." The fact is not necessarily the sweetest dream that *memory* knows. The interchapters are about the deployment of aesthetics, about the inevitable shaping and designing and judging that accompanies truth telling or, rather, truth making.

McCarthy's fiction and literary criticism, especially her *Ideas and the Novel*, have encouraged many readers to stress her debt to the forms and sensibilities of eighteenth- and nineteenth-century writers. It was during the eighteenth century, after all, when the term *aesthetics* was coined to describe a relatively autonomous sphere of experience—free, it was hoped, from the encumbrances of the minister, the monarch, and the marketplace. (Scholars disagree about whether the influence of aesthetic experience was enhanced or weakened as a result.) This process and its consequences for modern writers and critics provides the broad context of which one of the more memorable incidents within *Memories of a Catholic Girlhood* can be read as allegorical. I refer to the memorable episode involving the tin butterfly. Readers will recall that Mary's youngest brother, Sheridan (he of the "fair-red curls," envied for being "the only blond among us"), loses a painted tin butterfly he had earlier fished out of a Cracker Jack box given him by the children's detestable guardian Uncle Myers. What was unique about the object, reports McCarthy, was not its intrinsic value but the fact that it was the only toy in the house bestowed on a single child; every other toy was "socialized," as McCarthy puts it—that is, shared by all four children. (In this respect, McCarthy's butterfly differs from Owen Warland's in Hawthorne's "The Artist of the Beautiful." But in other respects, both butterflies, however different, represent the fate of aesthetic experience in a society that assigns greater value to iron and tin.) One day, Mary's aunt enters her room, asks her whether she's seen the toy, and proceeds to enlist Mary's help in searching it out. Failing to find it, Aunt Mary gives way to Aunt Margaret, who directs Mary on another fruitless search, informing her afterward that her Uncle Myers has suspected her all along of stealing it. Mary dramatically professes her innocence before joining the rest for dinner, but after dinner, the tin butterfly is found—pinned to the table pad right by Mary's place. She suffers several beatings, during which she defiantly maintains her innocence. Looking back, McCarthy recalls the powerful feeling of righteousness, almost beatitude, that washed over her once the beatings relented in the wake of her stubborn refusal to recant. Years later, although her brother Preston himself could not confirm it, Mary uncertainly recalled him having revealed that he had seen the evil Uncle Myers steal into the dining room and lift the tablecloth with the tin butterfly in his hand.

With this vignette, McCarthy presents the modern aesthetic problematic, in which capital (here personified by Uncle Myers) exercises control over the distribution of beauty (through commodities such as the tin butterfly), thus removing fine art from the scope of the common or community life and privatizing it (Uncle Myers gives the tin butterfly to Sheridan). As conditions of the market increasingly place art and beauty on a remote pedestal, so that they seem to become lost even to capital itself, those cultivated individuals associated with art, including academics, are accused of hoarding, even pilfering, as is the young Mary. When she denies any association with the tin butterfly, she resembles the contemporary academic literati that deliberately dissociate themselves from beautiful objects, even when those objects are placed within their precincts by the institutions in which they labor. Mary, of course, was wholly innocent of any trafficking in tin butterflies (although she did traffic in real butterflies); but literary academics, despite their protestations to the contrary, continually value and judge textual and literary objects, even if they do so tacitly. We may wish to be inclusive and egalitarian in our judgments, but as John Guillory has observed, it is futile to try to make judgment disappear instead of reforming the conditions of its practice.

Regarding this matter, Mary McCarthy has always been an exemplary writer and critic, because she understood the necessary relationship among judgments of quality in literature, art, and politics and because she understood that democracies benefit by a literate, cultivated citizenry. This was most amply evidenced in her purest political book, *Vietnam*, in which she condemned American involvement not mainly for historical or policy reasons but for essentially aesthetic reasons: the hawks were not so much historically or politically wrong as unintelligible. Her descriptions stressed their mental disarray, moral imbalance, and incoherent idiom. Their crimes were seen to originate in loose habits of mind, even in forms of illiteracy. Moreover, the areas under their control were unsightly, and the Vietnamese they had allegedly liberated were uniformly listless.

Mary McCarthy did not express an aesthetic sensibility; she deployed it. It became a rhetorical act. With *Vietnam*, her deployment most obviously involved military matters. Perhaps it was her militancy about beauty that was or should have been responsible for her reputation for ferocity. At any rate, that is something about Mary McCarthy we may want to embrace. For her, the aesthetic, understood as an aspect of literacy, is a privileged site for reimagining the design of our social life. Reading her encourages us to defend the aesthetic and to deploy or spread it to the point that it no longer makes up a privileged site at all. But this is easier said than done. Despite her commitment to beauty and her belief that experiencing beauty is an essential part of any life worth living, she is acutely aware of the ways in which beauty gets appropriated by power, privilege, and subversion. Her lecture "Art Values and the Value of Art," published as "Living with Beautiful Things" in her final collection of criticism, *Occasional Prose* (1985), provides ample evidence of this. It offers a catalog of ways in which art collectors, curators, art historians, forgers, thieves, and radicals appropriate beauty for unattractive purposes. Delivered at the University of Aberdeen, Scotland, in 1974, the lecture became, at the urging of McCarthy's close friend Hannah Arendt, who had attended, the basis for McCarthy's final novel, *Cannibals and Missionaries* (1979). In the novel, the hijackers of an airliner headed for Iran realize that a group of wealthy art collectors on board are more useful to them than the other onboard group—liberals investigating allegations of torture by the shah. McCarthy directs her attention in the novel to the political uses to which art was increasingly being put during that decade (and, as we now know, beyond). It is symptomatic of our times that her remarkable lecture provoked no commentary by either of her two major biographers, Carol Gelderman in *Mary McCarthy* (1988) and Carol Brightman in *Writing Dangerously* (1992). Both biographies appeared during a period of American literary studies when aesthetic considerations were no longer part of the scholarly agenda, making McCarthy's lecture one of the last serious discussions of beauty before that subject all but disappeared as a legitimate subject among American intellectuals and scholars for more or less the next thirty years. When, in 1993, Dave Hickey wrote his book on beauty, he appropriately titled it *The Invisible Dragon: Four Essays on Beauty*. In his opening pages, he comments on the situation: "Simply put, if you broached the issue of beauty in the American art world of 1988, you could not incite a conversation about rhetoric—or efficacy—or pleasure—or politics—or even Bellini. You ignited a conversation about the market. That, at the time, was the 'signified' of beauty."[7]

"Living with Beautiful Things" chronicles the then-recent dramatic rise in the number of assaults on art and museums around the world since the 1960s, including an incident at the Tokyo National Museum in which a young woman sprayed the glass case containing the *Mona Lisa* with red paint to protest the museum's policy of excluding the disabled, a damaging attack on Michelangelo's *Pietà* by a psychotic Australian wielding a hammer, a Vermeer cut from its frame in the Rijksmuseum in Amsterdam, another Vermeer stolen from the Kenwood House in England and held for ransom of a half-million pounds to be distributed among the Caribbean poor, the theft of Schongauer's *Virgin of the Rose Garden* from Colmar Cathedral in Alsace, the disappearance of a Breughel and a Van Dyck from Poland, a bizarre incident at the Uffizi when someone went through the first three rooms piercing tiny holes in the eyes of pictured saints with a sharp pointed object, acid thrown at a Rubens in the

Pinakothek in Munich, a brazen raid on a collection in Ireland that resulted in demands for ransom and the transfer of four Irish Republican Army prisoners from England to Ulster, and the defacement of Rubens's *Adoration of the Magi* at King's College Chapel, Cambridge. McCarthy also refers to a handbill distributed in front of the Tokyo National Museum that claimed the exhibition of the *Mona Lisa* discriminated not only against the disabled but against working women. McCarthy attributes these brazen crimes, including a spate of forgeries, in part to the greatly expanded publicity given art sales, whose scandalously ballooning prices were a shock to common sense and even "common decency." That so much "artistic capital" was being exported to affluent Americans was causing alarm in nations seeing their patrimony vanishing, and this was generating public campaigns to save great art by keeping it at home. McCarthy refers to these campaigns as "mass movements" and part of a democratizing process, for never before had the public been so fascinated with what were to be understood as unprecedented levels of protest "against accepted art names and art values."[8]

McCarthy notes that none of the actions described resulted in the successful reappropriation of art: every one of the stolen art objects was eventually recovered or returned, an indication that the thieves had not developed plans that were well thought-out. Rather than to destroy art, she surmises, the intention was more likely to seek publicity. The "ensemble of burglary and vandalism" were best seen as "advertisements."[9] Moreover, the wish to end the exclusion of the weakest was probably not a central motivation; rather, there was "murkier umbrage" taken, perhaps at the disproportionate attention paid to art objects, perhaps at the prevailing standards (which McCarthy admits to sharing) by which the life of a rare painting is thought to be more valuable than an actual human life. A Vermeer, after all, cannot be replaced, but a cadre in the struggle will be, summarily. Or perhaps umbrage was taken at the "mysterious" moral privilege art confers on owners who do not deserve their possessions. This is clearly not the case when it comes to jewelry, fancy cars, or yachts. We may consider these things odious or harbor hopes of having them ourselves, but, as McCarthy observes, "there is no virtue in them, no magical property that we sense as communicable, no aura beyond that of wealth."[10]

It is widely the case, then, that "most people like to think that beauty is not only a good in itself but is good *for* something."[11] But that something is elusive. Many believe that were they surrounded by beautiful things (ideally from birth), they, too, would become beautiful; they are certain that at least some beauty would rub off on them. Though McCarthy labels this "wistful imagining," she acknowledges that the daily encounter with beautiful things "conduces to decorum; it is a rite, a kind of communion, as we notice whenever we wash a fine wine glass as opposed, say, to a jelly jar. Nearly everybody, even the most insensitive, has had some hair-raising encounter with the aesthetic present in man-made things, just as nearly everybody, even the most irreligious, can attest to some brush with the supernatural, if only in the form of thought-transference."[12]

McCarthy pauses here to ask whether there exists any empirical foundation for the belief that direct contact with visual beauty is life-enhancing. This is an interesting question indeed, not only because it is rare for any critic of the arts to seek empirical verification of such things, but because it demonstrates McCarthy's proximity to the art world of Manhattan, a relationship easy to criticize, in retrospect, for its provincialism, yet broader, for all that, than the academic perspective from which such criticism usually emanates. But McCarthy's empiricism, refreshing as it is, is limited by its subjective, anecdotal nature. Surveying the art dealers, museum curators, art historians and critics, and, finally, art owners she knows, she finds that these cohorts seem not to be much improved by their regular exposure to beautiful things. Art dealers, she testifies, as mere buyers and sellers of product, "are not morally better than butchers or dentists; certainly they have a worse reputation." Museum curators fare only slightly better, and here, too, McCarthy discerns no beneficial moral effect from their regular exposure to art. Though better educated and possessed of better manners than dealers, curators must do more than their share of flattering and "sucking up," because a good part of their business is promotion and public relations. "Association with beauty," McCarthy observes, "has not given the mass of curators large hearts or soaring minds."[13]

Art historians and critics offer yet more improvement, though slight. Divinely inspired and rapturous critics at the lectern notwithstanding (McCarthy knows some in the field of art but points out she knows others in other fields), many critics and historians surround themselves at home with tasteless, utilitarian decor, not unlike the radicals in Henry James's The Bostonians. Art critics' relationship with beauty is also compromised by "quasi-commercial factors. The calling is highly competitive and productive of jealousy and vicious backbiting."[14] Frequent hobnobbing with the rich inevitably "uglif[ies] the uneasy recipient" of their favors.[15] Clearly, McCarthy writes of an era, now long passed, when critics and historians could not rely on the academy to supply them with tenure and a good salary, requisites (though by no means guarantees) of independence and integrity.

Finally, there are owners. Most of us own at least some art objects, but however fine they are, we tend to ignore them after time. "There are pictures," reveals McCarthy, "on my walls and little objects on my mantelpiece that I do not 'see' for weeks, maybe months, at a time just as you cease to hear a clock ticking in a room." A Rembrandt or a Goya may elicit a different response: instead of ignoring them for weeks or months at a time, we might ignore them merely for days at a time. In any event, regular neglect ought to be a reason to get rid of the neglected object, but no one does: "with a dress, yes, but with a vase or a drawing, no."[16] But perhaps the influence is subliminal. To consider the possibility, McCarthy turns to "big" collectors "who should be subject to more influences." Once again, she sees no evidence of moral uplift: "Think of Goering," she declares. Recalling gentle, mild, and philanthropic collectors, "even one or two who are liberals (in the American sense, i.e. slightly to the left) in politics and devoted to human rights—this is a very rare species. The majority, I must say, are not very nice people. Living with beautiful things has not enlarged them; one could almost think the opposite." McCarthy wonders about the progress or regress of individuals—whether and how the acquisition of beautiful things changes the collector: "Was he small, narrow, selfish, and deeply reactionary to start with or did devotion to his *things* bring those traits out in him?" How does a big collector compare with an ordinary wealthy philistine? "My guess," she says, "would be worse, though he may be a little easier to talk to, at least at the start." How does such a collector compare to a bookish rich man? McCarthy is of the opinion that those attracted to the visual arts are "poisonous people," whereas those attracted to literature are likely to be "humane and responsive."[17] Even an omnivorous reader, she observes, will not be greedy, for he does not deprive anyone else of his share, and this is an important difference. Bibliophiles, however, are similar to art collectors. According to McCarthy, the single significant residue left on big art collectors by beautiful things is taste: "Sooner or later, those who are covetous of beauty, whether they are Renaissance popes or tyrants or modern collectors, generally develop a faculty of discriminating that often extends to other departments of life . . . [t]hough not to the moral or intellectual sphere." Taste enhances but one sort of power: the ability to select more beautiful things with which to surround oneself. "That is all," claims McCarthy, "a rather vicious circle."[18]

The discussion is then taken to another level, from private ownership and individual experience to culture at large. A city with ample parks, numerous public squares and statuary, distinctively designed buildings, and handsome homes must support a higher quality of life than a shantytown—and not just because it is healthier and more pleasing to the eye. "Such a city ought to inculcate virtue," declares McCarthy. Certainly the ancients thought so, and the architects of the great churches, and Machiavelli. But during the Industrial Revolution, the cities got bigger and uglier, and the buildings and squares that had been thought to nurture virtue were replaced by nature and its beneficent powers. Natural beauty came to be experienced as soul making. The idea remains, but too often "in terms of vacations, camp, pack trips, sailing."[19] That the connection between beauty and civic life has been broken is evident even in Paris, according to McCarthy, where André Malraux, as minister of culture during De Gaulle's regime, placed twentieth-century statuary from the Louvre in the Tuileries Garden for the pleasure of the public. But the effort to get art out of the museums and into the lives of ordinary citizens without them having to pay admission, wait in line, and fight crowds was not a success. The statues were not meant for the garden, and they looked "pathetic and absurd plumped down on the grass."[20] Not a single government official followed this project with additional ones.

As is the case with most good lecturers and essayists, McCarthy's inquiry undulates. Now she retreats to what so many of us know from our individual, empirical experience: beauty brings immediate, revelatory happiness: "Seeing a spring apple orchard, a field of wild flowers, a Greek temple, a Renaissance fresco, a Henry Moore makes us feel not only good but 'good.'"[21] Can there be any doubt that a society that encourages such experiences is better than one that does not? Well, yes, McCarthy responds, and she cites Germany as her test case, a country whose most beautiful regions—Bavaria and the Rhineland—are absolute treasures for their natural loveliness, the design and architecture of their towns and cities, and their centrality to the arts in general. Yet they were also home to the worst of the Nazis. Bavaria was still, in the 1970s, a neo-Nazi stronghold. A similar correlation existed in Italy, where the most fanatical fascists hailed from Florence, Machiavelli's city.

All of these enigmatic facets of living with beautiful things finally cause McCarthy to declare the essential mystery of the encounter and its effects. If it is good *for* something, that something remains elusive. If it is useless, McCarthy speculates that perhaps this is the reason so many "are letting it disappear with so little regret."[22] So McCarthy left her readers to trouble over the fate of beauty in an age when whatever sensuous, moral, or spiritual value beauty engendered was dismissed as either ill-defined or nonexistent. This, of course, was the beginning of an era of spreading aesthetic illiteracy, in part encouraged by trends in criticism and theory that mirrored the rest of contem-

porary life by placing exclusive importance on understanding beauty's mone-
tary and political value alone.

I have used the term *aesthetic illiteracy,* by which I mean simply the inability to identify and appreciate or otherwise judge artistry in man-made objects
or to recognize and respond to natural beauty. But, of course, there is nothing
"simple" about aesthetics, because for some people, every word in the description I just gave is a lie, including, to paraphrase Mary McCarthy's famous 1980
attack on Lillian Hellman on the Dick Cavett Show, *and* and *the.* Whose appreciation is at issue? Where and how is that appreciation expressed? What is
its connection to money and power? What is beauty—as if we could isolate it
from the interests and ideologies of the beholder? Is *taste* not just another
word for the preferences of elites with particular values that lead to the pursuit
of valu*ables?* Mary McCarthy addresses each of these questions, and her keen
understanding of the ways of her world cause her to acknowledge the many
modalities by which beauty is wedded to power, wealth, and the status quo. To
paraphrase Lionel Trilling, she burns away the soft tissue of too-easy satisfaction when it comes to beauty's effects. But her refusal to reduce undeniably engaging, fulfilling, and transformative aesthetic experience to self-interest or
class ideology immunizes her against cynicism.

I have been reminded of this cynicism on several occasions. A number of
years ago, during a departmental discussion about graduate curriculum, a colleague stated emphatically and with no small amount of defiance that she did
not think it part of her job description to teach students to appreciate or be inspired by literature. I confess I was taken aback by my colleague's blunt repu-
diation of this aspect of aesthetics in the classroom. I have never felt that teaching literature contextually and encouraging political awareness—pertaining to
class, gender, sexuality, race, ethnicity, and certainly ongoing political movements, parties, constituencies, and positions—rules out experiencing the pleasures of good writing or trying to enhance my students' capacity for such pleasure. As a former labor organizer and someone who has been involved in
progressive politics for some time, I have always felt that, on the contrary, an
appreciation for aesthetic quality never vitiated but, in fact, complemented
both an appreciation for and the struggle for a better society. Struggles for social change are by definition, after all, actions taken in order to enhance the
quality of one's social world. Their goals reflect judgments that a better quality
of life, however defined, is possible and that its pursuit is preferable to enduring the limitations of the present. Surely, the process of making judgments
about the quality of life one desires for the future bears an important relation

to—that is, can be improved by—perceiving quality in the things we experience in our present life.

The second reminder of the prevailing mood regarding aesthetics occurred
when a graduate student in my seminar "What Is American Literature?" described a session of the composition class she was teaching for the first time.
Her students were discussing a text (I cannot remember which one), and they
were massacring it with arbitrary interpretations. My student finally could not
endure any more, stepped in, and set her students on course by offering what
she considered a more acceptable interpretation. What stunned me was her attitude: she abjectly apologized for her failure and expressed profound regret
for what she called her "elitism" and her "authoritarian" teaching methods.
The issue here was interpretive, not aesthetic, but it had to do with different
levels of judgment, competence, and sensitivity to the text—the very things
skeptics of aesthetics believe to be invidious, discriminatory, or exclusionary
when applied to considering the quality of different literary texts.

Ironically, these are the same skeptics who, if they are worth their salt as
teachers (and many are), take great care constructively to correct, comment
on, and grade their students' essays, which are, after all, imperfect examples of
"literary texts." Though few of us would describe our students' essays as "beautiful," we evaluate them by responding to several aspects that include aesthetic
ones, such as clarity of expression, the shape of an argument, felicitous phras-
ing, elegance, and wit. For the skeptics who believe that the enjoyment of skill
and craft is elitist, that objective or even reliable standards of judgment are
fraught with self-interest and therefore dangerous, and that ranking the
achievements of writers is restrictive and oppressive, it becomes difficult not
only to teach effective writing properly but to provide a rationale that would
justify teaching it in the first place. Thus, many in the field of composition have
jettisoned the teaching of writing as an art or craft and chosen instead to teach
rhetorical strategies, political and ideological awareness, and respect for
(though, crucially, not mastery of) modes of writing that are alternatives to
Standard English. Although such strategies no doubt impart useful knowledge, the results have not been encouraging. Nowhere—certainly not at my institution—has convincing evidence shown this approach to result in a discernible, systematic improvement in the quality of writing. To the contrary,
the approach has more often contributed to the decline in writing skills at-
tested to by a growing consensus of educators. The inevitable result of ignoring aesthetics in one's teaching practice (ignoring it in one's scholarship produces it own disastrous consequences) is ineffectiveness. Despite the desperate

search for alternatives, in part generated in recent years by composition programs intent on challenging the hegemony of English departments, none has proven an effective substitute for teaching the art of writing. The real challenge is to take advantage of the connections composition programs have often made to their surrounding communities, with their diverse constituencies and various modes of discourse, and to link this to a full exploration of the aesthetic experiences and practices found within those communities. That would produce a new respect on the part of students for the many skilled craftspeople who surround them, and it would encourage students to want to emulate these people in their own written work.

Mary McCarthy reminds us that though it may be difficult to ascertain the precise effects of living with beautiful things, especially in the context of the increasing number of aggressions against the notion of beauty as something that bestows superiority, actions or agendas that would make an enemy of beauty are doomed to failure. Traditionally, writers and artists are asked by states, movements, organizations, and academics, "What have you contributed to the struggle for social and economic justice?" The force of Mary McCarthy's inquiries would have us reverse the question and ask what states, movements, organizations, and academics have contributed to writers and artists. Since the 1960s, she has been joined in her rebuttal of the cross-examination of beauty by Susan Sontag, another distinguished public intellectual who devoted a career to defending the necessity of aesthetic experience. In one of her last essays, "An Argument about Beauty," she, like McCarthy, lists the ways beauty has been appropriated to serve dubious causes. These include what was perhaps the occasion for her essay, a Vatican bent on managing the worldwide crisis brought on by revelations of systematic child abuse by predatory priests. Speaking of the Roman Catholic Church, Pope John Paul II told a group of American cardinals, "A great work of art may be blemished but its beauty remains." As Sontag hastens to point out, "Beauty, as a term signifying (like health) an indisputable excellence, has been a perennial resource in the issuing of peremptory evaluations."[23] In this case, as in many others, the most important attribute of beauty is alleged to be permanence, but as Sontag observes, it is really evanescence, of which the Japanese, for instance, are well aware, as signified by their annual, elegiac, rite of viewing cherry blossoms. "To make beauty in some sense imperishable," comments Sontag, "require[s] a lot of conceptual tinkering and transposing." Thus, as beauty's meanings both multiplied and stratified, the ascendant values of "intellectual" and "spiritual beauty" took precedence over what is ordinarily understood as beautiful: "a gladness to the senses." In the meantime, the beauty of face and body, often de-bunked by the arbiters of taste, remains "the most commonly visited sites of the beautiful."[24]

In light of the appropriation of beauty by institutions of authority, it comes as little surprise that modernism, dedicated as it was to radical projects of innovation, should have discredited beauty as a quality of serious art. Gertrude Stein, Sontag reminds us, said that to call something beautiful was to say it was dead: "there was no more vapid or philistine compliment."[25] Lovers of beauty like Oscar Wilde and defenders of taste like Kant notwithstanding, both beauty and judgment have taken their lumps. Sontag observes that a corollary to the failure of the notion of beauty has been "the discrediting of the prestige of judgment itself, as something that could conceivably be impartial or objective, not always self-serving or self-referring." Nowhere is this more obvious than in the literary academy. Sontag writes of the current dispensa-tion, in which the celebration of the defeat of snobbery is manifested as the tri-umph of bad taste. It is not that academics admit to having it, only that more and more of them regard difficult art and literature as old-fashioned while they give the green light to mass culture and the preferences it elicits among the multitudes. Among the experts, "interesting" has replaced "beautiful," and the reason is precisely to avoid making a judgment of value. The "interesting," according to Sontag, is essentially a consumerist concept, "bent on enlarging its domain" and banishing the "boring," the great enemy of the successful com-modity. Sontag closes her essay with the single line "Imagine saying, 'That sun-set is interesting.'"[26]

Before concluding, Sontag makes two central claims on behalf of beauty that will inform the rest of this book. The first is that beauty bears a relation-ship to knowledge and goodness: "The wisdom that becomes available over a deep, lifelong engagement with the aesthetic cannot, I venture to say, be dupli-cated by any other kind of seriousness." The second speaks to the tenacity, if not the ubiquity, of aesthetic experience: "Unlike beauty, often fragile and im-permanent, the capacity to be overwhelmed by the beautiful is astonishingly sturdy and survives amidst the harshest distractions. Even war, even the prospect of certain death, cannot expunge it."[27] To conclude, Sontag observes that "the best theory of beauty is its history. Thinking about the history of beauty means focusing on its deployment in the hands of specific communi-ties."[28] The following chapters will look at two such communities: the academy and the heretofore unobserved "community" of common citizens that staff it and surround it.

CHAPTER 6

The Decline of Aesthetic Literacy and the New Aesthetics

The term *aesthetic literacy* was suggested to me by the late Richard Kroll, a former colleague at Princeton and, until his recent untimely death, a distinguished scholar of the eighteenth century at the University of California, Irvine. I was blabbering on about my students' inability to respond to the felicities of craft in the literature they were reading—skillful narrative design; use of sound, syntax, or imagery; figurative language; and so on. Richard offhandedly responded by saying something on the order of "Mine lack aesthetic literacy as well." Perhaps it took someone who had devoted a career to understanding what was behind the very creation of the word *aesthetic* in the eighteenth century and the particular experiences it denoted to state so succinctly what it was I was talking about. At any rate, a light went on as I considered both the importance of the phenomenon we were encountering and the seeming lack of public concern about it. As a society, we may not care enough about conventional illiteracy to do much about reducing it, but at least we are aware of it by the grim statistics available. No such concern is directed toward what seems, at least anecdotally, to be the widespread diminished capacity to take pleasure in the art of writing. I am very well aware of the enhanced sensibilities of many of my students and my own children when it comes to certain kinds of visual experiences and electronic forms of writing—movies, videos, e-mailing, texting, and twittering all have their own set of skills and pleasures. When it comes to longer and longer-lasting forms of writing, however, the response to the specificities of craft seems uniformly less eager and acute.

These growing deficiencies, if this is what they are, do not arise from new modes of technological expression alone. They arise from priorities within the schools and from an educational system that increasingly marginalizes the arts. When we do teach the arts, we usually teach them as though they are merely ornamental or else as disguised social documents whose fundamental interest is historical, political, or ideological in nature. Within our English departments, it is little exaggeration to say that two cultures have coexisted since the dual absorption of theory, on the one hand, and the proliferation of creative writing programs, on the other. It would seem that Alfred Kazin's observation that "scholars were one class and writers quite another" when he went to college during the 1930s is as germane to today's English department as it once was to society as a whole.[1] In many university departments, there is the culture of criticism, theory, and scholarship and the culture of creative writing. Much was made during the 1960s about the split between the cultures of the humanities and of science, which C. P. Snow made famous in his *The Two Cultures* (1959). I do not wish to be nearly as portentous as Snow, but the division of which I speak is real, and it deserves our attention.

Too many university English departments are divided between its faculty of scholars and its faculty of creative writers. Although both groups involve themselves with literature most of the time, they perform their jobs in quite different ways. Scholars write articles for specialized professional journals and publish monographs; writers write for small literary magazines and/or commercial magazines and publish novels, collections of short stories, or volumes of poetry. As for reading, relatively few writers subscribe to *Critical Inquiry, American Literary History,* or any such professional journal; relatively few scholars subscribe to the *New Yorker,* the *New York Review of Books,* or any commercial literary publication. Scholars attend the annual convention of the Modern Language Association (MLA), which features relatively few writers; writers attend the annual conference of the Association of Writers and Writing Programs (AWP), which features few scholars. On campus, the scholars attend poetry or fiction readings only intermittently, and the writers rarely attend scholarly lectures. Often, the two groups have separate administrative staffs, although they coexist under a departmental rubric. Representatives of one of these groups often do not serve on hiring committees of the other; even less often will there be any representation of one group on the graduate admissions committee of the other. The occasional switch-hitters notwithstanding, the two groups teach different kinds of courses within different programs that have different requirements. The central matter at hand—the consideration of craft, assessing the skill and quality of writing, deepening and discussing aesthetic experience—is almost entirely reserved for the writing workshops or other courses taught by creative writers. Rarely will students be educated in these areas if they stick to the courses offered by the scholars, and these students remain the great majority in most English departments today. The sad reality is that the teaching of aesthetic literacy goes on in a relatively small number of our courses and is taught by a minority of the literary professoriat. At the end of *The Program Era,*

Mark McGurl's fascinating new book about the rise of creative writing programs and the literature they have produced, McGurl playfully speculates about the possibility of "convert[ing] historical materialism into a mode of aesthetic judgment," while granting that today "there is no way for a literary scholar to engage in strenuous aesthetic appreciation without sounding goofily anachronistic."[2] In this chapter, I sketch out some of the reasons for these disjunctions, many of which I believe to be unnecessary and debilitating for our students and ourselves. Indeed, literary evaluation has all but disappeared from literary scholarship and therefore from most English classes. But fortunately, some scholars are finally looking for alternatives.

In charting the retreat from aesthetic literacy, I will focus my attention primarily on two widely influential and symptomatic studies from the 1980s and 1990s: Barbara Herrnstein Smith's *Contingencies of Value* (1988), which provided conceptual ballast for the move, and Michael Denning's *The Cultural Front* (1996), which helped solidify the turn in American studies away from aesthetic and even literary considerations. Of course, the turn from aesthetics was very much a part of the turn to theory beginning in the 1960s: some readers will recall the title of one of the more influential texts of the period, *The Anti-Aesthetic*, edited by Hal Foster. Whatever the particular mode of analysis—structuralism, semiotics, reader-response theory, deconstructionism, Marxism, psychoanalysis, feminism, cultural studies, queer studies, ethnic studies, race studies, New Historicism—the general tendency or emphatic insistence was either to attack the very grounding of aesthetics and literary evaluation in particular or to ground them in something other than conscious, experienced, sensitive, and unencumbered responses to artistic skill. That grounding was variously described as linguistic or ideological codes or systems, the indeterminacy and play of language, political and economic social structures, revealed or repressed elements of the unconscious, the experiences of marginalized groups, or fluid and unpredictable cultural and economic exchange. Although these theoretical projects added important perspectives regarding the many factors that influence and are in turn influenced by aesthetics, they brought excessive critical pressure on the idea that aesthetics could be something other than cultural production as ideological work. We see excess as well in the effort to "demystify" the belief in objective literary judgment and the cult of connoisseurship that was thought to have infected the academy under the reign of the New Criticism. In many cases, this was part of a larger effort to destroy the very category of the "literary." Two of the most important studies of aesthetics that came out of this milieu were, of course, Pierre Bourdieu's *La Distinction: Critique sociale du jugement* (1979; translated as *Distinction* in 1984) and Terry Eagleton's *The Ideology of the Aesthetic* (1990).

As I argue elsewhere, a good number of these contextual perspectives ought to be pursued through a range of empirical research projects that bring literary scholars face-to-face with some of the very "subjects" said to be affected by literary and cultural evaluation or, for that matter, by the whole range of political and ideological issues that have interested literary theorists. This would be the next and logical step toward a process of verifying or rejecting theoretical insights; it would be based on testing hypotheses by bringing to bear empirical evidence obtained using acceptable protocols and procedures developed largely by scholars in other disciplines. As I indicated, such ventures could illuminate a whole range of issues, not just those having to do with the aesthetic and evaluative issues that interest me and that I pursue in later chapters. For the moment, I want to identify some of the more regnant tendencies within the broad body of theory I have mentioned, not by offering a sketchy survey, but by spending a bit of time on two influential studies that arose out of the theoretical milieu from which we are emerging.

As her title indicates, Smith's *Contingencies of Value* focuses on the value question. According to her, "all value is radically contingent, being neither a fixed attribute, an inherent quality, or an objective property of things but, rather, an effect of multiple continuously changing, and continuously interacting variables." It is, in fact, "a changing function of multiple variables," the "product of the dynamics of a system, specifically an *economic* system" that is made up of market and personal economies.[3] These variables are indeed multiple—so much so that it is hard to see any aspect of social or biological existence that Smith rules out as irrelevant. Indeed, in her words, "our experience of 'the value of the work' is equivalent to *our experience of the work in relation to the total economy of our existence.*"[4] Her theoretical framework is all-encompassing: it includes biophysiological factors; the general and specific social and institutional contexts of the producer(s) of the object in question, of the evaluator, and of the reader(s) or listener(s); the "structure of interests" that generates and shapes the entire "social/verbal transaction" in which the evaluator contributes; and an acknowledged inexhaustible set of variables that affect both the "social, cultural, and verbal histories of those involved" and the specific perspectives from which they derive their judgments.

For Smith, we evaluate "a) by articulating an estimate of how well a work will serve implicitly defined functions; b) for a specific implicitly defined audience, c) who are conceived as experiencing the work under certain implicitly defined conditions."[5] Canonical texts become canonical not because of intrinsic worth, design, craft, or other literary properties but because the power and inertia of social and cultural elites have kept them in circulation. It is typical that these elites naturalize and universalize their own tastes, thereby marginalizing other tastes and texts, often in the name of sophistication or cosmopolitanism. For Smith, cosmopolitanism is often another name for cultural imperialism, for when it enlarges its purview "from China to Peru, it may become all the more imperialistic, seeing in every horizon of difference new peripheries of its own centrality, new pathologies through which its own normality may be defined and must be asserted."[6]

Radical historicism of this kind has become our current staple, our orthodoxy. When Smith's book appeared over twenty years ago, its own cultural capital appreciated quickly and substantially despite its self-described subversiveness. Its luster accrued partly because of the author's professional stature: at the time of publication, Smith was president of the MLA, and she was also the only "pure" theoretician on the all-star team that Duke University was then assembling. Lest you think that by bringing this sort of thing up, I am somehow reducing the value of Smith's book, I would only remind you that this is precisely what Smith herself suggests we do, because these very factors are the essential ones that determine value. If you are uncomfortable with my observations about Smith's place and power in the profession, then perhaps you are uncomfortable with Smith's understanding of value's contingency. That is OK; I think you should be uncomfortable. Before I point out why, I want to make clear my belief that her historicist approach to the value question, broadly shared by an entire generation of scholars, has yielded substantial gains. Rarely does anyone claim that beauty or value is inherent in a given artifact or that value resides in a small collection of supernal masterpieces whose sublime subtleties can only be appreciated by a necessarily select, highly cultivated elite. No longer do many scholars claim that measures of value that contribute to excluding a good amount of work produced by historically marginalized groups and authors are preferable to measures of value that encourage catholic tastes and a more inclusive canon. Skepticism about pure aesthetics that disguise their actual contingency is appropriate; such skepticism has reshaped literary studies in ways that will continue to be appreciated.

This said, I want to identify a few of the problems with Smith's position. Despite her momentary acknowledgment that "the current value of a work . . . is by no means independent of authorial design, labor, and skill,"[7] she discusses value nearly exclusively in terms of functions fulfilled, usually ideological functions fulfilled. What is conspicuously absent in her analysis is the actual site of judgment, the interactive encounter between reader and text, observer and artwork, listener and performance or recording, and so on. In the words of John Guillory, "the exploding of [the] fictions of intrinsic, universal, or transcendent value, which was a necessary means of recovering a sense of the historicity of judgment, does not necessarily clarify the actual circumstances in which judgments are made and have effects."[8] In fact, Smith's account of the aesthetic function of art is disappointing because she denies the existence of aesthetic value as something distinct in the first place. She claims that "since there are no functions performed by artworks that may be specified as generically unique and also no way to distinguish the 'rewards' provided by art from those provided by innumerable other kinds of experience, any distinction between aesthetic and non-aesthetic value must be regarded as fundamentally problematic." She gives the following example to illustrate her point: "Is my airplane neighbor reading *Rebecca* enjoying it less than I am enjoying *Emma*? Is there any way (by the difference in our EEG waves? rates of heartbeat? muscle tone?) it could be demonstrated that the teenager listening to Pink Floyd is not feeling as good as I do when I listen to *Parsifal*?"[9]

These are good questions, but the difficulty of measuring levels of individual satisfaction does not mean that individual pleasures and preferences cannot be compared through collective conversations and debates and cannot result in the consensus of thoughtful, sensitive people. In his review of Smith's study, Martin Mueller would have us take the case of "an infant playing peek-a-boo and deriving intense emotional and cognitive satisfaction from its manipulation of presence and absence. Perhaps no pleasure compares to this activity. But what parent would not be disturbed if their teenage children were still seriously playing . . . peek-a-boo?" According to Mueller, there are "infantile, childish, perhaps even adolescent pleasures," and there is at least something to the "common idea of a teleologically directed 'normal' maturing of aesthetic tastes and judgments." He continues,

> Implicit in [Smith's] remarks is a preference for a possible world of incommensurable, non developmental, non hierarchical economies of enjoyment that would remain in peaceful equilibrium were it not for the sin of privilege. . . . But the demystification of aesthetic autonomy as a disguise rests on a remarkably impoverished and ungenerous vision of human interests in all their variety. . . . Only rarely, and never with enthusiasm, does she hold the view that

approval, fame, canonization, etc. are often justified and appropriate responses to the qualities and virtues of particular human activities or artifacts. . . .

And yet, in any field of human activity there will be some people who are particularly, often spectacularly, good at it, whether "it" is throwing or catching a ball, dancing, making pottery, singing songs, or telling stories. Their fellow men are typically quite good at recognizing such talents and their productions. This is especially apparent in the work of craftsmen and athletes.[10]

I read someone who observed that people pay lots of money and spend lots of time watching great athletes but that no one was going to pay to watch him lumber around the track twelve times in twenty-two minutes flat. On occasion, this person put his mind to composing poetry, but when he read Yeats he knew he could not do anything like it if he had his whole life to live over again. He responded the way the amateur carpenter Robert Hughes responds to the vastly superior skill of Japanese woodworking: without resentment, with pleasure and reverence.

By most accounts, Shakespeare was good at writing. Smith tells us she has been reading his sonnets for thirty years and teaching them for fifteen, yet she maintains that she cannot evaluate Shakespeare's sonnets, in part because, she claims, she "know[s] them too well"[11] and in part because she is all too aware of the variable nature of both their value over the centuries and her own attitude toward the poems. Almost equally astonishing is her claim that she can no longer see "the form, style, logic, figurative language, or structure of the poems" because "they have been absorbed or reabsorbed into the art of the whole and my experience of it."[12] After a lengthy catalog of the numerous sources that have been responsible for evaluating the sonnets—Shakespeare himself, readers, publishers, printers, purchasers, editors, anthologists, critics, and scholars—Smith disqualifies herself as a judge and refuses to commit herself to any explicit assessment as to the sonnets' value. She demurs despite the fact that her close attachment to them over the decades indicates without doubt that she values them very highly. We might be tempted to call her modesty or coyness a mere eccentricity were it not so damaging to her overall argument. In immersing herself solely in the consideration of all the possible circumstances that might shape evaluation, she forgets not only the objects being evaluated but the specific subjective response of the evaluator as well.

Although Smith presents herself as writing within a pragmatist tradition, her version of pragmatism borrows heavily, perhaps too heavily, from the sort of mechanical version of materialism that Marx himself inveighed against in *Theses on Feuerbach* (in which human subjectivity, what Marx calls "practical, human-sensuous activity," is fatally diminished) and from a Foucauldian instrumentalism that theorizes no space for judgments irreducible to ubiquitous power relations. This pragmatism has drifted a rather long way from that of Dewey and Rorty, for whom aesthetic experience and considered judgment are central to the workings of a democratic society because they are qualities that are necessary to active citizenship. Smith's agnosticism when it comes to evaluation is a fatal flaw because it yields not a single example of what she considers an appropriate, acceptable evaluative process and conclusion. Her book in fact suggests that contingency is sufficiently limitless as to render legitimate evaluation impossible. This would seem to fly in the face of Smith's stated intention of providing a basis for enlightened, self-conscious, and progressive evaluation and returning literary judgment to the academic agenda after decades of neglect. But her book makes it amply clear that literary evaluation has everything to do with the ensemble of social relations and little to do with literature or aesthetic experience. Her own testimony is revealing: she cannot judge the quality of Shakespeare's sonnets because the past has thrown up extreme variability. This is like arguing that the uncountable, infinitesimal, and ever-changing shifts in atmospheric conditions means we cannot talk about the weather or that the myriad uncertain variables of the battlefield preclude attack. With regard to the first analogy, effective pragmatism, like the kind practiced by Wallace Stevens, must talk about the weather, precisely because it offers a way to ground persuasive, adequate evaluation in contingency. With regard to the second, Smith is the McClellan of the literary theater: when it comes to actually committing herself to a judgment, she seems paralyzed by a persistent case of "the slows."

The second problem with Smith's historicist view—again, shared by many—is its reliance on subcommunities. For Smith, the all-important social values expressed in a canonical work are ideological manifestations of the dominant culture. In the case of noncanonical works, what gives value are the ideological manifestations of oppositional cultures and subcultures. Because noncanonical works are usually valued more highly by left and liberal critics today, there tends to be a great deal of attention paid to these cultures and subcultures. But regardless of the amount of attention, the model remains the same for dominant and oppositional (or hegemonic and counterhegemonic) cultures: *all* communities construct objects of value (like canons) that can only be properly valued within the particular community that produces the object.

Thus, the value of the classics is produced by white male Europeans, and to explain and/or share those values, one must understand fully or identify fully with that community, as large and diverse as it is. By the same token, to properly value novels written by, say, radical women writers of the 1930s, one must identify oneself as fully as possible with the subculture that has produced these works. We will see that for Michael Denning as well, appreciation and value arise from full immersion, thick description, and adopting a local rationale for making judgments. But aside from the fact that a literary text is a material object with a force of its own and is not a cipher to be valued wholly extrinsically, there are problems on the extrinsic end as well. Although the intention of breaking down cultures and communities into progressively smaller entities is to disintegrate an all-encompassing national entity, what it actually establishes is a distinct, ideal, and homogeneous oppositional source of identity replete with its own set of values and valued texts. Thus, each valuing subcommunity and subculture expresses a kind of local universality that brooks little dissent or diversity. In this model, there exists no explanation that accounts for differences within the subcommunity. More specifically, the perspective is not capable of describing the cause or effect of a value judgment that deliberately disputes the normative judgment of such an oppositional community.

Let me return to radical women writers of the 1930s. This subcommunity has produced no text that has become part of the dominant culture's canon, although Tillie Olsen's *Yonnondio* once seemed like it might be on the way toward attaining such status (Zora Neale Hurston's canonical *Their Eyes Were Watching God* is considered the product of the African American community). The rest (including, among others, Meridel LeSueur's *The Girl*, Myra Page's *Gathering Storm*, Tess Slesinger's *The Unpossessed*, Josephine Herbst's *Rope of Gold*, and Clara Weatherwax's *Marching! Marching!*) constitute an alternative canon that is said to represent an overlooked and maligned subcommunity of radicalized working-class (white) women. This affiliation alone is what gives these books legitimacy. However, why these books are in print while others written by women within the same community are not remains an unanswered question. Amid the very critique of aesthetic judgment, such judgments apparently *are* made, albeit very quietly, in the privacy of one's own study or editorial office, so to speak. This is entirely inevitable. There is no escaping, finally, preferences and hierarchies, even when it comes to the literary productions of subcommunities championed by academics eager to show their solidarity. As to how aesthetics get smuggled into these preferences, no one's willing to "bliss and tell."

Regarding the canon of radical women writers of the 1930s, there is the revealing case of Mary McCarthy's *The Company She Keeps,* a radical novel written in the late thirties and published in 1942, whose psychological insights,
middle-class characters, critique of political cant, and Augustan sentences all
conspire to create a very different kind of book than those I have mentioned.
How do critics who share Smith's views account for such mutants? They usually declare such a book the product of a different community. In the case of
The Company She Keeps, the novel has been associated, until very recently, with
the New York Intellectuals, despite the fact that McCarthy, like these other
women, was a woman and a radical who wrote during the 1930s. No doubt,
within the various imagined, valuing communities, such as that of radical
women writers of the 1930s, there is a great deal of exclusivity. There are white
male values, fundamentalist Christian values, African American values, lesbian
values, and so on. As John Guillory points out, "In practice . . . a 'valuing community' is impossible to conceive at all without recourse to the local universal-
ization of its local values; such communities, once constituted, seldom refrain
from policing differences within themselves as a logical consequence of the
fact that they must exalt the difference of the community from other communities."[13] In the end, like most other attempts to historicize values by seeking
causal factors exclusively outside the close interaction between reader and text,
Smith's effort can account for neither similar contingencies that produce dissimilar values nor dissimilar contingencies that produce similar values.

It turns out that, paradoxically, by dismissing the aesthetic as a "universal"
discourse that suppresses difference, historicists remove any basis for apprehending the text as the objectification not of subcommunities or subcultures
but of the relations between groups and subjects. Here, I come to my last quar-
rel with Smith's position: in her endless sensitivity to falsely universalist claims
from above, she barely acknowledges that there are compelling shared experiences by those who live at or near the bottom. The category of class becomes
extremely important here, for as Guillory astutely observes, "the fact of class
determines whether and how individuals gain access to the means of literary
production. Indeed the system regulating such access is a much more efficient
mechanism of social exclusion than acts of judgment."[14] This system, of
course, operates in large measure through the schools, which regulate and distribute cultural capital unequally. Indeed, what Smith and most others do not
do is seriously challenge the location of the canon debate in the university. Unfortunately, the culturally dispossessed outside the university "have little occasion to rejoice at being 'represented' in the canon."[15] The situation is not all

that different from that depicted in Rebecca Harding Davis's classic 1861 novella *Life in the Iron Mills*, arguably the first work of realism in the United States. In that graphic depiction of a miserably exploited ironworker whose unique aesthetic sensibility is systematically suppressed by capitalist industrialism, we find this ironworker wandering into a church in which a radical minister, his heart warm with charity for the dispossessed, preaches for reform. But, Davis writes,

> his words passed far over the furnace-tender's grasp, toned to suit another class of culture; they sounded in his ears a very pleasant song in an unknown tongue. [The preacher] meant to cure this world-cancer with a steady eye that had never glared with hunger, and a hand that neither poverty nor whiskey had taught to shake. In this morbid, distorted heart of the Welsh puddler he had failed.[16]

What is particularly distressing about the current situation is not only that the ideological content of texts is almost uniformly thought to count much more than the unequal distribution of cultural capital but that so few have been interested in making the comparison.

Michael Denning's *The Cultural Front: The Laboring of American Culture in the Twentieth Century* was written from an overtly leftist perspective. It attempted, to paraphrase E. P. Thompson, to rescue the cultural achievements of the American Left from the enormous condescension of posterity. Denning informs us that the redoubtable doctors Spock and Seuss began their careers as Popular Front writers, that the Left once published a popular tabloid known as *PM*, that Frank Sinatra was "fairly close to the Communist Party line" (in the words of a friend),[17] that Billie Holiday sang the antilynching song "Strange Fruit" at Popular Front rallies and was harassed by the FBI for her political songs, that Communist Party associates ran a nightclub called Café Society that featured many of the jazz greats of the thirties and forties, and that the Popular Front included film stars Paul Muni, Joan Crawford, Bette Davis, Humphrey Bogart, Rita Hayworth, and John Garfield; musicians Benny Goodman, Count Basie, Duke Ellington, Artie Shaw, Cab Calloway, Sidney Bechet, Dizzy Gillespie, Miles Davis, and Charlie Parker; baseball players Satchel Paige, Josh Gibson, Red Rolfe, and Ripper Collins; and boxer Joe Louis. Denning's book means not only to retrieve a forgotten past for an academic constituency that might use it to correct the record but, beyond this, to provide the public with a history of accomplishments in cultural democracy that could help change our own times. I suspect that this pride in the past and concern for the future quietly kindles his book, making it so affectionately embracing yet, at times, so oddly indiscriminate in its judgments.

Denning claims that the cultural front "reshaped American culture. Just as the radical movements of abolition, utopian socialism, and women's rights sparked the antebellum American Renaissance, so the communisms of the depression triggered a deep and lasting transformation of American modernism and mass culture."[18] The achievements were most pronounced in the musical theater, cabaret blues, film, animation, and especially literature. With regard to the latter, Denning makes very large claims for the proletarian literary movement, which

> left a profound and lasting mark on American literature. The writers who emerged from the movement have proved to be the central figures of their generation, and the formal and aesthetic issues with which they grappled inflected the work of many other writers of their generation as well. . . . Moreover, the movement produced at least as many enduring and valuable works of fiction as any other literary movement or school in the twentieth century. . . . [T]he proletarian literature movement has had far greater influence on the subsequent half century of American fiction than the experimental modernism of Stein and Hemingway.[19]

To be sure, Denning's treatment of this movement contains fascinating material linking it to both the grotesque and the pastoral traditions; moreover, he offers fresh, discerning readings of such key texts as John Dos Passos's *U.S.A.* trilogy, Tillie Olsen's *Yonnondio,* and Mike Gold's *Jews without Money.* But his rather astonishing claims for the subgenre are badly out of proportion to its noteworthy but comparatively modest accomplishments. What enables Denning to entertain such extravagant claims is a bit of theoretical prestidigitation, by which a body of literature is transformed into a "formation," thereby creating a new and rather arbitrary canon, one that includes, among others, Richard Wright's *Native Son,* Ralph Ellison's *Invisible Man* (actually an *anti*proletarian novel), and even Henry Roth's *Call It Sleep.*[20] But even with this canon full of new ammunition, any claim that this new front line has somehow defeated the modernist juggernaut is, well, "unreal city." Experimental modernism triumphed because it transformed the means of artistic production while persuading its readers that its revolution was deeply grained, authentic, and moving. Arguing for the superiority of proletarian literature would involve making careful distinctions of quality. This Denning does not do, because he implies that aesthetic judgment is merely festooned ideology and, thus, that the work of the historically informed literary critic is to offer context, description, and local rationale as the real grounds for identification and appreciation. This leads him to make some unreliable literary judgments, such as calling *Yonnondio* "the lyric masterpiece of the Popular Front"[21] while neglecting the more accomplished efforts of Henry Roth, James Agee, and Richard Wright, all of whom achieved in their best work an unmatched level of psychological complexity, fully convincing stylistic and formal innovation, and political intelligence, albeit of the kind that increases awareness of the limitations of politics.

The Cultural Front would shift attention away from what Denning calls the "melodrama" of largely individual artistic and political choices, in favor of a deeper recognition of the preestablished social and aesthetic contingencies that determine those choices (hence his preference for Raymond Williams's category of "alignment" over "commitment"). This preference allows him to present a richly detailed map of the Left's midcentury cultural work, but it also prevents him from considering the impress of the individual sensibility upon art, morality, and politics. Thus, the quality of the specific aesthetic, ethical, and political choices that were made within the cultural front does not elicit enough of Denning's interest. For all its accumulated information, *The Cultural Front* does not get to the heart of things. In the end, we are still wanting for a precise account of not just the content but the character and quality of the cultural life he explores.

" 'Beauty is difficult,' as Beardsley says in one of Pound's *Cantos*. It seems a self-evident value and to brook no question. It thrives on keeping quiet and never explains itself"—so writes Denis Donoghue on the first page of *Speaking of Beauty*, a lovely book that gives voice to beauty by amplifying important conversations *about* beauty. Donoghue's book appeared in 2003 and has become part of a new body of work that places aesthetics back on the agenda and that even, in some cases, revives discussion about its subset beauty, which, since the 1960s and until recently, has been the ravished bride of quietness. I call this body of scholarly work the "new aesthetics," although it remains to be seen just how enduring and influential it will be. I cannot be certain as to the date or the particular text that inaugurated this development. Surely, there were powerful outliers who wrote rebuttals on behalf of aesthetics and even beauty during the height of the skeptical attacks on them. I think of Robert Alter's *The Pleasures of Reading in an Ideological Age* (1989), the several collections of William Gass's exemplary essays on form,[22] and Helen Vendler's persistent and broad-minded formalist studies of modern poetry.[23] As I have shown, *Contingencies of Value* (1988) ostensibly sought to rectify the neglect of evaluation in literary studies, even if, in practice, the results may have discouraged interest in actually doing evaluation. Certainly, the early and mid-1990s saw some initial momentum generated by studies that challenged the orthodoxy then (and still) prevailing. One of the earliest of the period was Richard Shusterman's *Pragmatist Aesthetics: Living Beauty, Rethinking Art* (1992), a maverick philosophical and cultural application of an updated Deweyan aesthetic to funk and hip-hop, among other things. Dave Hickey's *The Invisible Dragon: Essays on Beauty* (1993; recently reprinted in a revised edition by the University of Chicago Press) produced perhaps the opening salvo, at least so far as the visual arts are concerned. Among the earliest, if not the earliest of these efforts among literary scholars was George Levine's edited volume *Aesthetics and Ideology* (1994), a collection of compelling revisionary essays by an impressive group of scholars. Richard Rorty delivered his controversial "The Inspirational Value of Great Works of Literature" to a skeptical MLA audience in 1995. In the same year, Wendy Steiner produced *The Scandal of Pleasure: Art in an Age of Fundamentalism,* a ringing endorsement of art's empowering and relatively free virtualism. Several additional studies appeared in the late 1990s, including Gene H. Bell-Villada's *Art For Art's Sake and Literary Life* (1996), which offered a broad historical challenge to the eclipse of aesthetics in the academy; Jerrold Levinson's *The Pleasures of Aesthetics: Philosophical Essays* (1996); *Negotiating Rapture,* edited by Richard Francis (1996); *Aesthetics,* edited by Susan Feagin and Patrick Maynard (1997), one of the first of several readers in aesthetics that would appear in the coming decade; *Uncontrollable Beauty: Toward a New Aesthetics,* edited by Bill Beckley (1998); Philip Jackson's *John Dewey and the Lessons of Art* (1998), an effort to return art to an important place in a progressive educational system; James Kirwan's *Beauty* (1999); Gérard Genette's *The Aesthetic Relation* (1999); and Elaine Scarry's *On Beauty and Being Just* (1999), perhaps the most influential book of all.

After the advent of the new millennium, books on aesthetics proliferated.[24] What distinguishes the "new" aesthetics from the "old"? The following characteristics are shared by many, though not necessarily all, of the recent attempts to simultaneously return to and revise aesthetics. First, the new aesthetics repudiates any correspondence between its conspicuous interest in form or appreciation for craft and political conservatism, defense of the status quo, bourgeois mystification, and the like. Second, both old and new agree that, in the words of George Levine, the aesthetic is a "mode that operates differently from others and contributes in distinctive ways to the possibilities of human fulfillment and connection,"[25] but the new insists that aesthetics (particularly beauty) is not transcendent, ahistorical, or wholly separate from society, ideology, and politics. The new aesthetics seeks to restore the connection between the aesthetic and what Alexander Nehamas refers to as "the sensual, practical, and ethical issues that were the center of Plato's concern"[26] before being isolated, in part by the legacy of Kant. It engages robustly and complexly with political and moral problems by allowing for experience without direct consequence. Such experience is variously described as vicarious, virtual, free space, free play, utopian, and so on, because it affords a perspective that encourages awareness and judgment of one's own and others' interests. If such experience is not purely disinterested in the Kantian sense, neither is it a direct production of interest, nor does it necessarily reproduce that interest. Third, the new aesthetics discovers aesthetic life in a broader range of experiences than did the old. Not compelled to search for beauty exclusively in incomparable works of art, the new aesthetics finds it in all manner of recreation and work, in "low" as well as "high" culture, and in the commercial and entertainment spheres. Fourth, part of this greater capaciousness is a willingness to consider the spiritual dimensions of aesthetics, not as religion per se, but as deeply personal and intimate intensities that bear relationships to the more material aspects of the surrounding world. Fifth, unlike the old aesthetics the new is not committed to the notion that aesthetics emanates from the art object—that it is fundamentally a quality of the formal properties of the object—or to the notion that it is wholly a product of the artist's genius. The new aesthetics generally understands aesthetics to be a phenomenon produced through the interaction of both extrinsic and intrinsic factors, the boundary between them being porous. It rejects the idea that the art object and its specific powers are essentially nullities whose effects are wholly determined by contingencies. Sixth, the new aesthetics is interested in encouraging individually and socially aware affective experience among readers and observers as a powerful accompaniment to cognitive experience. It places greater stress on and gives greater validity to pleasure, appreciation (as distinct from worship), and judgment among readers in general and students in particular. Seventh, the new aesthetics is more broadly interdisciplinary than the old. Whereas the old often combined the insights of the two disciplines of literary criticism and philosophy, the new has ventured out farther to add to these cultural studies, psychology, biology, anthropology, and sociology.

One thing the old and new aesthetics continue to have in common is that neither, as yet, has concerned itself with the aesthetic experiences of people who live outside their academic and artistic worlds. Part of the reason Denis Donoghue is able to allude to beauty's quietness without fear of contradiction is that we have not asked very many people about beauty. Yet when I spoke with ordinary people about their aesthetic experiences—or, more precisely, their "encounters with beauty," as I phrased it—they were surprisingly pleased to have been asked and were eager to tell about beauty in their lives. The next vital step in the process of understanding aesthetics is to explore its presence in the world and not just in the advertising, cosmetic, and commercial sectors. Evaluation, as Barbara Herrnstein Smith observes, is a fundamental and indispensable part of existence; so is aesthetic experience in general, and it is time to seek it out, as John Dewey once suggested, "in the raw." It is to this task that I now turn.

CHAPTER 7

When Everyone Misreads the Same Book

My office at Syracuse University is in the Hall of Languages, the oldest build-ing on campus and allegedly the model for the Addams Family's macabre mansion. Rumor has it that former English major Charles Addams thought his professors overlooked his considerable talents, so he took his revenge by caricaturing the distinctive campus building that housed the English Depart-ment. It turns out that this is indeed rumor: Addams attended Colgate for two years and then the University of Pennsylvania for two years where similar apocryphal architectural stories are told. In any event, the Hall of Languages does bear some resemblance to the Addams mansion, and when I open my office door, it creaks. Once safely ensconced inside, I often glance at a banal poster entitled "American Writers," which has remained on my wall for years despite my perennial intention to redecorate. Like many professors, I want something on my office door or walls—a print, poster, quote, or motto—to infuse in my charges at least a love of literature and, even more ambitious, to do what the Torso of Apollo did for Rilke: inspire the epiphanic response "You must change your life." Like many of my colleagues, I have not quite found the right decor. The poster includes portraits of Nathaniel Hawthorne, Emily Dickinson, F. Scott Fitzgerald, Richard Wright, Walt Whitman, Mark Twain, Edgar Allan Poe, Edith Wharton, Henry David Thoreau, Herman Melville, and John Steinbeck.

There are three interesting facts about Steinbeck's presence on this poster: (1) measured by book sales, he is the most popular among all the writers pic-tured, even more popular than Twain; (2) he is the only Nobel Prize winner among them; and (3) he is the one writer in the group who lacks a critical con-sensus supporting his major status, and thus, for many critics, he does not be-long. Invariably, depending on whom you ask, they would suggest a worthier replacement—perhaps Henry James, T. S. Eliot, Wallace Stevens, William Faulkner, Zora Neale Hurston, Ralph Ellison, Flannery O'Connor, or Saul Bel-low, among others. His reputation, or case, dramatizes the differences between the experts and the common reader and offers an opportunity to explore the relationship between these two groups—one professional and often academic;

the other public, passionate, and often, like their professional counterparts, politically liberal or progressive.

This is especially true for readers of *The Grapes of Wrath*, Steinbeck's best-known novel. In 2004–5, they could be found in abundance in the Syracuse area because the CNY Reads campaign made *The Grapes of Wrath* its selection. CNY Reads was launched in central New York in 2002 as a "One City, One Book" or "If Everyone Reads the Same Book" campaign. Its first choice was Ernest Gaines's *A Lesson before Dying*, read in conjunction with a stage adaptation mounted at Syracuse Stage, the area's accomplished regional theater. In the following year, it chose Arthur Miller's *All My Sons*, but the campaign stumbled when Miller had to cancel his visit to Syracuse for health reasons. Then, *The Grapes of Wrath* was chosen by the campaign's selection committee in 2004. Like the earlier decisions, it was not chosen with an eye toward the intrinsic qualities of the book. It, too, was chosen in coordination with Syracuse Stage, which had scheduled a stage version of the novel for the following spring. The decision was made despite the fact that many on the selection committee had not read the novel or had read it so long ago that their memory of the novel was weak.

CNY Reads is one of a proliferating number of programs around the country that attempt to promote literacy, fellowship, and discussion within a self-defined "community" by inviting common readers to read a book in common. Begun by librarian Nancy Pearl in 1998 in Seattle, the idea has spread rapidly to cities as large as Chicago and as small as Plinkit, Oregon. In an interview, Pearl told me her original goal, in conjunction with a grant from the Lila Wallace–Reader's Digest Fund, was to increase the readership for literature.

> We chose literature because a book discussion should be about everything that a writer hasn't said, all those white spaces on the page. If it's a work of non-fiction, what you're talking about is the subject, and that's a different kind of discussion. I wanted a discussion that focused on why the author chose to do what he did. Why, in Russell Banks' book [*The Sweet Hereafter*], is the story told from four different points of view? I wanted these discussions to get into the whole creative process. It's fair to say we wanted readers to pay attention to craft, artistry, and those things that make literary texts something else in addition to being social documents. We didn't want a text that was subservient to some *idea*.

Another goal of Pearl's was the creation of community. "Our society is increasingly diverse, increasingly divisive," she observed.

When we look at people we see differences rather than commonalities. Today you can easily go through a whole day without having a meaningful conversation with anyone outside maybe your partner. You pump your own gas and check out your own groceries. There's a hunger in many people for some connection to another person. I wanted to bring people together. I think those connections can most meaningfully be made in a public space, like a library or a community center. Bringing together people of different genders, ethnicities, races, sexual orientations, and ages and having them talk about a piece of literature seemed to be a way of developing a common vocabulary.[1]

One cannot help but think these efforts are a response to the same circumstances that gave rise to Oprah's Book Club, which has been choosing books read by hundreds of thousands of women (and some men) since 1996. Oprah's choices have at times been controversial, for neither she nor her staff seem to possess any distinctive professional qualifications as writers or critics. Nonetheless, Oprah has chosen some very good books, such as Jonathan Franzen's *The Corrections,* Gabriel García Márquez's *One Hundred Years of Solitude,* and Toni Morrison's *Song of Solomon.* Indeed, following a brief hiatus, the club reemerged to place greater emphasis on "the classics": its selections have included Tolstoy's *Anna Karenina* and, in the summer of 2005, three novels by William Faulkner.

Oprah offers guidance and suggestions to readers beleaguered by a marketplace that includes an impossibly wide array of books and by the publicity and advertising machines that make it difficult to know what is really good. Her book club provides a service that others no longer provide. Among other things, she fills a void left by the decline of the public intellectual, who, until the 1960s, provided the common reader with discerning reviews of a large number of new books and accessible, high-powered essays on a range of literary and cultural issues. Whether public intellectuals in significant number might again serve today's much more diverse cultural world remains to be seen; if such a turn of events occurs, it will mean a reconsideration of academia's relationship to the general public. Today, most academics write for each other, often despite the widespread egalitarian sentiments found inside many English and humanities departments. As for the reading public, it is much more heterogeneous than it once was (indeed, some critics insist there is no single public but only publics): since the 1960s, the public has been made multiple by racial and ethnic inclusiveness, the empowerment of women, skepticism of cultural and political authority, identity politics, diversified interests, and niche publishing. Certainly one of the goals of Oprah's Book Club and "If Everyone Reads the Same Book" (or "One City, One Book") campaigns has been to create or re-create community.

In centuries past, everyone *was* reading the same book: the Good Book. In the nineteenth century, entire communities turned out to hear sermons lasting two to three hours. Home libraries commonly contained many of the same books: the Bible, of course, and Shakespeare, Bunyan's *Pilgrim's Progress*, Stowe's *Uncle Tom's Cabin*, Byron, Dickens, and Pope. As late as the mid-twentieth century, many people for whom art and ideas were of central importance were reading the same magazines. Susan Sontag, by way of example, tells of her excitement when, each month, she would make the trip from North Hollywood to the newsstand at Hollywood and Vine to get her copy of *Partisan Review*, for many years the most influential among a small number of publications that aspired to cover our intellectual and cultural life as it then existed in whatever breadth it was understood to have.

Today, no commonly acknowledged, comparable publications exist to which a large proportion of the educated readership turns. Different sectors of the public turn to their own specialized publications and, more important, to different media for whatever cultural sustenance they may find. The reasons for this changed state of affairs are many: fewer books reviewed in the dailies; intensified competition among an increasingly attractive array of other forms of leisure activity, from cable TV to convenient multiplex theaters to the Web to computer games to DVDs to iPods; the steady incorporation of culture into a shrinking number of multinational media leviathans that are market and profit driven and thus reluctant to publish new, experimental, or difficult writers; suburbanization and the decline of neighborhood centers with their independent bookstores.

So programs like CNY Reads are up against it. Are they working? To answer this question, we first need to see how these programs work. How are readers reading? What are they experiencing? What are they discussing? What are they learning? Are they enticed to read more, and if so, more of what? I set out to find answers to these questions—somewhat methodically but not scientifically. I did something academics rarely do but need to do: I spent time talking with readers. I did this instead of doing what academics have been doing for a century: read the book myself and write an analysis based on what the ideal reader thinks—the ideal reader being me, of course. The results of my inquiries reveal some fairly serious problems with the CNY campaign, problems that I imagine are not unique to one campaign but, rather, typical of campaigns nationwide.

So I went to the campaign kickoff event at the local Barnes & Noble. It was attended by approximately fifty people, most of them middle-aged or older, seemingly middle-class, and white. The master of ceremonies was the deputy county executive of Onondaga County, who began by quoting William James, who apparently once said that the most beautiful words in the English language are "summer afternoon." He then introduced Liverpool High School teacher Julia Bliven. She spoke briefly about the need to oppose censorship, explaining that *The Grapes of Wrath* has had a long history as a banned book. She followed this by quoting her students, who had read the book that summer and written about why it was worth reading. Here are the reasons they gave:

- Ma Joad is a strong female character, keeps the family together, and therefore shows the importance of women.
- The novel emphasizes the importance of the American Dream and the dignity of work.
- The novel shows man's inhumanity to man.
- Tom Joad's hard work, his dedication, and the fact that he never gives up hope is inspiring.
- The novel depicts the rich vs. poor.
- The novel teaches that we should never take our comfortable lifestyles for granted.
- The novel shows the importance of family and community.
- The novel makes us see that, by comparison, people today quit when things get hard.
- The novel helps us understand the Depression.
- The novel shows how Okies were victims of stereotyping.
- The novel reminds us of factory closings and unemployment in Syracuse.
- The novel offers an intimate depiction of character.

Bliven was followed by a brief dramatization of the famous farewell scene between Ma and Tom Joad, performed by two students from the Syracuse University Drama Department. The event concluded with a brief talk by Joyce Latham, the head of Onondaga County Public Library, who recounted the history of banning *The Grapes of Wrath* from public libraries.

I would make two observations about the event: (1) as an event centered on a Depression novel that focused on exposing oppressive social conditions and evoking sympathy for migrant farmers, it naturally seized on issues of social import; (2) it focused attention on these matters almost exclusively, thus construing the text fundamentally as a social document. The event did not consider the novel as a literary and artistic object (the sole exception being the student who commented on the vivid characterization). In fact, in all of my subsequent conversations with readers of the novel, this distinction loomed large, for nearly all readers developed their most compelling connection to the social and political messages embedded in the novel.

After the kickoff, there were many events scheduled in conjunction with the campaign. Several—displays at the local museum and community college and at Syracuse University Library—focused on artwork, photography, and/or books of the era. Several focused on censorship: Bird Library at Syracuse presented "Dirty Books and Dangerous Ideas," and the city's public library organized "Symposium: Censorship and *Grapes of Wrath*." The novel has indeed been a favorite target of the censors, burned on the steps of the Salinas Public Library in California and censored or targeted for any number of reasons—its critical depiction of the California growers or the state of Oklahoma, its alleged left-wing politics, its sexuality, or its controversial ending. The CNY Reads events enthusiastically emphasized the links between the novel and its historical and cultural surroundings and exuberantly explored how hostile readers have read or misread the ideological content and effect of the novel. But the particular "literariness" of the novel was not of crucial concern.

Rather typical of this approach was the performance of a Steinbeck impersonator at a local suburban library before some thirty people. Wearing brown slacks, a brown plaid shirt buttoned to the throat, a brown corduroy car coat, and a brown Stetson and holding a smokeless pipe—I believe it, too, was brown—the impersonator spoke in the first person about Steinbeck's life, about the regrettable censorship campaigns in California, about the impoverished migrant farmers with their poor housing and lack of adequate healthcare, and about the callous and bullying agricultural combines. Afterward, audience members asked about the dust bowl, sharecropping, Steinbeck's wife's role in helping to write the book (she supplied the title), the racial makeup of the tenant farmers, schooling for the children of the migrants, the impact of the novel, and Steinbeck's reputation abroad. Following questions, the discussion moderator, Lorraine Weicker, an English teacher at Eagle Hill Middle School, dramatically shifted the focus of the discussion to the artistry of the novel: "Everyone's into the discussion," she acknowledged, "but I don't want to miss the beauty of his language." She then read several of her favorite passages, including the famous "turtle-crossing-the-road" scene, commenting along the way on the powerful images found in the novel's impressionistic intercalary chapters.

I next visited Julia Bliven's tenth-grade English class and eleventh-grade Honors English class at Liverpool High School. The tenth-grade class had recently read selections from *The Grapes of Wrath*, and the eleventh-grade class had read the entire novel the previous summer. I spent most of my time with the eleventh graders. Initially I had hoped to record conversations with individual students and perhaps with the class as a whole, but I was told by school officials that the days of ready access to sixteen-year-old girls and boys without parental consent are well behind us, so instead of bringing my tape recorder, I came equipped with questionnaires, which the students filled out anonymously. Twenty-nine students were questioned. The results of the first two questions follow.

Question: On a scale of 1–10, how much did you enjoy *Grapes of Wrath*?	Frequency
10	1
9	1
8	3
7	8
6	2
5	6
4	4
3	2
2	1
1	1

Question: On a scale of 1–10, how would you rank John Steinbeck as a writer?[2]	Frequency
10	3
9	6
8	11
7	4
6	1
5	3

When asked about enjoyment, the mean score of the students was 5.7; when asked to rank Steinbeck, the mean score jumped to 7.9, a rather large discrepancy. That many students were willing to rank Steinbeck highly as a writer while at the same time registering an enjoyment level below that ranking suggests their awareness that the degree of pleasure one derives from reading is not necessarily correlated to the quality of writing. We all, I think, recognize that we may at times take less pleasure from a writer we admire than we think we ought. I would like to think that this realization impels many of us to become more responsive and maybe, therefore, more responsible readers (because we would be supporting the work of more deserving writers) by cultivating our taste. By not measuring quality solely on the basis of enjoyment, these students signaled at least the potential for further cultivation. I say this because had they insisted that a writer's worth be measured by the degree to which he or she entertains, any goad to self-improvement would be absent: writers who fed their appetite would be valued, and writers who left them unamused would be considered inferior. In my conversation with them, some students commented on Steinbeck's "greatness" and, modestly, their own inexperience when it came to reading such long and important books. These responses suggest awarenesses that ought to be expanded by emphasizing aesthetic literacy in the classroom, by which I mean the ability to understand how forms and craft contribute to meaning and evoke pleasure.

The questionnaire continued with the following two queries.

Question: What did you most like about the novel?	Frequency
Realism (the times, American Dream, discrimination against Okies, the language)	17
Family (strength, unity)	9
Theme of human solidarity	2
Themes	1
Formal elements (imagery, interchapters, voice)	5

Question: What did you like least about the novel?	Frequency
Too long (dragged, slow)	22
Too much description (the dust, the turtle, "too much diction")	12
Complex language (too many symbols, metaphors, images, complex sentences)	3
Dialect (old-fashioned, hard to read)	3

Context (didn't know or wasn't interested)	2
Nothing	1

Both sets of answers suggest the strong attraction that thematic material held for the students. Of the thirty-four separate answers given to the question about the sources of their enjoyment of the novel (students were allowed more than one answer each), the vast majority were related to thematics. Elements of form were explicitly cited only five times and were implied by the one student who praised the novel's realism because of the characters' true-to-life language. Concomitantly, most students cited elements that can best be understood as formal—length, pace, symbols, metaphors, images, sentence structure, dialect—when describing what they liked least. Clearly, whatever the intentions of their teacher (whom I shall discuss shortly), the students were overwhelmingly partial to the novel's ostensible subject matter and expressed little interest in or indulgence for those elements of language that, broadly speaking, make a novel a novel and not another kind of social text.

In an attempt to learn something of the students' actual experience with the novel,

I asked the following question.

Question: Do you remember any parts of the novel to which you had a stronger response than usual? Describe your response. What did Steinbeck do as a writer to elicit it? Indicate if you can't remember or didn't have any such responses.	Frequency
The ending (shocking, moving, repulsive at first)	11
Can't remember	6
Had no response	5
Turtle	2
Flood, Tom/Casy dialogues, death of grandma and Ma's restraint, Joad's removal from land	1 each
Descriptions of their responses	0

It is disappointing that nearly half the students either had no strong response to any portion of the novel or could not remember having had a strong response and did not answer. More troubling is the fact that not a single student was willing or able to provide a description of a response beyond a single adjective, in every case represented as an abstraction and not as an emotion or feeling that they experienced personally. For instance, students described the famous ending of the novel, in which a lactating Rose of Sharon offers her breast to a man dying of hunger, as "shocking," "moving," or "repulsive," but none wrote that he or she was shocked, moved, or repulsed. Perhaps this reluctance even anonymously to describe personal experience to a stranger was due to teenage insecurity or modesty; perhaps it was a result of being taught not to personalize responses (many of my own students, for instance, express surprise when I inform them that using "I" in an analytical essay is perfectly acceptable). Whatever the reason, it seems that students are not being encouraged to explore, with any degree of self-consciousness, their own responses, whether cognitive or affective, and therefore their own sensibilities. If the responses I received were actual intensities of intellect, they seemed to be of the abstract analytical sort exclusively; otherwise, I was likely being treated to the gestures of dull ritual.

This reluctance or inability to value a complex personal response to literature, a response, of course, that need not avoid analytical precision, seemed to inform student responses to my next question as well.

Question: What's accomplished, if anything, by reading literature?	Frequency
Learning about the world, others	13
Learning to apply lessons	6
Gaining knowledge in general	4
Enjoyment, entertainment	3
Expand imagination	4
Learn about writing techniques, new words	2
Help express feelings	1

Here, a large majority of the students cited gaining knowledge (about the world, about lessons, or in general) as the chief benefit to be derived from reading literature, thereby signaling literature's value in terms of its power to provide social knowledge rather than, say, stir the soul. It is not that gaining knowledge about society cannot engross one's entire self, evoke powerful feelings, or generate pleasure. Perhaps these responses are implicit in the students' claims about learning and gaining knowledge, but I doubt it. In only a small number of answers (eight, to be exact) did students explicitly point to the personal effects of encountering literature. Among these, a smaller number might be described as aesthetic responses. It would seem we have much to do to ensure that our young people attain aesthetic literacy.

The students' teacher Julia Bliven received her BA in English from the State University of New York at Oswego and has been teaching English ever since—for thirty years now. She is passionate about literature, enjoys reading immensely, and sees herself as trying to teach literature both as a source of social knowledge and aesthetic experience. She found herself thoroughly absorbed by *The Grapes of Wrath,* which she had read twice before, as a first-year college student and as a young teacher. "I got lost in Steinbeck's language and writing style. I let myself fall into the writing, the weaving of the words and sentences around each other," she exclaimed. Most evocative to her were the "staccato, fast-paced" intercalary chapters and the scene in the first government camp in which starving children surround Ma Joad as she cooks the meager portions meant for her own family. In the early class discussions, she had stressed the historical context of the novel, with particular attention paid to the Depression and the unusual weather patterns that gave rise to the dust bowl. But these conversations, at least in her honors course, led to discussions of images such as the tractor, which Steinbeck uses to sharply distinguish machines from men and to distinguish the uses of technology from people and their needs. On several occasions, the students broke down individual paragraphs in what Bliven called "stimulating" conversations about the writing style and language. According to Bliven, these discussions did not include judgments about the quality of the writing. The only time Steinbeck's power or limitation as a writer came up was in the context of explaining why some have sought to censor the novel.

One of the reasons it is easier to teach the themes, Bliven maintained, is that students are not encouraged to think about writing as an art. This was made amply evident in the study guides and material provided by the sponsors of the CNY Reads program, nearly all of which emphasized the social ramifications of the novel. For instance, Syracuse Stage's extensive Web site (no longer active) included a plot summary and the following Web pages: "Steinbeck's Life," "The Dust Bowl" (including a video of an actual dust storm), "Migrant Life," "Voices of Dissent during the Depression," "Route 66," and "The Mixed Critical Response." By including only book reviews from the dailies and weeklies, the last Web page missed a prime opportunity to address crucial debates. There was no mention of major critics who have weighed in on the novel—Malcolm Cowley, Kenneth Burke, Edmund Wilson, Lionel

Trilling, Alfred Kazin, Harold Bloom—all of whom wrote influential and memorable reviews and essays. Is it important that the most trenchant critical conversations of the past sixty-odd years were not part of the current conversation? I think so. If we are going to encourage the public discussion of the arts, it seems obvious that some of the deeply interesting responses of the past ought to be known and allowed to provoke our thoughts.

The critical background to the novel began with the fanfare surrounding its publication, which was the biggest literary event of 1939. The novel appeared in March, and within a month, 2,500 copies were selling each day. Steinbeck won the National Book Award and the Pulitzer in 1940; the movie rights immediately sold, and the now-famous film version directed by John Ford and starring Henry Fonda, Jane Darwell, and John Carradine appeared only nine months later. In 1982, the *New York Times* reported that *The Grapes of Wrath* was the second best-selling literary novel in paper ever, with sales of over 14,600,000 copies.

Yet the status of the novel among the critics was and remains uncertain. Though Steinbeck was abundantly honored during the course of his career— he received the U.S. Medal of Freedom and the Nobel Prize—and though his popularity as a novelist still endures, his critical reputation has never reached the heights of his public acclaim and, in fact, has suffered a considerable decline. Harold Bloom, for instance, has said that *The Grapes of Wrath* is a "very problematical work, and very difficult to judge. As story . . . it lacks invention, and its characters are not persuasive representations of human inwardness. . . . He gives us a vision of the Oklahoma dustbowl, and it is effective enough. . . . It has social and economic meaning, but as a vision of loss it lacks spiritual and personal intensity. Steinbeck is more overtly biblical than Hemingway, but too obviously so. Steinbeck is not an original, or even an adequate stylist; he lacks skill in plot, and power in the mimesis of character."[3] In his classic *On Native Grounds,* Alfred Kazin combines an assessment of *The Grapes of Wrath*'s strengths and limitations.

> Though the book was as urgent and as obvious a social tract for its time as *Uncle Tom's Cabin* had been for another, it was also the first novel of its kind to dramatize the inflictions of the crisis without mechanical violence and hatred [as had many proletarian novels]. The bitterness was there, as it should have been, the sense of unspeakable human waste and privation and pain. But in the light of Steinbeck's strong sense of fellowship, his simple indignation at so

much suffering, the Joads, while essentially marionettes, did illuminate more than the desperation of the time: they became a living and challenging part of the forgotten American procession. . . . Though [Steinbeck's] interests have carried him squarely into certain central truths about the nature of life, he has not been able to establish them in human character. Nothing in his books is so dim as the human beings who live in them, and few of them are intensely imagined as human beings at all.[4]

Finally, Lionel Trilling observed of the novel,

If we are to talk about literature in its relation with social good and the future of democracy we ought to be aware of how harmful literature can be. A book like *The Grapes of Wrath* cockers-up the self-righteousness of the liberal middle-class: it is so easy to feel virtuous in our love for such *good* poor people! The social emotions can provide a safe escape from our own lives and from the pressures of self-criticism and generously feed our little aggressions and grandiosities. Shelley says that it would have been a pity if the philosophers of the Enlightenment had never lived, but, he goes on, "it exceeds all imagination to conceive what would have been the moral condition of the world if neither. . . . Dante, Petrarch, Boccaccio, Chaucer, Shakespeare, Calderon, . . . nor Milton had ever existed." Some of these men were proud, even arrogant, in the ways they conceived their poethood; others were simple, humble or casual; all made their effect by being the men they were, by the tone and style of their utterance, not by setting out to fulfill their societal function. It is conceivable that books like Steinbeck's have an immediate useful effect by rallying people to the right side. But ultimately they leave hollowness and confusion.[5]

Elsewhere, Trilling was equally provocative.

John Steinbeck is generally praised for his reality and his warmheartedness, but [his] lower-class characters receive a doctrinaire affection in proportion to the suffering [that defines] their existence, while the ill-observed middle-class characters are made to submit not only to moral judgment but to the withdrawal of all fellow-feeling, being mocked for their very misfortunes and almost for their susceptibility to death. Only a little thought or even less feeling is required to perceive that the basis of his creation is the coldest response to abstract ideas.[6]

These views, part of a much larger critical conversation that includes many responses more favorable to the novel, tend to reflect my own ambivalence about the novel. But even were this not the case, I would still argue for their continued importance and relevance to the kinds of public conversations it seems to me we want to encourage. Common readers ought to be encouraged to take part in critical, evaluative conversations. We should not assume that politics, notions of good citizenship, or social sympathy and solidarity have nothing to do with the recognition of literary artistry or with the capacity to discern superior expression and take pleasure in that expression. Such recognitions and widened capacities might lead us to expect and require the same from those in power, from institutions, from our fellow citizens, and from ourselves. Some of our best critics have raised some fundamental questions relating to the novel and to us. In our quest for active citizenship, community, and social justice, how well did Steinbeck know and how well do we know our perceived adversaries? How well did Steinbeck know and how well do we know our perceived allies, the excluded and afflicted? How much do we want to know them? What are our actual relations with them? To what extent is our sympathy for them the result of vital ongoing civic engagement with them? Considering the so-called red state/blue state divide—more accurately a rural/urban divide—which persisted, though with less intensity, during the 2008 presidential elections, are we academics, who tend to be middle-class liberals and progressives, adequately reaching out to all sectors of the population, regardless of their political and social views, in order to have inclusive conversations about books and the issues they raise?

CNY Reads and the dozens of other "One City, One Book" campaigns across the country have accomplished a good deal. They have revived notions of citizenship and community and created occasions and settings in which people of different ages, incomes, and races encounter literature and, through that literature, one another. But might we infuse our discussion of Steinbeck's novel and others with fewer proper sentiments and comforting pieties and more debate and argument, so that we get closer to the grain of our democracy? Community, after all, depends on the narratives by which people make sense of their condition and interpret the common life they share. At its best, even political deliberation is not about competing policies alone but also about competing interpretations of the character of a community, of its purposes and ends, of its understanding of quality in two related senses: quality of expression and quality of life. This, in particular, is why aesthetic literacy is of vital importance to our democracy. Democratic pluralism, as the philosopher

John Rawls never tired of reminding us, must be a pluralism of *incompatible* yet reasonable comprehensive doctrines. That means we need to create conditions that encourage constructive disagreement.

We have gotten used to talking about "interrogating" texts. But of course, good books interrogate us. They force us, with their incorporeal coaxing, into self-examination, useful doubt, and occasional retractions and confessions. One example comes from Harold Bloom, whom I quoted earlier. He had second thoughts about *The Grapes of Wrath,* and his willingness to turn back upon himself has always struck me as one of the more admirable gestures I know among critics.

> I remain uneasy about my own experience of rereading *The Grapes of Wrath.* Steinbeck is not one of the inescapable American novelists. Yet there are no canonical standards worthy of human respect that could exclude *The Grapes of Wrath* from a serious reader's esteem. Compassionate narrative that addresses itself so directly to the great social questions of its era is simply too substantial a human achievement to be dismissed. Whether a human strength, however generously worked through, is also an aesthetic value in a literary narrative, is one of those large issues that literary criticism scarcely knows how to decide. One might desire *The Grapes of Wrath* to be composed differently, whether as plot or as characterization, but wisdom compels one to be grateful for the novel's continued existence.[7]

The *Grapes of Wrath* campaign was followed by several others, in which CNY Reads chose two novels, a work of nonfiction, and a volume of selected poems as its featured books. With the close of the *Grapes of Wrath* campaign, the Syracuse University Library Associates took over administration of CNY Reads. Its planning board promptly chose as its next book a formulaic work of historical fiction with a mystery overlay, *North Star Conspiracy* by the regional author Miriam Grace Monfredo. The novel is set during the 1850s in Seneca Falls, New York, where the protagonist, a feminist librarian, helps an enslaved young woman escape on the Underground Railroad. Monfredo trots out the likes of Susan B. Anthony, Elizabeth Cady Stanton, and Frederick Douglass to lend star power to the impeccable, if rather predictable, politics that no doubt delighted the progressive portion of her suddenly expanded readership (the novel had actually been out of print at the time it was selected). To be sure, the book proved to be, in the words of Gregory Griffin, then the program's director, "a catalyst for community-wide discussion about important issues," including issues of authority and justice, race relations, and women's rights.[8] To its credit, the new leadership encouraged many new local organizations to join—the CNY Reads consortium grew to over forty members—and sponsored over fifty events relating to *North Star Conspiracy*.

This was no mean feat, but I questioned the wisdom of choosing competent but undistinguished writing—*North Star Conspiracy* is pulp fiction with a conscience—as the basis for such an impressive number of community events and conversations. Like the writers of "soap operas for social change" and certain telenovelas that deliver to working-class viewers important social messages such as condom use and respect for women, Monfredo was officious about sending progressive political messages couched in romantic and family drama. Although hard to measure, the CNY Reads campaign likely did some service to the community by helping hundreds of Central New Yorkers confirm and reconfirm their progressive views. But this service ought to be provided by politicians, religious leaders, movement activists, and progressive history and government teachers, not necessarily advocates of books and reading as a basis for building community. When "One City, One Book" campaigns take it on themselves to cater to particular constituencies and promote particular political values, they limit themselves to serving but a portion of the population. Those who have conservative views of authority or justice or who do not hold enlightened views of race or gender relations as progressives have defined them are not sought after, do not take part in the conversation, and thus are not involved in the "community-building" process. Indeed, commitment to progressive values is no guarantee of solidarity with the victims of inequality or injustice, who are as often conservative as they are liberal. One reason Nancy Pearl placed a premium on literature was her belief in the unique nature of this art as a creative medium that subordinates ideas to complex experience rather than the reverse and renders that experience in discerning and pleasing ways. Literature thus appeals to diverse communities that might not otherwise communicate or that communicate adversarially with perceived enemies. *The Grapes of Wrath* at least had generated a sustained and often profound critical conversation over many decades, to which the public ought to have been made privy; with *North Star Conspiracy*, no such critical response existed, because the quality of its writing and subtlety of its thought were not sufficient to provoke one. It is no small irony that a program under the auspices of a university had, by its choice of text, essentially rendered its literature faculty useless. Any public-minded scholar willing to take the time to join the campaign would have had to be content either with dwelling on the rather obvious historical and political thematics of *North Star Conspiracy* or with explaining to bewildered audiences (not to mention angry organizers and author) why the writing lacked distinction. Such would have been an unenviable task, though certainly not a worthless one. Not surprisingly, there were no takers.

The next choice of CNY Reads was *The Kite Runner.* I had not read it at the time and did not vote for it. My vote went to Grace Paley's *Collected Stories,* which did not make the short list. I did not involve myself with the *Kite Runner* campaign other than to devote a session of my first-year honor's seminar to a discussion of the prodigious best seller. (Anonymous literary brokers within the Syracuse University administration had chosen the book as required reading for all incoming first-year students—without consulting faculty in the Creative Writing Program, the English Department, or our equivalent of a comparative literature department.) Like my colleague, novelist Arthur Flowers, who thankfully had the temerity to point out some of the novel's artistic limitations during his speech at the fall convocation, I admired aspects of the novel and felt it would impart valuable information about Afghanistan to a largely uninformed audience, but I had reservations about its literary merit. I felt that any book chosen to be read by so many ought to be distinctive and not just popular; it needed more to recommend it than its depiction of an unfamiliar social world, no matter how relevant to current events—it had to possess a level of achievement that would delight readers then and long after its topical interest waned.

So I took a pass on *The Kite Runner,* partly for these reasons and partly because I was overwhelmed with other scholarly and administrative responsibilities. Just as with my earlier decision to bow out of the campaign featuring *North Star Conspiracy,* I agonized over my decision. In both cases, I felt there was little expertise I could contribute to the public discussions: I was an expert neither in nineteenth-century American history nor in Afghan culture. I certainly could have joined the public conversation by debunking the books chosen and explaining their deficiencies, but I was reluctant to reinforce attitudes about the elitism of the academy by playing the perceived role of ogre, regardless of how diplomatic I might be in my effort to encourage readers to expect more.

But no matter how reasonable these explanations seemed under the circumstances, perhaps my decisions to retreat back to the academy were ill-considered after all. For if "going public" is to mean developing with nonacademic communities *sustainable* relationships marked by the kind of commitment and loyalty we show our students, it would seem we need to find ways to engage the public through thick and thin, as it were—to cultivate styles of dialogue and forms of partnerships that allow for difficult as well as comfortable interaction. This might be thought of as a new type of relationship with the public. Whereas the traditional way of engaging the public has been through criticism and commentary by public intellectuals—absolutely vital, time-honored efforts that have been an indispensable component of the nation's cultural life, not to speak of what exists of its democratic political life—perhaps there is room now for an additional modality of public engagement, in which a more regular, more immediately reciprocal and collaborative relationship is built between the academy and the common reader.

CHAPTER 8

Reading Simic in Syracuse

It was not my idea. It was hatched by Phil Memmer, poet and director of Syracuse's Downtown YMCA Writer's Center. In the previous year, I had suggested Elizabeth Bishop as CNY Reads' featured author, but I had never considered a contemporary poet, no less one as odd as Charles Simic. But Phil was charged up: he had already booked Simic for a fall reading, which meant Simic would be in town twice because he would also be reading for the Creative Writing Program as part of the Raymond Carver Reading Series on the Syracuse University campus.[1] In addition, Simic had just been appointed the fifteenth poet laureate of the United States. So we quickly patched together a presentation to the CNY Reads board, in which we gave some background on Simic, read a couple of his more accessible poems—"Country Fair" and "Fork"—and offered ideas for programming. Much to our amazement, the board members voted to place Simic on their short list and eventually chose him as the featured author for 2008–9. CNY Reads thus became the first "One City, One Book" consortium ever to choose an individual poet (and there are hundreds of these groups that, together, have likely made thousands of choices over the past decade and a half). The Seattle group, I believe, once selected Bill Moyers's *The Language of Life,* a collection of contemporary poems by a range of poets, but none has ever chosen a single poet. Simic's agent reported that when he first heard the news, Simic was convinced it was a joke.

After the vote, Phil and I looked at each other: "Now what?" We had succeeded in championing a seventy-year-old poet who was born and raised in Belgrade; suffered through the hell of Nazi occupation during World War II and Stalinism afterward (he once quipped that Hitler and Stalin were his travel agents); moved with this history in his marrow to a country where history is bunk; writes funny casual poems about atrocity or, worse, sex; owes a debt to surrealism and Serbian folktales; and possesses no conventional religious sensibility. How were we going to bring this poet into our community and schools and find interested readers there?

We would bring his poetry to the local mall, of course, the heart and soul of American cultural life. I had read in Joan Rubin's *Songs of Ourselves* that, some years ago, they had celebrated the first National Poetry Month at the Mall of America outside Minneapolis by having shoppers compose poems using magnetic letters on refrigerators supplied by Sears. I called the business office of our local mall, which includes a Best Buy, and asked about the possibility of doing the same here. The initial response of the officious young associate over the phone was not encouraging: there would likely be insurance issues, we might interfere with pedestrian traffic, there were no free dates until after the holiday season, and moving refrigerators through the mall could be a problem. Sensing imminent defeat, I changed tactics, drove to the mall, and walked into the Best Buy store. Four months earlier, I had had a nasty run-in with a snotty store manager there with a Napoleon complex, over a condensation-damaged digital camera he refused to take back even though my wife and I had paid extra for an extended warranty. I made sure I avoided him and was soon introduced to another manager, who, when I introduced myself as an English professor and said I wanted to propose an unusual new way to sell refrigerators, politely escorted me up a staircase, through a locker room, and into his cinder-block office. There I laid out my plan, asking for a dozen large fridges to be wheeled out to the center of the mall, which would not only have poems composed on their doors but price tags on them as well. I mentioned the insurance concerns of the mall administration. Much to my surprise and pleasure, this young manager, who worked for a chain store with an aggressive corporate culture that left as little to chance as possible, said that it sounded like a good idea and that he would do it. Armed with Best Buy's support, I contacted the mall associate, who, after consulting with his team, informed me we could have our Poetry Palooza in January, after the holiday season was over.

Back on campus, I was teaching an Introduction to Poetry class to twenty-five students. It was the first time I had ventured to teach an introductory course in poetry after years of teaching Twentieth-Century American Poetry to seniors or graduate students, and it turned out to be one of the worst classes of my twenty-five-year career. Perhaps it was the chemistry of this particular group, the fact that so many young people seem to lack the patience to slow down and read carefully, or just plain poor teaching. To wake up my dozing students, I devoted a class to listening to hip-hop lyrics and viewing videos of poetry slams. This led to my suggesting that in lieu of a traditional analytical final essay, students could involve themselves in some sort of public scholarly project. Having just received the green light from the mall, I told them about the idea, and several students picked up on it and resolved to organize a trial-run Poetry Palooza event at the student center during an afternoon a couple days before Thanksgiving. The students procured six mini-fridges from the storeroom where they are rented out to students living in dorms, Barnes & Noble donated magnetic words, the university bookstore set up a table full of Charles Simic's poetry, and a few other students made up a game in which players were asked to match poets and poems.

I had visions of my students standing alone for four hours in the student center lobby, but as it turned out, I had nothing to worry about: although it would be an exaggeration to say students flocked to the event, there was never a time when at least one student was not busy composing a poem. Much of the time, all six mini-fridges were being used, and in the end, there were some thirty poems submitted for prizes, poems that my entire class judged to determine the winners. The stage was set for the citywide event at the mall, scheduled for two weeks into the next semester, when I would be teaching Twentieth-Century American Poetry, an upper-division course.

Whereas the previous class had been one of my worst, this may very well have been my most enjoyable course ever. The first class included a half-dozen students who resented having to read poetry closely and analyze its meanings, because they thought poetry was exclusively about authentic emotion that must, to paraphrase Wordsworth, be murdered to dissect. The latter class included several talented poets and many poetry lovers. Having anticipated the possibility that some of these students would be interested in getting involved in the CNY Reads campaign, I assigned Simic's *Sixty Poems* as the first volume of the semester. I also offered students three tracks to choose from to satisfy the writing requirements for the course: they could choose to write a traditional analytical midterm and final essay, they could produce a half-dozen two-page response papers in which they would emphasize emotional and intellectual responses to the poetry, or they could produce a publicly engaged piece of scholarship that centered around poetry in the community. Nine of twenty-four students chose the last, track three, and all of them opted to get involved in the effort by CNY Reads to bring the poetry of Charles Simic to the wider community. The first event they would work on would be the Carousel Mall Poetry Palooza.

The event took place on a Saturday, from 10:00 a.m. to 5:00 p.m. I arrived early and was immediately faced with a quandary: we were given permission to set up in a somewhat out-of-the-way location on the ground floor, but only twenty-five feet away was the floor of the mall's central atrium, which would have given us much more visibility. Should we set up there even though we were told we would impede shoppers in that area? Once we were told that the mall official I had been in communication with would not be coming to work that day, we took our chances and set up in the atrium. It turned out we did not impede traffic and never did hear from any angry mall officials.

Once the refrigerators were wheeled in to make a large circle (our "Maytag Stonehenge," as my student David Medeiros put it), my students began to drift in. I assigned two to conduct a "mix-and-match" poetry contest, each of the others to a pair of refrigerators where they would explain the rules, oversee the poets, and photograph each poem with their cell phone cameras and also record them the old-fashioned way—on paper. The rules were quite simple: poets would compose their poems using the available words plus words they could write onto blank magnetic strips. There was no time limit—indeed, several poets lingered over their compositions for nearly an hour—and previously composed poems were not allowed. There would be Barnes & Noble and Borders gift cards for the winners in three different groups: a children's group for ages up to twelve, a teen group for ages thirteen to seventeen, and an adult group for ages eighteen and above.

To our chagrin and, as it turned out, our great disadvantage, the microphone we requested was not provided. Thus, our intention of reading Charles Simic poems throughout the day was only partially realized. As loud as we read, we could not be heard by shoppers who did not walk directly toward us, and this significantly reduced our audience. Nevertheless, the event attracted an impressive number of people and very active participation. From noon until late in the afternoon, nearly every refrigerator was taken, and by the end of the day, local poets had composed over eighty poems. Many had tested their knowledge by playing a poetry matching game, and a few had purchased volumes of Simic's poetry from a table that the Syracuse University Bookstore set up. Best Buy even sold a refrigerator. We received impressive local media coverage: the local National Public Radio station aired a piece, as did several of the local network television stations, and the local press covered the event.

Not only had we met hundreds of poetry enthusiasts from the community, but my students spent a day at the mall that, by their own testimony, they will not soon forget. None of them had ever taken part in an event such as this, and they had no idea what to expect. Most were skeptical and were not expecting much, anticipating an awkward day hawking poetry to indifferent shoppers. All were surprised at the public response, and many were quite taken by the degree of interest, if not downright passion, that many people showed. At semester's end, the students evaluated their experience in assigned reflection papers, and these revealed the extent to which the event caused them to think deeply about a number of issues that had to do with poetry, society, and higher education. The comments of two of the students follow.

After seven semesters of undergraduate study, I find it increasingly rare that I come across something completely novel. Of the three options on the syllabus, track three stood out from anything I had done before. . . . I had probably written a hundred essays and papers as an undergraduate, but nothing remotely like this; it was simultaneously educational, subversive, and political. There was something disruptively playful about it and my curiosity wouldn't let me miss such an opportunity. Looking back, I learned a great deal about how people interact with poetry—lessons I may not have picked up in the classroom.

Poetry Palooza engaged the community by inserting itself into distinctly nonacademic space. The circle of refrigerators in the center atrium must have been a confusing sight to those used to seeing S[yracuse] U[niversity] students in roving packs of consumers in the mall. . . . None of this would be particularly remarkable on University Hill, but this was largely unprompted and in the middle of a mall. With few exceptions these people were caught in the middle of their chores—some not having devoted a thought to poetry in months or years. Yet many shook off the rust and took to the task. Anyone who questions that great poetry has a power to move people's emotions and nestle in their memories would have been shaken in their disbelief. I'm tempted to doubt that the reaction would have been the same had it been a "Trigonometry Palooza."

Though I was primarily stationed at the "mix-and-match" game, I did get several opportunities to work the refrigerators. There, people were invited to compose original poems using a provided set of magnetic words. Among the remarkable phenomena that emerged from this part of the palooza was the apparent gulf in quality along the age axis. Despite a roughly equivalent size of the age-group submissions, the consensus of the judges agreed that the children's submissions were more accomplished than those of the two elder groups.

While I won't pretend to understand the reasons for this outcome, this experience leads me to believe that the perception of poetry as uniquely difficult and inaccessible is largely a myth. If anything, the teens and adults seemed to be the ones struggling to express themselves creatively in poetry. Where the children created candid narratives, the adults often layered their poems with scatterbrained excesses and nonsense. The adult poems either gushed about love to the point of being overwhelming or had no discernible structure or meaning. One got the sense of the adult notions of what poetry was expected to be. I, for one, will never look at children's poetry the same way again.

The great thing about the track three assignments, though, was that in many cases we were able to force people past that initial resistance. Interrupting someone's shopping habits by literally standing in their way or demanding that a student work through a difficult poem was entirely unlike my previous experiences with poetry. What I had considered a private, contemplative pursuit was suddenly thrust into a much more public light. The most revolutionary aspect of the project, however, was the setting. For all of the talk of "scholarship in action" around Syracuse University, too many projects carrying that tag only engage those who wish to be engaged; no one takes students off the hill against their will or drags townspeople onto campus. The flat-footed participants made for a far better experiment than could have been had with the self-selecting crowd that would have shown up had these been held at the university. Unwilling participants though they were, I was struck by how much the locals were generally pleased to see us students in their everyday context. The track three assignments worked to demystify poetry by taking it out of the academy and taking it to the people directly.[2]

At the beginning of the semester, I was not really sure what I was getting into. . . . I assumed we might need to attend a neighborhood poetry reading or visit a high school or elementary school—maybe get to know a few more people outside of the S[yracuse] U[niversity] community. But I definitely did not expect to come home from the Poetry Palooza feeling eager to relax with friends and let go of/try to make sense of a few major off-putting thoughts that had built up in my head during the day.

I partly came away from the mall event not expecting to feel so awkward having to present myself as a "university student" (at an expensive private college) before the "general public." And maybe I am engineering some of this in my own head, but at the beginning of the day, I sensed an awkward disconnect between my efforts and how the rest of the community might perceive them. I honestly was worried that the public might assume we put on the event for "charity" or to "exploit" them for their "banality" and "cute" attempt at poetry. Truly, for the first time in a long while, I was very put off by the journalists—I wanted to tell them to go away and find something else to film. Their presence almost seemed to cheaply reward my assumed "generous" efforts to get off campus and talk to some people less educated than me and my peers. The cameras seemed to make us into celebrities, recording the proof that we, the self-assumed "educated elite," in fact do care about other people out there.

At the palooza, I really had a hard time walking up to people in the beginning. If I did approach a family/person/couple, I hoped we could share ideas equally—as if no one knew more than the other—like talking to my friends. Looking back, I feel silly thinking these things and making assumptions about other people's perceptions of me. I really now hope that the people I approached frankly could have cared less I was from SU studying poetry in an academic class. I hope all they wanted to do was write a poem because it was how they felt at the moment. Maybe they just had something they wanted to say and I merely had the supplies to help them do it.

Aside from my own self-doubts, I was really moved by the many displays of pride and self-accomplishment from young and old after finishing a poem. I remember one very young girl running up to the turn-in area so impatient to read her work to me and other people. She just beamed with delight and excitement and reminded me of myself when I was little. I was also impressed that many people labored for almost an hour at the refrigerator—and when they were finally finished, all they really wanted was for me or someone else to say, "Are you done?" then write the poem down, maybe read it aloud or quietly, and finally nod in approval. But, as I said before, this sense of approval, or even sense of me taking on the role of "approver," gets awkward for me to handle. Yes, we learn ways to interpret and study poetry in class. And yes, I think some poems have more depth, originality, and interest than others. But, in this type of situation, who am I to tell someone, based on my education, that his or her poem is good or not as good as someone else's. Once I assume the role of "literary judge," I somehow seem intellectually/socially "better" and unintentionally above them.[3]

The author of the last comments is a young Caucasian woman from a fairly well-to-do family, and the anxieties she registers are typical of many sensitive but protected middle- and upper-class students I have asked over the years to do publicly engaged scholarship. These students must be encouraged to have serious encounters with literature during their college careers, and sometimes this can best be accomplished with one foot in academia and one foot in the world that books most often describe and in which they arise and are read. Once out of the literary and theory hothouse that English departments have sometimes become, students are able to confront issues of class, taste, and judgment head-on, and the press of consequence deepens their experience. In many cases, the problems they identify and the solutions they seek add considerably to personal and social knowledge and also lead to a greater understanding of differences in quality and judgment and of how to translate this awareness into tactful, judicious, and appreciated acts of evaluation. The humanities in general and good books in particular are in great need of readers *and* ambassadors. The vast majority of our students will leave academia within a few short years, and we have an obligation to them and to literature to prepare them for comfortably entering and skillfully improving the cultural world they find there. That my student grappled with her privileged status and comparatively cultivated tastes while simultaneously interacting with the public and with me, her professor, meant she could retreat neither into snobbery nor into the self-abnegation common among sensitive, guilt-ridden and publicly inactive academics and their students. Because she would eventually serve on the selection committee that chose the winning poems in the three age-groups I have mentioned, she was required to examine and adjust her attitudes according to the requirements of fair judgment as she was best able to determine them under the circumstances and by her best lights. In such a context, where her goodwill and the interests of her fellow citizens were at stake, my student's wringing hands were compelled to grab the wheel and drive.

Five of the nine students who helped put on the mall event served on the committee to select the best poems. We met for a couple hours one evening at my home, and our conversations about the poetry were among the most insightful and useful of the entire semester from a pedagogic perspective. Faced with a job that needed doing, whatever reluctance the students may have had about making value judgments—due to either their "elite" status or their uncertainty about their powers of discrimination—was transformed from abstract and paralyzing anxiety into acts of judgment that combined awareness of skill with awareness of possible bias. Our conversations were most often centered around such things as diction, rhythm, sound, sense, and syntax (which, by the way, in classroom settings rarely elicit the kind of focused attention they did here), but our backgrounds and values sometimes insinuated themselves into our deliberations and occasionally affected our judgment. What is most important is that students learned to make decisions and live with them. Reading dozens of poems written by passionate poetry lovers who often lacked much training and usually had not read widely or deeply exposed my students to a large number of conventional and thus somewhat similar poems. They became aware that common presuppositions about poetry—that it ought either to rhyme strictly or dispense with rhyme and directed use of sound or rhythm altogether, that it should be pretty, and that it should be up-lifting—rarely lead to interesting poems. They found themselves not just seek-ing out freshness, unpredictability, originality, and competence but describing these qualities using specific examples from the poems. Giving my students re-sponsibility was revelatory: they realized they had taste, as did others; that everyone's taste was not the same; and that even with these differences, con-sensus would usually develop.

The second major project I involved my students in was to bring Simic's poetry into the local community and high schools. The previous semester, along with the trial run of the Poetry Palooza on campus, I had encouraged two students from my Introduction to Poetry course to plan a public scholar-ship project in lieu of a final interpretive essay. One of the students, Carina En-gleberg, led a couple of poetry activities with students who had read Simic's *Sixty Poems* in Mrs. Doreen Miori-Merola's Advanced Placement English Lit-erature and Composition class at Solvay High School. One of the activities was a competition in which two teams attempted to organize strips of paper, each containing a single line of verse, into a cohesive poem. The other student, Lara Rolo, performed a montage of Simic's verse and created a short sketch by de-livering the poetry in two voices. These presentations served as valuable pilots for the larger projects of the next semester.

In one of the projects of the second semester, a talented young poet, Gina Keicher, who has since been accepted into the MFA Program at Syracuse, led Nancy Dafoe's Advanced Placement English class of thirteen at East Syra-cuse–Minoa High School in a discussion of Sylvia Plath and confessional po-etry. Gina focused on the little-known "Mad Girl's Love Song" and proceeded to teach "Daddy" and "The Disquieting Muses," the latter of which the stu-dents had not read before class. Gina did a marvelous job, commanding the students' respect because she introduced herself as a practicing poet, spoke confidently and insightfully, and wore her tattoos and piercings proudly. In her assessment of her experiences, she wrote about how much her engagement with the public and these students meant to her.

The experiences of Poetry Palooza and teaching the Advanced Placement class have caused me to reflect deeply on poetry's place in culture. Despite knowing my own personal connection to the art is strong, at times I used to question just how relevant poetry is to other people, if it still mattered. The night before Poetry Palooza, I spoke with a writer for *The Daily Orange* about the event and she asked me my thoughts on poetry. I shared that I certainly don't think poetry is, as many say, "a dying art." I told her about a recent visit to Borders when I was disappointed to see the *Twilight* book and merchandise display was much larger than the poetry section, but then I recalled the number of people I'd been in contact with as we all waited for our acceptance and rejection letters from MFA programs across the country, and in some cases the world. If anything, these experiences have been eye-opening; the community involvement at the mall, the encouraging teacher at the high school, and the students sharing their insight on the harsh German language in Plath's "Daddy" each have their own way of showing that poetry is certainly significant and more than relevant in contemporary culture.[4]

My students and I visited two other classes taught by Ms. Dafoe: an Advanced Placement English class with twelve students and a Creative Writing class with twenty-five students. In the former, my student Dan Vallejo taught Robert Lowell's "The Quaker Graveyard in Nantucket," and Lindsay Morgan led a discussion of Elizabeth Bishop's "The Fish," "In the Waiting Room," and "The Man-Moth." In the Creative Writing course, after introducing myself and my three students Josh Frackleton, Marty Gottlieb-Hollis, and Tim Woolworth, I explained why we were there and gave a very brief biography of Simic. We then divided the class into three groups of eight students, each one led by one of my students. The groups discussed as many of the following poems by Simic as time would allow: "Country Fair," "Factory," "The Prodigal," "Have You Met Miss Jones," "The Secret," "Night Clerk in a Roach Motel," "Sunday Papers," and "Paradise Motel." In a final project, I visited Patty Farrington's Creative Writing course at Cicero–North Syracuse High School with three of my students: Steven Deutsch, David Medeiros, and Kate Overholt. Some fifteen students awaited us, mostly juniors I believe, including one student who was committed to silence in observation of gay and lesbian solidarity day. As one could almost predict, class was interrupted by a fire drill, during which we were required to march out of the building and wait under atypical Syracuse blue skies for ten minutes.

All of my students were quite anxious about what amounted to the first formal teaching any of them had ever done. They had each studied the chosen poems and prepared outlines of what they would want to say about them in the classroom. On the evening before our visit, we met at my home, where, together, we discussed each of the poems. The effort was to find ways to make the poems accessible to sixteen- and seventeen-year-olds and also to encourage the students to direct some of their attention to language—to the sounds, rhythms, images, metaphors, and diction that worked to elicit the thoughts and feelings they had while reading. For instance, with one group, I discussed a strategy for teaching the poem "Factory," which follows.

The machines were gone, and so were those who worked them.
A single high-backed chair stood like a throne
In all that empty space.
I was on the floor making myself comfortable
For a long night of little sleep and much thinking.

An empty birdcage hung from a steam pipe.
In it I kept an apple and a small paring knife.
I placed newspapers all around me on the floor
So I could jump at the slightest rustle.
It was like the scratching of a pen,
The silence of the night writing in its diary.

Of rats who came to pay me a visit
I had the highest opinion.
They'd stand on two feet
As if about to make a polite request
On a matter of great importance.

Many other strange things came to pass.
Once a naked woman climbed on the chair
To reach the apple in the cage.
I was on the floor watching her go on tiptoe,
Her hand fluttering in the cage like a bird.

On other days, the sun peeked through dusty windowpanes
To see what time it was. But there was no clock,
Only the knife in the cage, glinting like a mirror,
And the chair in the far corner
Where someone once sat facing the brick wall.

We discussed connecting the poem to the many abandoned factories that littered the area in which the students lived. We considered some of the thoughts and feelings the poem would likely evoke—of joblessness, homelessness, fear, morbidity, oppression—and pointed out that none of these actually had much direct relation to the circumstances surrounding the composition of the poem. At one of his readings, Simic had introduced the poem by recalling the many abandoned factories in the Soho area of Manhattan, now a gentrified and highly commercialized neighborhood. Back in the 1970s, Simic recalled, a number of his friends purchased these factories at rock-bottom prices and turned them into comfortable lofts that are now worth a fortune. Simic said he was tempted to do this, but when he tried to spend a night in one of the buildings, he was haunted by the experience and could not bring himself to make a purchase. So the poem was not generated out of an acute awareness of the casualties of a postindustrial world, it was not meant to symbolize the shattered dream of an all-powerful industrial proletariat, nor was it a depiction of the rampant homelessness one finds in our country or in refugee Europe after World War II. Yet, we observed, the poem could profitably be discussed as an insightful commentary on any of these phenomena. It could equally serve as a nice illustration of the vicissitudes of biographical and contextual readings, which can never finally capture the strange unpredictability of resonant works of literary art.

Armed with the knowledge gleaned from our group discussion of the previous night, their own insights, and chests full of nerves, my students took their seats at the heads of their respective groups of utterly unknown high school students. The only rule was that any poem they discussed had first to be read aloud. Considering everyone's inexperience with this sort of thing (including my own), the results were satisfying indeed and yielded some rich teaching and learning moments for me and my students and for the high school students and their teacher. An assessment by one of my students follows.

> My classroom experience in a creative writing class at Cicero–North Syracuse High School was my first real teaching experience, and it helped to have the instant respect that a poet laureate carries. Simic writes without pushing vocabulary beyond that available to a high school student, and his lack of emphasis on rhyme scheme and structure meant that I was able to encourage the students to perform a close reading of the poems as they would with a piece of prose fiction. They seemed to go for this approach, and often made observations from my lesson plan before I was able to bring them up. By the end of our session the group of six students I was assigned had begun to look at the poems with a more acute critical eye. The progress was discernible and rewarding.
>
> One of the more important lessons from my time leading the discussion came at the end of our session. I asked my group if their feelings about Simic

had changed since the class began. One of the female students said flatly that she didn't care for his poetry anymore. For her, our review had shown Simic to be frightening, violent, and historically dense. At first I was taken aback and maybe a little insulted; if I had known beforehand that I would be turning a student off to Simic I might not have even tried. As time passed, though, I came to look at her position differently. Despite my sense of entitlement, it was the student's right to dislike Simic.

Indeed, if an hour-long critical discussion had shaken her earlier appreciation of Simic, it must not have been a profound appreciation to begin with. That kind of callow deference looks more like fear than respect—I had seen it in the eyes of the people walking around the refrigerators. This was not what I was witnessing. No, she felt secure enough to make her own decision without accepting quality on authority. She was no longer intimidated.[5]

These forays into the high schools represent preliminary steps in a process in which, by taking literature into the community, we initiate our fellow citizens into the best forms of social life and into modes of associated experience characteristic of a functioning democracy. The role of the university should be precisely to engender the broadest possible collective of full participation and, to use a phrase of Dewey's, "conjoint communicated experience," in which personal experience becomes a mode of social experience and in which sympathy and moral reasoning prevail. Students and citizens in general respond well to assumptions of their maturity and significance; taking the challenging poetry of Charles Simic into their midst proved that "the formulation of values and ideals, the production of articulate and suggestive thinking,"[6] are not beyond their abilities and aspirations. My students and their students rose to the occasion as they labored over poems that almost never appear in the prescribed curricula put together by our state and local bureaucracies, where emphasis on test scores, technical proficiency, and good manners in politics does not encourage conversation. We in higher education are not doing what we ought to remedy this and educate our unprepared young people for the intellectual and moral work that an active democracy requires. I have proposed these modes of publicly engaged scholarship for consideration as possible solutions. Not unlike the uses to which literature was put as reported by Azar Nafisi in her best-selling memoir *Reading Lolita in Tehran* (on which I based my title for this chapter), we, too, must find ways to make full use of the transformative power of literature in opposition to our own nation's strategies for domesticating intellect and spirit.

PART 3

Aesthetics "in the Raw"

CHAPTER 9

Dialogues on Aesthetics and Politics

In over a century of academic literary study in the United States, few scholars have ventured forth into the public sphere to produce research based on meaningful dialogue with common readers. Many, of course, have written about their teaching, but this is different. Though "professing" is all about interacting with students who are part of the public, literature has its effect on populations far larger than student bodies. Considering the influence of reader-response theory within the academy these past several decades and the widespread commitment to transgressing boundaries and giving voice to the silenced, it is surprising that there have been so few efforts to reach out to ordinary readers. Cultural studies has only partially rectified the situation. The salutary influence of the Birmingham Centre for Contemporary Cultural Studies in the 1980s—spurred on by the arguments of Richard Hoggart, Raymond Williams, E. P. Thompson, Stuart Hall, and others—encouraged American cultural studies scholars to add an important ethnographic dimension to their work. What ensued was a cottage industry of subcultural studies—books on punk, fanzines, working-class culture, immigrant communities, Goths, and so on. But rarely did this scholarship entail research into literary or aesthetic experience. Most often, the focus was on the ideology of popular culture, usually understood as the political effects that accrue when historical subjects actively engage with social texts understood as the products of belief systems and structures of determination and domination. Because much of cultural studies has been bent on unmasking the aesthetics of the privileged, emphasis has been placed on cultural assaults from below whose goal is to subvert elite taste, not on developing an understanding of the affirmative aesthetic experiences of their subaltern subjects.

In 1984, simultaneous with Birmingham but unconnected, Janice Radway published *Reading the Romance: Women, Patriarchy, and Popular Literature,* a book I have taught numerous times over the years with some success, only in part because I ask my students to read Kathleen Woodiwiss's *The Flame and the Flower* (1972), the romance novel considered singular by the women Radway wrote about. Radway's book resembled the subcultural studies of the

Birmingham Centre insofar as it, too, challenged the then-regnant view of popular culture—heavily influenced by the work of Theodor Adorno and Max Horkheimer—that popular culture (or, more properly, "mass" culture) was a manipulative assault on the critical capacities of the masses and worked to secure their docile acceptance of the established institutions of domination. But *Reading the Romance* achieved something very few other studies at the time or since have: Radway queried individual readers about their personal reading experiences, and she even pressed them, though unsuccessfully, to discuss their aesthetic responses. This is a vital line of inquiry that we might more emphatically pursue today.

The reasons for this, as I have indicated previously, have to do with the widespread rejection during the 1960s of the New Critical academic regime. The specific set of aesthetic criteria installed by that regime produced a literary canon that, for all its revisionist and modernist energy, excluded traditionally marginalized writers like women and authors of color. With the rejection of that regime, white men preferring white male writers came to be seen as unacceptable. Not only was the criteria they used to determine literary achievement rejected, but, as I have previously indicated, the entire enterprise of judging, valuing, and ranking literature came under such deep suspicion that these activities themselves, so fundamental to literary criticism, were pushed to the wayside by a battalion of literary theorists bent on proving that all judgment, valuation, and canon making is necessarily ideological in nature.

Insofar as Radway took seriously not only popular culture—romance novels no less, the literary genre that is lowest of the low—but the experiences of middle- and working-class women, her scholarship was consistent with some of the intellectual trends of the 1980s and 1990s. But what set *Reading the Romance* apart was its commitment to ethnographic and especially to empirical research, which very much went against the grain of the prevailing skepticism within the literary academy of scientific claims (including social-scientific claims) or, for that matter, any claims of objectivity or disinterested inquiry. Indeed, one detects a defensive and even occasionally an apologetic tone in the introduction Radway wrote for the second edition of *Reading the Romance* in 1991. At a time when she was nearly alone in pioneering an empirical approach to the reading experience, we find her trimming her earlier ambitious claims about empirical research and assuring her colleagues that such research should never replace "*all* intuitively conducted interpretation in cultural study"—as if this were ever a serious claim or position. Instead of assertively challenging the legion of literary academics who granted no legitimacy to empirical research, she appropriated their oft-repeated and frankly unpersuasive declarations regarding the limitations of empirical research modes and turned them on her own work. Thus, looking back from the vantage point of the early 1990s, she dutifully repeated the mantra of the day. "I would therefore now want to emphasize more insistently," she confessed, "Angela McRobbie's assertion that 'representations are interpretations.' They can never be pure mirror images of some objective reality . . . but exist always as a result of 'a whole set of selective devices, such as highlighting, editing, cutting, transcribing, and inflecting.'"[1]

Who, exactly, in 1991 or any other time, believed representations could be "pure mirror images of some objective reality" remained a secret. Anyone foolish enough to make such a claim would not be worth refuting in the first place. The real issue was and continues to be how a set of analytical protocols, what Radway referred to as "selecting devices," can be refined so as to produce an adequate representation as determined by a considered evaluative experience involving analyst, subject(s), and a relevant community of scholars. The best critiques of naively objectivist anthropology, by now accepted and incorporated into the discipline, understand this and require sophisticated protocols to minimize undue projection on the ethnographer's part. These refinements have significantly improved the possibilities that ethnography, skillfully done, can contribute to the effort to understand how literature and culture are experienced by the general population. Radway's more reasonable adjusted claim that ethnographies of reading could be part of a variegated approach that attempted to understand "the ways historical subjects understand and partially control their own behavior in a social and cultural context that has powerful determining effects on individual social action"[2] failed to address the sometimes sophistical anti-empirical sentiments that carried the day in 1991 and that in many respects still do. This, of course, was and continues to be the real issue within a disciplinary context that finds almost no room for the kind of research that Radway conducted so compellingly and that modesty perhaps prevented her from advocating more forcefully.

Today, scholars continue to ignore the following exhortation by John Dewey from nearly three-quarters of a century ago.

In order to *understand* the esthetic in its ultimate and approved forms, one must begin with it in the raw; in the events and scenes that hold the attentive eye and ear of man, arousing his interest and affording him enjoyment as he looks and listens; the sights that hold the crowd—the fire-engine rushing by; the machines excavating enormous holes in the earth; the human-fly climbing the steeple-side; the men perched high in air on girders, throwing and catching red-hot bolts. The sources of art in human experience will be learned by him who sees how the tense grace of a ball-player infects the onlooking crowd; who notes the delight of the housewife in tending her plants, and the intent interest of her Goodman in tending the patch of green in front of the house; the zest of the spectator in poking the wood burning on the hearth and in watching the darting flames and crumbling coals.[3]

When I first encountered them, Dewey's words provided me with much-needed encouragement to complete a project I had only just begun. Having spent the first years of my life living in a working-class Bronx tenement, having grown up in a middle-class suburb in the San Fernando Valley, and then having spent some six years working in Chicago factories, I was inured at an early age to romantic, condescending, and dismissive attitudes toward "the masses." It became second nature to avoid making assumptions about "ordinary" people. Instead, I plunged into exploring their experiences with them so as to better understand their attitudes and values. In this and the following sections, I present the words of ordinary Syracusans who have talked with me at some point during the past few years about their encounters with beauty, and I offer some commentary to suggest how these encounters might help us understand long-standing aesthetic problems and issues.

Marshall Blake has been a labor organizer for over twenty years. When I spoke with him, he represented the Service Employees International Union (SEIU), as director of the Syracuse Labor Council, and was an enthusiastic opera fan. This will strike many readers as an odd combination, but in interviewing several dozen people, I discovered that a surprising number were at least partially interested in "serious" arts or crafts, whether classical music, ceramics, the ballet, painting, or design. Moreover, those whose interests leaned toward the more "popular" arts—auto restoration, knitting, fashion—were equally aware of and interested in assessing either their own or other people's levels of achievement within their chosen interests. Making aesthetic judgments—determining bad, worse, and worst as well as good, better, and best—is not only prevalent outside the literary academy, where it is generally thought to be tertiary at best and pernicious at worst; it is considered by many to be absolutely vital to their well-being.

I begin with Blake because his experiences put pressure on the dominant view of aesthetics, beauty in particular, within the academy today, an ostensibly leftist view deeply suspicious of notions of artistic accomplishment and superiority for their easy commerce with elite taste, cultural hierarchy, and habits of exclusion. Blake tells of his upbringing in what he terms an "unaesthetic" environment and of the impact of a teacher who introduced him to classical music and helped him to become a lifelong devotee. Blake then extended his interest to painting. "My taste evolved," he recalls,

> toward Beethoven and Mozart, still the core of my interest in classical music, and Dvorak, Bartok, and Stravinsky as well, although I'm much more interested in opera. So there has been some evolution in my taste. There certainly has been in painting. I mean I still like Orozco, Rivera, Kahlo, and that whole group of painters. But I have much "rangier" taste now in terms of Western art. I think there are only one or two major museums in the Western world that I haven't spent time in.

I asked Blake repeatedly about the relevance of his interest in the arts to his job and his politics. His response, given the beliefs and values that inform much academic literary thinking, might be received dismissively by some of my colleagues.

> I think there is some intersection between my love for the arts and my job, but I guess I can't think of where it is. I don't know. I think my reaction to art that appeals to me is that it makes me feel more centered, more grounded, more connected to sort of a spiritual dimension of our existence, whereas my work doesn't make me feel that way. My work is different. It's about action and devotion . . . and distraction to some extent. It is the other piece of what I do. In some respects my work is all about distraction. And it is appealing because of that. I am always in motion. Maybe this is an extension of the way I was in grammar school. It is always moving about; it is always action. Art centers me, and quiets me down, and relaxes me. It refreshes me. It's been a long time since I read Lenin on art and literature [laughs]. Socialist realist art has never been very appealing to me. To me—and I am not making a religious point—art lets me touch some more spiritual fundamental; it lets me touch some more spiritual aspect of either my character or the larger universe of which I am a part. And to that extent I certainly wish everybody had those opportunities.

So much for art as criticism, negation, indeterminacy, transgression, insurgency, rebellion, or revolution—all highly valued qualities attributed to art during the twentieth century by modernism and within the academic humanities today. Hard as I might try, I could not get Blake to add even a smidgen of subversion to his account of what he thinks art is or does. On the contrary, Blake describes art's role in his life in ways that elicit scorn from most leftists, academic and otherwise, who associate his stress on art's calming and recuperative effects with powerful and privileged elites eager to encourage passive contentment among the masses. But given Blake's commitment to activism and social change, it is not so easy to dismiss his description of how art works for him. Is art that calms and restores quietistic if it reinvigorates, refreshes, and enables an individual to reenter the fray and function more effectively? People like Blake tend to be ignored because academics rarely talk to working-class activists. Does he not deserve a bit of the enthusiasm that we customarily reserve for art that subverts or transgresses? Or would we, given the opportunity, simply tell him that "refreshment" is what you get from soft drinks, while art must go about the serious business of unmasking the power and privilege of elites? Encounters with beauty function for many as a mode of productive relaxation—Keats's phrase for this power of passivity was "diligent Indolence," a form of passivity distinct from laziness, self-indulgence, or apathy and instead, as Lionel Trilling once observed, a source of "conception, incubation, gestation."[4] Without it, those who are politically engaged risk being consumed and eventually exhausted by their difficult labors. For some, the heat of beauty prevents burnout. In an age such as ours, when active citizenship is aggressively discouraged by a whole set of institutional networks and circumstances, those interested in social change would do well to explore the nature and potential of passivity and its actual proximity to action, rather than continuing to romanticize assertive, militant, fierce political styles that are demonstrably unappealing to so many. Citizens need to be brought into civic engagement through alternative styles and modalities.

Karen Mihalyi has devoted her adult life to serving the cause of social justice. When I spoke with her, she was director of the Syracuse Community Choir, a position she had held for over ten years. In this capacity, she nurtured both her group and the surrounding community in the furtherance of egalitarian and inclusive values. She has been particularly keen to develop a strong feminist, multiracial, and multiethnic outlook that both empowers and inspires ordinary people. In the process, she has shaped her music and made it available to help meet the needs of various sectors of the progressive movement: the feminist, gay and lesbian, peace, and environmental sectors. Yet, although Mihalyi has come to believe in the inseparability of art and politics, she does not believe they are equivalent, convertible, or without defensible boundaries. Her music reflects her politics, but her music possesses an integrity of its own that must be served. So, it seems, must her own subjective needs be fulfilled by her music, and when she encounters beauty, what is aroused are not political passions (though such passions may be indirectly satisfied) but a kind of personal rapture that she is comfortable calling spiritual and that makes her want to forge connection with others. When I asked her what it feels like to be in the presence of beautiful things, she hesitated before she said,

What I first thought of when you asked that was my grandmother's garden. She had a beautiful flower garden and there were a number of early memories of being in this huge bed of tulips—red vibrating sunlight tulips, and feeling like "Oh, there's something sacred here. There's something that's so beautiful about this that I can't even put words into it." That is something that I feel often. It doesn't have to be with people. I can feel it walking along the beach or in my own flower garden, hearing some music or looking at a painting. It's almost too much to take in, like a lilac. There's something about that much joy. At the same time, art doesn't necessarily bring joy. You can look at something and feel agitated. I've been working on this quilt that I have been making for my daughter. She picked out a lot of this stuff. It's right there; I can show you. When I was in Florida, we were working on it together. I had been out walking, and I saw dolphins. I thought, "This is *so beautiful*." We were touching it. It was connection with her. We were creating something beautiful, and I felt the same tingle that I felt with the tulips when I was really little, a tingling in my body.

As Blake and Mihalyi suggest, art serves to prepare and equip active citizens for progressive civic engagement through solitary experience as well as connectedness, or through centering as well as decentering. Thus, perhaps we need to find other ways to talk about the politics of art. At the very least, it would seem that if we wish to assess the effects of art, perhaps especially its political and ideological effects, we will want to turn our attention to how art influences actual people in actual political and ideological situations. This will entail withholding judgment as to what these influences might be, until familiarity with the art object and its context is matched by familiarity with art's respondents and their circumstances of life.

When I spoke with Lauren Austin, she was director of the Syracuse Community Folk Art Center, located in a poor African American section of the city. Austin is a passionate advocate of African American culture, a student and teacher of non-Western art and attitudes toward art, and someone keenly attuned to the politics of art. Throughout our conversation, she challenged what she perceived to be unexamined assumptions behind the questions I posed to her, assumptions she characterized as "white" and "Western." From her perspective, these were founded on accepted notions regarding the separation of art and ordinary life, the division of art into "high" and "low," the need to inculcate artistic principles rather than cultivate creativity, and the privileges of taste and taste making. Yet, although Austin is vociferous in her condemnation of traditional thinking and practice in the arts, she emphasized the importance of proper unconventional training and judgment that reflect the achievements of powerful, albeit subordinate, cultural traditions. In her narrative of her own training in the craft of quilting, she speaks of learning skills within the context of everyday life and under the tutelage of ordinary people. For Austin and her circle of friends and family members, becoming technically skilled and aesthetically literate brings a vital sense of satisfaction and well-being.

> My grandmother's friends would quilt together, and they would meet sometimes at her house. I learned through them. It's not taught like a class. When I say "taught," I think I mean something different than when other people say "taught." I mean that things were being made, and you watched and you participated, and someone might say, "Well, I would do it this way," and then you would see how that way was done. Or you might try something and it's "Hmm, I don't know about that," and then they take it out and you do it again. But it's not teaching the way teaching is done now. I think it's a very African way of learning. I have seen similar things when I lived in Uruguay. I had friends in the Afro-Uruguayan community who took part in these groups called *comparsas,* which are drumming groups that do drumming and singing together, and they meet once a year and have a contest to see who's better, who's louder, who's more on rhythm, who's more creative. It's a big festival, and the way that you learn is you are in a group from the time you are small and you watch; you get to carry the drum. Maybe you get to clean the drum afterwards and you go and get coffee and latte for the drummers and you get to run messages back and forth, and you don't really get to participate until you have reached the level that everybody feels that you're okay. But it's not like you take a test or something; you just grow up in it. And to me that was very similar to how I learned to quilt. I would try things out, and I would make stitches and they would be taken out. My grandmother did this with me crocheting, and that's why I don't crochet. I would crochet along and she'd look and say, "No, take it out." Finally I was just so frustrated with it that I just stopped doing it. But one of my grandmother's friends

was very different. She would say, "Oh, that's good, very good. You're getting along, you're coming along." And then I would go home and I would think, "Oh great, I'm going to be part of this community quilt project" or whatever it was we were working on. And years later my grandmother told me, "The owner, she would just take it out after you were gone [*laughs*] and do it herself, you know."

These experiences serve to expose the inconsistency that occurs when relatively privileged academics, themselves trained in how to recognize the presence or absence of craft (manifested, for instance, every time an English professor corrects and grades a student essay), declare that judging levels of artistic achievement is self-referential, self-serving, and dangerous. In failing or, more often, refusing to cultivate their students' sensibilities and powers of judgment concerning aesthetic achievement, they perpetuate the monopoly on taste enjoyed by the privileged. Worse, they deprive their students of the many satisfactions and powers that accrue from the direct experience of art, either as producers or recipients.

Austin's views of art would likely sound familiar to academics, for she stresses the politics that shape art at every turn. When I asked her, for instance, what the phrase "coming together through art" meant to her—the phrase appeared in the pamphlet of the Community Folk Art Center—she replied,

Art is an activity of cultural expression. It can be political or ideological—it depends on what you want to say. I think that cultural expression, when done by people from groups that have not been allowed to express their cultures, *when* they talk is very political. When you speak when you're not supposed to, that's a very political act. I think maybe all art is political if it's trying to say something, if it's trying to persuade.

Yet Austin's emphasis on politics did not explain everything, most particularly her personal response to art. When I asked her to describe the sensation of being pleased by art, she first said that she feels pride. But she followed this up in an unexpected way in our exchange.

Describe your subjective reaction when you see a painting like this.
I thought that was what I was doing [*laughs*], but I guess I wasn't. I think pride.
I think what you gave me are the reasons for your reaction. But I'd like you, if possible, to describe the reaction itself.

I do a happy dance. Pride. I laugh. I tend to want to walk right up to it and
touch it. I've been thrown out of many museums because of that. Really.
Now what I do is befriend the guards. I talk to the guards first and tell
them that I have this uncontrollable urge to touch the work.
Does this mean you secretly violate the "Do not touch" signs in your own gallery?
Well no, I get that out of me while we're putting work up [*laughs*].

Elsewhere in our conversation, Austin described her reaction to attractive art.

It's just "Whoa, that's really nice! How did you do that? I wanna do that!" That's
what I think it makes you do. It makes me do that. I would think so. Why not?
I mean it goes back to the idea that art [isn't] something for some people, and
separate from everyday life and everyday people.

Austin sets up an interesting undulatory movement here between intense
aesthetic experiences—sensory acuity, joy, pride, enthusiasm, even rhap-
sody—and a desire to reach out to other works of art and other individuals.
For Austin, as with many others I spoke with, cohabiting with beautiful objects
induces a quality of attention and regard that is consistent with the high state
of alertness toward injustice that ought to be shared by citizens in a democracy. Invariably, my subjects speak of beauty's power to strengthen connections with others; they acknowledge the highly personal, solitary, other-
worldly, or transcendent quality of the encounter but also testify to its
powerfully sociable afterlife. When Austin experiences the immediacy of art,
she does so quite consciously as part of a larger social and political world. A
constant theme in her comments is that art is ordinary and must not be separated from everyday life. But when she talks about her own encounters with
art, she does not subordinate them to surrounding social circumstances. These
encounters retain a degree of spontaneity and autonomy and must be approached as unique experiences not easily assimilable to particular political
agendas. In Austin's case, the encounter with beauty is consistent with her politics but not reduced to them. Her encounters cause her to seek to emulate
what she sees ("How did you do that? I wanna do that!") and to respond sen-
suously to it ("I do a happy dance. . . . I tend to want to walk right up to it and
touch it"). Elaine Scarry makes the case that the felt experience of beauty induces, even demands, an act of replication. She does not mean only the act of
begetting children, although that is not an insignificant result. She means the
desire to reproduce beauty—by one's own hand, through further pursuit of it,

by encouraging others to experience it. Austin states or implies that all three of these considerations are at play when she experiences beauty.

Gus Newport hails from nearby Rochester. He joined the civil rights movement in that city in the early 1960s, became a friend of Malcolm X, and served as mayor of Berkeley, California, in the late 1970s and early 1980s. He continues to organize in disadvantaged urban neighborhoods, lectures, consults on urban issues, and is considered a national authority on grassroots politics. I first learned of Newport's unique and effective strategies when I came across a piece some years ago in the *Nation*. That piece, by Jay Walljasper, was entitled "When Activists Win: The Renaissance of Dudley St." Dudley Street winds through Boston's Roxbury district, and the area suffers the usual problems of the inner city: poverty, redlining, unemployment, racism, inadequate public services, poor schools, drugs, crime, neglect. According to Newport, the surprising key to mobilizing a community such as Roxbury to fight for its many political and economic needs is to address its cultural needs, specifically the craving for beauty, which, when satisfied, provides the pleasure, pride, and vision needed to bind together and help direct community members toward common goals. Here is the way Newport described it to me:

The arts are very much a part of it. It's about being able to maintain their own culture and their own language, too—which we never think about . . . and I don't think about until I run into these things. I've been to the Basque country a couple times, and it's really interesting how they eat and celebrate . . . and how they maintain the look of an area. The maintenance of beauty for a lot of people, too, prevents others from stripping them of what's essential. Aesthetics turned out to be the best organizing tool in community building in blighted communities across this country. People went door-to-door early on asking what neighbors wanted to see in a new Dudley Street. They said that they wanted to clean up all this illegal dumping and debris that happened because of the illegal dumping done by developers and people that take advantage of poor communities that don't have any political clout. They also wanted to make sure that all the streetlights were fixed and working. There were a lot of vacant lots owned by the city they wanted cleaned up. The public policy people and the sociologists will say the first thing people in this community want are jobs. The sad reality is that as much as a job means, it's not necessarily the primary thing that people are looking for. They're looking for a sense of aesthetics and beauty. I'll give you two examples. On Dudley Street the people decided that we want to be as creative as we want and get all this illegal dumping out of here and clean up these lots. They tried to get the city to respond because people kept bringing in all this illegal dumping, but they wouldn't. So when Ray Flynn, who had claimed he wanted to be the mayor of the neighborhoods, was running for reelection, they came up with the scheme to go down to his campaign office and say, "We want to work for you, Mr. Mayor," and they picked up about a thousand bumper stickers. And a lot of people dumping illegal debris would also park cars that would die right in these streets. So they took the bumper stickers and put them on everything that was dead and caused blight, and they called the television. TV came out and took pictures of all this, and here's Ray Flynn's signs on all of them. His campaign hurried up and responded. He created a hotline, and he said, "Jesus Christ, these people cleaned all that shit out of there!" And he began to cite people doing illegal acts. And then the community said, "Now bring some trucks down here so we can clean out all this stuff and grow wildflowers until we can determine what we want to put in these lots."

From the start, members of the Dudley Street Neighborhood Initiative consulted with community members to identify what they wanted. During an eight-month period, they organized a series of meetings that produced a plan stressing a new community spirit as much as new housing. According to Walljasper, among the goals the group came up with were, of course, pressing economic needs, like jobs, but also bike paths, apple orchards, outdoor cafés, community gardens, fountains, art programs, and a town common with concerts.[5] Much of the success of the initiative was, in fact, due to the common vision of cultural well-being and beauty that bound the community together.

A century ago, W. E. B. DuBois rose to address the NAACP at its yearly gathering. His subject was art and beauty, and he immediately challenged those in his audience of activists to rid themselves of their preconceived notions regarding the separation of beauty and politics. He identified two groups within his audience: those who considered art to be completely irrelevant to the miserably oppressed and those who were willing to turn away from their concerns to be momentarily pleased by "sit[ting] and dream[ing] of something which leaves a nice taste in the mouth."[6] To both, DuBois posed an alternative that was striking for its dramatic combination of aesthetic and political commitment. "The thing we are talking about tonight," he began,

> is part of the great fight we are carrying on and it represents a forward and an upward look—a pushing onward. You and I have been breasting hills; we have

been climbing upward; there has been progress and we can see it day by day looking back along blood-filled paths. But as you go through the valleys and over the foothills, so long as you are climbing, the direction—north, south, east, or west—is of less importance. But when gradually the vista widens and you begin to see the world at your feet and the far horizon, then it is time to know precisely whither you are going and what you really want.[7]

For DuBois, as well as for Newport, art and beauty provide the best present experience of future happiness—happiness to be secured through the political actions of active citizens. Art and beauty address ultimate questions of the quality of life that individuals and movements aspire to. For DuBois and Newport both, movements for social change neglect beauty at their peril.

CHAPTER 10

Dialogues on Aesthetics and Judgment

The tension between egalitarian political values opposed to hierarchy and the recognition that all things are not created equal in art ran through all of my conversations with activists, yet one does not find among my subjects what Susan Sontag has called the "discrediting of the prestige of judgment itself," so widespread within the academic humanities.[1] On the contrary, each of my subjects reserves a vital place for making comparative judgments of quality. Marshall Blake does so by valuing some of the classics of music and literature over examples from popular culture. Karen Mihalyi takes pride in the openness of her choir to all comers, even those with little talent, and she acknowledges that extra-aesthetic considerations often go into the program choices she makes in consultation with others. She is skeptical of those who would privilege "higher" forms of art and more "serious" forms of music, and she is critical of the elitism of "high" culture and the disproportionate resources directed its way. Yet, despite all this, she is vitally concerned with improving the skills of the members of her choir and improving the quality of the choir's performances. At times, her egalitarian values are in tension with fulfilling the highest standards of her art, but she is nonetheless certain that standards exist. Mihalyi is aware that the way to resolve this tension is through greater participation in the critical process of judgment. This is reflected in her commitment to collective evaluation on the part of the entire choir, though she also realizes, somewhat reluctantly, that those with greater expertise will sometimes have to step in and make artistic decisions. Her implicit view is that both full participation and qualified, accountable leadership must be part of any genuine vision of cultural democracy.

In her influential book *On Beauty and Being Just*, Elaine Scarry makes a number of claims about beauty that my dialogues tend to corroborate. One is that, contrary to the views of theorists who disparage beauty, encountering beauty in one thing does not lead to intolerance and exclusion of other things; on the contrary, it enhances the acuity with which one encounters other things, and moreover, it stimulates the search for them. My subjects express little hesitation when it comes to recognizing skill, craft, or artistry in others.

This recognition rarely leads them to make invidious comparisons; much more often, it leads to appreciation, inspiration, and aspiration. Making judgments of quality proves to be an essential, empowering act without which their lives would be less tolerable. Simply put, beauty makes life more vivid. It sustains and even saves lives. Most everyone I spoke with remarked on how deeply impoverished their lives would otherwise be without the cultivated capacity to be enthralled by the power of the art or craft that had become a part of their life. Much of their testimony belies the claims of theorists who maintain that disadvantaged populations are victimized by taste, which creates harmful hierarchies. But aesthetic discrimination bears no necessary relation to the older meaning of discrimination, and making distinctions does not necessarily create hierarchies based on undeserved authority. Value judgments per se would seem not to be the problem; their misuse is.

Janet Lutz is co-owner of Calico Gals, a quilting shop along the Erie Canal in Fayetteville, New York, just east of Syracuse. If all arts and crafts are at least partly shaped by surrounding social influences (what Barbara Herrnstein Smith calls "contingencies"), quilting must be one of the most powerfully circumscribed. Aside from the general influences of gender, education, family, and the like, the typical quilter's world is shot through by the market. Everything she works with is a commodity, and manufacturers, designers, advertisers, and retailers all exert themselves in an effort to influence her. More specifically, computerized sewing machines and an astounding array of tools, yarn, colors, fashions, styles, and patterns provide the choices available to quilters and thus play a significant role in shaping the craft. This said, it would be a mistake to conclude that quilting is wholly determined by corporate entities and is thus in the tight grip of capitalism or, less ominously, that the craft is overly influenced by corporate interests. Lutz claims that, to the contrary, manufacturers and their corporate companions have developed surprisingly close, reciprocal ties to quilters and that, rather than dictate or create the needs of their consumers, they eagerly consult with quilters and attempt to produce the products they desire. Marketing and advertising play an important part in creating new fashions, a process needed to sell new products. But as Lutz describes it, the process can also serve to refresh, enliven, and diversify the craft.

The relationship between designers and the women who actually buy the fabric? It depends on the designer. Let's use Alex Anderson as an example. Alex Anderson just came out with a line of redwork fabric. Redwork is a trend right now in stitching, and it's something that was popular back in the 1920s and

1930s. It's stitching with red thread on white fabric. You could also do it in blue—that's called bluework. It's a big trend right now, redwork. We've got a huge display of redwork down there. So Alex Anderson comes out with a line of redwork fabric. The trend was already there, and now we've added the name to it. Now teapots are big. So somebody's going to do a line of teapots. Hawaiian is becoming a trend right now. We have another friend who designs fabric, and we have her full line: very bright, big flowers, ladybugs . . . fun, fun, fun. She's an artist. She also has patterns. She will come and spend time in our shop and likes to talk to the women. She likes to watch them and see what they're buying. She's a businessperson, too. The fabric companies are always looking, too. They may say to a designer, "Teapots! We've got to have teapots!" [*laughs*]. They'll look at artists, too. Many artists do watercolors or such things with quilts in them. And so then they'll have them do fabrics. If we ever got a big name and we really branded our store well, undoubtedly a fabric company would come to us and say, "We'd like to have 'Calico Gals' on a fabric." I have *no idea* what we'd come up with [*laughs*], but it doesn't matter. Well, it does— they've got to like it to buy it. But they've got that selling point. I know my kids will wear anything if it says "Old Navy" on it. But then there's quality too. We're not going to sell it if it's inferior, no matter what it looks like. Sometimes there're flaws.

Lutz goes on to describe the sensory and tactile methods women use to assess the desirability of fabric.

Most quilters feel this is a very touchy business. They're going to touch. And it's visual. You go stand in the store and every woman . . . you have to touch it. You have to touch it right there. And if you love what you're touching, then you have to put that into a quilt, because a quilt is also something that you touch, unless it's an art quilt, and then it's something that you look at.

Although Lutz distinguishes between "art quilters" and "casual quilters" who quilt for fun or profit, maintaining that the two groups do not interact much, nevertheless artists do not inhabit a world of their own, nor are their achievements ignored by other quilters or, as she indicated in her preceding comments, by designers. Although artists employ unconventional materials and techniques to produce quilts that transcend fashion trends and that rarely sell well, they are not regarded as remote aesthetes who look down on the commercial side of their craft. Some may indeed scorn the business end of quilting, but from Lutz's perspective, artists in general do not constitute a disaffected or alienated grouping. Women seem to take notice of their work, learn from it, and admire it. Competition and judging are an important part of the quilting world, but Lutz understands this to mean that quilters are drawn to superior skill and do not regard rewarding that skill as privileging some and ignoring others.

We actually have my artist friend's work here and teach some classes in that. And we have shows here with some of their things. Oh, we love to see them. We all do. We're totally amazed that someone can do an entire landscape painting in fabric or that somebody can do a total abstract. We're blown away by this stuff. We know we can't do it. I personally don't even have the desire to do that. But it's within us to create. I think that many women don't even know what's in there because they've never had the opportunity. I might've been a great cello player, but how do I know, I never had the opportunity. Given the opportunity, they may start with a Debbie Mumm potholder, and then they go from there. Some of them didn't even know that it was within them. And they go to wonderful heights with what they do. They pick up skills and they see other people and they go to more shows and they're inspired.

Bob Warner owns a body shop and is one of the best-known auto restorers in the area. Typically, he'll take a car built in the 1930s or 1940s and rebuild it from the inside out, adding paint and design elements to produce a gleaming, eye-catching, contemporary look that adds to the venerated models of yesteryear. Contrary to what many readers may assume about an art they know little about, auto restorers in general are keenly aware of tradition, style, and developments within the craft. When I spoke with Warner, he was working on a 1939 coupe. He had restored the body and was preparing to do the artwork. I asked whether he comes up with ideas by himself or studies the work of other restorers. He answered that he is very much influenced by others. In fact, he added, "Before you came I probably had twenty-five magazines all over the floor because I had been trying to get some ideas. . . . Not that I'm trying to copy anybody. I wouldn't take any particular car and make exactly the same thing, but I'd get an idea from this car, an idea from that car, and I'd come up with my own creation to make it my car." The more we spoke, the more I appreciated Warner's particular vehicular aesthetic, which he is not reluctant to share with his customers. His tastes tend toward reproducing as much of the original as possible and toward consistency of design.

It's like anything else. If you go to a car show and you look at a particular car, you're thinking, "Man, what was this guy thinking when he built this thing?" The thing just looks terrible. Maybe the way they put the headlights in it, or maybe the way they two-toned the paint. It's not even that. The way they built the car, the way they put things together. Some of the stuff doesn't look real safe. And when I put something together, I try to put it together so everything is uniform, like the particular car that I've got right now. The car pretty much looks original other than the wheels. Don't open the hood on it [*laughs*]! But everything on that car is pretty much original. . . . [T]his car here: it's got the original mirrors on it, moldings, the grill, the headlights. . . . But with some of the cars, you take all the moldings off them and put on different mirrors, different headlights, custom grills. I believe if you're going to go one way, you follow through. If you're going to go another way, you follow through. I do it either way. I mean, if you're going to go custom, the sky's the limit. I usually go pretty radical on stuff, especially with the paint. Everything I've ever built for myself has had graphics, wild graphics.

Bob and his wife, Janet, frequently attend car shows, and although they do not go for the purpose of winning awards—Janet says they go to "be with people that enjoy cars"—they have competed for prizes, and Bob has served as judge. Although both are critical of perceived favoritism and the political nature of too much of the judging, they have continued to participate. When I asked them about the qualities of a good judge, Janet replied that one needs to love cars and know how they are built. Bob also emphasized experience: "Cars," after all, " are not just the top surface. You are looking at the underneath, the insides." Though he is extremely modest, it's clear that Bob's mastery of his craft brings him considerable pride. Janet had to pry it out of him and, at one point, speak for Bob about the matter.

Janet: It gives him a real sense of pride, I know that.
Bob: Especially when you get the job all done and you stand back and look at it. Just makes you feel real good that you were able to turn something around that was a piece of junk into something that's very beautiful, in my eyes anyway. You feel it the whole time you're doing it. People see how you're doing things and you get compliments on how you did this or how you did that.
Janet: I think it's most satisfactory to him when one of the guys from the club

wishes he had the foresight to do it the way that Bob did. We were at one of the local hangouts one night, and we were standing there on one side of the fence and these people are standing on the other side. And they're talking about this car that's out back. And he's talking to friends and I'm just kind of standing there listening to this guy. And he's talking about this car and he goes, "I got a car I want built. I've never met this man, but I've got to find Bob Warner because he's got the best car on the lot" [*laughs*]. You just kind of wonder. They stopped talking and I said, "Are you looking for Bob Warner? Well, he's right here" [*laughs*]. Then the guy said, "I don't care what it costs, I want you to build my car. I want it to be as nice, as perfect as your car is." And that's not the first time Bob's heard that. But anybody that knows Bob will tell you Bob's a very quiet guy. He never blows his own horn. He doesn't let it go to his head that he's as crafty at his art as he is.

Nat Tobin is one of the unsung heroes of the Syracuse community. Without public recognition by city leaders, media, or cultural organizations, he has quietly made an enormous contribution to the cultural life of the city by bringing to his two art houses—the only ones in the Syracuse area—the best films of the past dozen years.[2] Like Janet Lutz, Tobin must balance his taste in film with the bottom line, but because his bottom line is so much shallower than those of the commercial houses, he has much more latitude than the multiplex operators to choose films of quality that will appeal to a smaller audience. Tobin makes much of the distinction between commercial and art films, a distinction that has become more dramatic for him as he has watched more films. "I certainly have veered away from commercial products to a great extent," he observes.

There are very, very few commercial films that come down the pike that I want to see. They tend to be predictable, formulaic, boring. The films that I like have something to say to the audience. Generally not necessarily with a sledgehammer. I think a well-made film . . . hits you with a message, is able to entertain you, keeps you interested, and gives you something to think about afterwards. . . . I get emotionally involved in films. A film like *Mediterraneo*—it's like watching old friends up there on the screen and now at home on the TV screen. I enjoy the emotional attachment that I have to them; I don't think there's anything like it at all in the world. I think that the beauty of movies is that they are able to grab your emotions. And if a film can grab your emotions and then give you something to think about on top of that, you can't beat that. . . . [C]ertainly the mass of the moviegoing public are looking to escape when they walk into a theater. They're not looking to think about what they're watching. I think [with] most of the product that we show there's an intellectual quality to it that makes it rise a little bit above . . . , well, hopefully a lot above, the commercial product.

Oddly, perhaps defiantly, Tobin always refers to film as "product," a locution that is anathema to most film lovers but may be quite appropriate to film studies programs, most of which go to great lengths to unveil the commercial and ideological underside of film and thus give priority to socioeconomic considerations over aesthetic ones. Given his own disdain for conventional commercial movies—the blockbuster Hollywood releases and endless sequels that substitute for serious filmmaking—it is strange that he applies the term to art films as well. But Tobin never quite buys the binary between commerce and art, commodity and artifact. For him, a rather large number of films—not megareleases, but commercially viable limited releases appropriate for theaters such as his—are perfectly capable of eliciting intense and thoughtful pleasure from ordinary educated audiences, whether referred to as "product" or not. He is not embarrassed by his affection for or the success of films such as *My Big Fat Greek Wedding* or *Bend It Like Beckham,* which he insists are art films because of their limited number of circulating prints rather than because they are the refined triumphs of an auteur. Nor is he embarrassed by use of the word *entertainment* to describe a function of good movies. Tobin believes his business is to present well-crafted films to his audience and to entertain them. In doing so, he is both satisfying developed tastes and developing taste. An example he gives is the success of *My Big Fat Greek Wedding.*

There is a stigma about art product. You know, "You show a lot of sexy movies." I remember when I first came up here, the "art cinema" in Binghamton was a porno house [*laughs*]. But people think that way. They think that foreign product is more or less soft porn. People don't like to read their movies; they don't like to think. They don't think that an art film can be funny. And if you get them to come in, they're generally very surprised. That's one of the better things about showing a film like *My Big Fat Greek Wedding.* It brought about 15,000 over the course of twenty-two weeks into an art house! That's the longest run ever for me.

For Tobin, taste is not purely a matter of aesthetics—it has a moral dimension. Perhaps a better way to put it is that developing a taste for unique, well-crafted films is moral because an individual exposed to a range of high-quality films is in a better position to make good moral judgments. Here is Tobin's view of the matter: "I think, to be a moral person, you need options, and in order to have options, you need to be exposed to thought and to different forms of beauty." I did not press him to make the logical connections needed to articulate a fully formed argument, but certainly anyone familiar with views of scholars such as Martha Nussbaum and Wendy Steiner[3] will recognize the drift of Tobin's remarks. Good films provide moviegoers with exemplary virtual experiences that they may live out imaginatively and without risk; they can engage in vicarious emotion and thought experiments that provide powerful perspectives alternative to their own. Steiner aptly calls this "enlightened beguilement." Such experiences subsequently provide what Tobin calls "options" that are available when moral judgment is required.

Deborah Boughton owns and directs the Syracuse Center of Ballet and Dance Arts. She taught my older daughter ballet for ten years,[4] and during that time, I was regularly able to observe and admire her teaching skills. She has the rare ability of strictly upholding the highest standards of the art of ballet while passionately encouraging her students to perform to the peak of their potential. She is, in a sense, a throwback: there are no warm fuzzies in her studio, but lots of hard work, high expectations, demanding intensity, occasional rebukes, constant encouragement—these are the tools of her trade.

Throughout our conversation, Boughton made it very clear that she believes in the high standards that the art of ballet has refined over the past century. Because of these standards, Boughton readily admits, thousands of dancers are annually disqualified from dancing for the top companies in the United States and abroad. Dance skills aside, they are rejected because they are not slender enough, their legs are too short, their breasts are too large, their bottoms are too broad. It would appear this is exclusion with a vengeance, and for the dancers themselves, indeed it is. But Boughton points out that ballet offers dancers options beyond the elite companies.

I don't stress thinness or the glamour of it. Yes, I emphasize the line and how to get your body to attain the best line it can. But today there are so many other areas of dance that you can go into that don't look at that. They look at your expression and what you can do with the movement. This is not like ballet that emphasizes whether your feet are arched right, how high your leg can be, and

how turned out your leg can be. But that's just those very few classical companies like New York City Ballet or American Ballet Theatre, where they are looking for the body type because they want to do the old traditional classics and
make it look gorgeously perfect. But when you go to a company like Alvin Ailey, you're not seeing those perfect bodies. All of a sudden you're enjoying
dance because it looks like you could do it [*laughs*].

Boughton defends ballet's high standards of performance and aesthetic ap-
pearance. She believes the balletic line is inherently beautiful, just as she believes certain physical features are universally appealing.

There is fashion. But if you have a crowd of a hundred people looking for the
most attractive person, a majority of the time the same one or two people will
be chosen. It's maybe a natural, inherent sense of beauty. It's simple as that.
Take something I know nothing about: which is the prettiest horse in the pas-
ture? I'd probably come up with the same horse that a lot of other people looking at a hundred horses would choose. It might be the way it holds its head, the
color, or the shape of its legs. Something about it just says something to us
that's beautiful. I think the same natural feeling would be felt all around the
world. I think that's what happened in ballet, too. We find that the longer the
line, the prettier the line. Not short and stumpy. Because it sends your eye away
from you. It might change over time, but again, I really think that as we have
become more civilized, we're refining it down. Dance is very new. It doesn't really have a lot of history—ballet's very new on the scene. And it is a refining
from folk dancing. When Louis XIV started this whole thing, somebody had to
think about all this and find ways of forming a position that looked good. We're
still refining. Dance is now so good it's scary. I sometimes ask myself how it can
get better. How can this dancer get any better? And they just keep coming out
and it's so beautiful. Dancers today who are in the corps de ballet are doing so
much more than dancers a hundred years ago that were the best. Take Anna
Pavlova. I'd love to show some of the young kids old films of her dancing, but
they would say, "I can do that." But were they the *first* to do that? Were they innovative enough to come up with that idea, to make the change? But today's
dance is gorgeous, and yet you don't see the stars anymore. It's homogenized.

No doubt, Boughton's recourse to nature and universality to explain the
persistence of certain aesthetic preferences will provoke sneers from readers
who are convinced such preferences are, in fact, socially constructed and ideo-

logical in nature. But Boughton's account of balletic beauty deserves careful consideration, not only because it makes a kind of argument that is widely made by ordinary people with whom academic humanists need to communicate, but because it makes the sort of claim about universality that has gained credence from psychological research that indicates proportionate human physiognomies are highly valued in all cultures observed. Perhaps the balletic line described by Boughton and sought after by choreographers everywhere fulfills some general human attraction to clean geometric design, if not bodily symmetry and youthfulness. But whether this is the case or not, it is doubtful that we can comfortably regard the ubiquity of the attraction as a taste imposed by elite institutions, patriarchal values, or mandarin arbiters. The fact is that tens of thousands of ballet lovers, dancers, teachers, and choreographers cannot all be the products of a manipulative or conspiratorial system. Even Pierre Bourdieu, who spent a lifetime enumerating the multiple sources that determine taste, cannot explain why multiple contingencies so often produce similar tastes or, for that matter, why shared contingencies often produce differing tastes. But whether the ultimate impetus for these aesthetic judgments and experiences is natural or social, it would serve us well to get beyond this conundrum and eagerly explore the vast and varied experiences that these tastes produce.

What remains for scholars to investigate is a whole new territory, in which people's lives are transformed by—in the case of ballet—compellingly beautiful gestures, movements, and images. There are too many varieties of human beings, too many unpredictable and atypical constitutions, too much experience, and too many changeable situations for any one explanation of taste. Citing contingency merely states the obvious and answers no interesting moral, political, or aesthetic problems. As Mark Edmundson has pointed out (in *Why Read?*), there are myriad ways of apprehending experience, and realizing this coincides with a flourishing culture and broad democracy. The sign of support for their combination in a cultural democracy is direct interest in and proximity to the particulars of our fellow citizens' complex lives. These particulars often involve judgment and choice—whether of the moral, political, consumerist, or aesthetic kind—and they are crucial to the well-being of individuals and societies. They are the bedrock of one's quality of life. Their absence, as Amartya Sen argues—that is, the absence of the power to judge and choose and the lack of preparation to judge and choose well—contributes to the continuing oppression of so many of the world's powerless and poor. Indeed, as all of my subjects state or imply, discrimination, perhaps especially appreciation, is an art that is as demanding and difficult to master as it is indispensable. Perhaps surprisingly, the value judgments they make more resemble what Richard McKeon once called "appreciation for artistic, cultural, and intellectual values" than they do "the random . . . reflections which frequently pass for appreciation."[5] Taken seriously, the art of judgment, as Joyce Carol Oates has observed, is exacting and risky because always open to challenge. But whether serving customers, attracting audiences, or teaching students, the people I spoke with embraced aesthetic judgment and frankly relished whatever unexpected attention our conversations drew toward it. Every one of them was delighted to have had the chance to discuss this neglected but altogether crucial part of their lives.

CHAPTER 11

Dialogues on Aesthetics and Spirituality

One of the more important effects of beauty, according to Deborah Boughton, is that it increases compassion.

> I think the feeling of compassion that any artist feels widens, develops, is thrown back into relationships, without a doubt. All of your senses become ... well, more sensitive [*laughs*]. Therefore I think you never look at just the flat face of things because you see more. I think it was a politician who asked, "How is art going to help feed the homeless?" Well, in a way it just might, because people who have an appreciation for the finer things and for the details will have more compassion for those people and ultimately those people will be helped. So I definitely think that ballet, and not just ballet, but a general appreciation and the ability to see beauty in something, is going to help you become more compassionate.

Not to put too fine a point on it, Boughton's perspective is consistent with Elaine Scarry's in *On Beauty and Being Just*. Quoting John Rawls, Scarry claims that "beautiful things give rise to the notion of distribution, to a lifesaving reciprocity, to fairness not just in the sense of loveliness of aspect but in the sense of 'a symmetry of everyone's relation to one another.'"[1] Such symmetry is enhanced by an encounter with another's creation, an encounter marked by concentrated intensity and a full engagement of the mind and the senses. The active reciprocity of the exchange is symmetrical so long as the observer is willing to open himself or herself to the detailed dynamics—what Theodor Adorno called the "force-field"—of the object. For John Rawls, the single most influential theorist in the American academy for the past thirty years yet widely ignored in the humanities, the mark of a democracy is robust, respectful discourse among citizens who differ on fundamental values. Even in disagreement, they must be willing to contribute to a conversation in which all views, though not shared, are nevertheless respected and hence seriously regarded. This is why Rawls explicitly states that democracy cannot be based on community, for community implies shared experiences, perspectives, and values. The test of democracy, then, is to create conditions in which citizens conduct constructive negotiation with one another despite basic differences. As I argued in chapter 2, it would seem that despite its conspicuous absence from Rawls's *Theory of Justice* (and its revised version, *Justice as Fairness*), art provides some of the best opportunities to cultivate the habits of attention and expression needed for these kinds of exchanges, in which compassion, though not agreement necessarily, is a most welcome attribute.

When I spoke with Anthony Frisiello, he was manager at the Prints Plus store in the local mall. I had the sense that Frisiello's enthusiasm for his work was more than public relations hype: he took real pleasure in helping people choose among the thousands of prints available and enjoyed fashioning matting and frames that would add to the prints' attractiveness. Like many of those I spoke with, Frisiello eagerly discussed the details of his craft, pointing out along the way that the skills described were the source of a not negligible degree of aesthetic satisfaction.

> You could become a good framer in a month's time! You develop a knack for it very, very quickly. And it's fun to put a frame together or mount the print onto some foam core, put it through the vacuum press so it's permanent, put the mat on there, and also cut the frame, and then having the satisfaction of knowing that it fits like a hand in a glove, then stapling it in, taping it up, putting your little felt bumpers on the bottom, sewing tooth hangers on the top, and placing a little sticker on there that says, "Framed with pride by . . . ," and then you put your name on there plus the date and store number. I love it. There's a sense of such satisfaction. Especially when you're doing a custom frame, a custom molding, because they're very unique. The stuff that you're going to see in the stores displayed all the time, even that's nice. Once you get through with the whole thing and you put the shield cleaner on it, that thing's just gleaming at you and it looks so great! And you say, "Yeah, I did that." Your signature is on it and it's going to be the centerpiece in somebody's home for a very long time. So there's a lot of satisfaction involved in that.

As Frisiello spoke—with the same enthusiasm about pride in craft that others unfailingly felt—I was once again struck by how revelatory so many of my conversations have been despite the "ordinariness" of my subjects' experiences. On the occasions when we chatted after our recorded conversations, many expressed amazement that they had never had the opportunity to discuss these vital experiences with anyone before and joy finally to be able to do so. I continue to wonder why these conversations are so rare. Most Americans have more or less ready ways to communicate about their religious experience and, certainly, their jobs, their consumer interests, and their relationships. Even sensitive topics such as gender and race are discussed, however inadequately. But there seems to be no place for conversation about aesthetic experience. Whether this is less true in other cultures will only be answered through comparative research. The causes, certainly, remain ambiguous. Emerson and Tocqueville, in pointing to the overwhelming practical and commercial bent of the nation, identify one. But as has been the case with much of our intellectual life, the very dichotomy they thought they observed in the nation as a whole—between commercial and spiritual or cultural pursuit—was a duality they themselves did not completely escape. By placing so much emphasis on writers, artists, and intellectuals creating a new American culture that would transform the average citizen, they failed to encourage a culture built on the unarticulated but very real aesthetic experiences of common citizens—experiences that were fertile in their own right but could be deepened, extended, and made more meaningful in the interaction with established cultural figures. Had more attention been paid to ordinary aesthetic satisfaction in the past, perhaps a wider range of citizens would today contribute to its creation and would be less susceptible to the blandishments of the entertainment and culture industries.

When it comes to decorating his own house, Frisiello is partial to "original" artwork. His favorite painter is the ever-popular Thomas Kinkade, whose work graces the walls of Frisiello's home. I believe he had three Kinkades. When I asked why he was so partial to that painter, he replied with great passion.

I can come home at night and spend time with my wife and my stepchildren or, if I want to, just light up my little Kinkade village that I have up there with a fountain and just relax and look at that little thing in there and just take a nap, just be at peace in my mind. There I am at the cottage, and I can even smell the air, and I walk through that little archway over there to that garden where all those beautiful, beautiful flowers are. That's one of the things that turns me on about the painting and about life in general. There's so much *variety* of colors, and there's so much variety in *everything*. . . . So yeah, I could look at that Kinkade and just feel like I'm there; and yes, I could fantasize about it, and if I'm really, really at peace, there may be a time when I visit there. . . . I truly believe an artist such as Thomas Kinkade is inspired by God. And that's why he does such a wonderful job at what he does. But I also believe that encountering Kinkade's painting . . . it's a *very personal thing.*

Like many others I spoke with, Frisiello's encounters produced an overwhelming sense of equipoise, a sense of peacefulness both spiritually fulfilling and restorative. As a born-again Christian, Frisiello talks about his aesthetic experiences as though they are supplements to and even extensions of his religious beliefs. If we compare Frisiello's experiences with those of Marshall Blake or Karen Mihalyi, whose beliefs and values are otherwise quite different from his, we note similarities insofar as all describe aesthetic experience in spiritual terms (Frisiello, of course, uses explicitly religious terms). For example, Mihalyi explained,

> What floods through me isn't a physical thing, it's a mental thing: a number of many, many old feelings of joy, like going to my grandmother's house or going to school with my parents where I grew up or walking in the woods where I grew up. There'll just be a flood of what I consider to be joy but also sacred. And then there'll be this fullness. You listen and feel. Sometimes there's an aura. That will happen sometimes when I'm seeing something beautiful. I think, for me, beauty—and creating beauty—is very sacred. And that creation of beauty is not just about art necessarily. It's about connection—to the earth, connection to each other, connection to something deep inside of us where that creative stuff comes from. I would say it's spiritual. I'm not really sure what that means. I'm pretty sure that for me it means a deep place in me. Probably everybody has that potential to be connected deeply to the earth.

Needless to say, the academic study of literature and the arts has shown very little interest in the spirituality of aesthetic experience; on the contrary, for nearly fifty years, the prevailing tendency among scholars has been to challenge the notion that either spirituality, religiosity, or other modes of inspiration have anything important to tell us about the nature of literature and the arts. In fact, the main effort has been to disparage, to the point of effacing, these effects, so that their underlying material and ideological causes and consequences might finally be revealed as the true constituents of our responses to the arts after centuries of neglect. When Richard Rorty delivered a talk at the Modern Language Association in 1995 with a title most outside the academy would consider unremarkable, "The Inspirational Value of Great Works of Literature," he was ridiculed for his hopeless naïveté and reactionary sentiments.[2] No doubt, no small number in Rorty's audience remembered the days of the New Critical orthodoxy and earlier, when fuzzy words like *great* and *inspiring* gathered immense authority, in part because of their mystifying vagueness and their association with the critical standards of a privileged, highly exclusive cultural elite.

Rorty, however, makes it clear that he does not wish us to rebuild the cultural pyramid. He argues, in fact, that the systematic dismissal of the experience of inspiration and judgment of greatness is itself symptomatic of an elitist professionalized academy that has lost touch with the citizens who surround it. It is no coincidence that he takes his definition of "inspirational value" from Dorothy Allison, a writer known for giving voice to the experiences of working people. Rorty begins,

> Let me explain what I mean by the term "inspirational value." I can do so most easily by citing an essay by the novelist Dorothy Allison: "Believing in Literature." There she describes what she calls her "atheist's religion"—a religion shaped, she says, by "literature" and by "her own dream of writing." Toward the close of the essay she writes:
> "There is a place where we are always alone with our own mortality, where we must simply have something greater than ourselves to hold onto—God or history or politics or literature or a belief in the healing power of love, or even righteous anger. Sometimes I think they are all the same. A reason to believe, a way to take the world by the throat and insist that there is more to this life than we ever imagined."[3]

With this example, Rorty invites us to consider the very real possibility that inspiration may take many forms, possess many meanings, and produce many effects, some of them affirming and liberating. To ignore or otherwise diminish these key components of the experiences of the arts—experiences that, ironically, have been central to the lives and career choices of most academics themselves, despite a widespread reluctance to acknowledge them and build a knowledge base on them—constitutes a refusal that adds considerable distance between academic and public culture. Moreover, it often makes it difficult for academics effectively to understand the experiences and advocate for the needs of ordinary people who lack their cultural authority.

Both Frisiello and Mihalyi speak, in terms cognate with Allison's, of the highly personal, even intimate nature of their experiences, and all three link them to something larger or higher. Their accounts make it obvious that any simplistic understanding of spirituality or inspiration as sentimental, bourgeois, or individualistic ideology disables cultural analysis, for it rules out an exploration of the relationship between intensified individual experience and the awareness of connection to the divine and to others, whether they be family members, fellow citizens, or generally those in need. Granted, without a strong civil social sphere, many of these impulses toward adhesiveness remain unfulfilled and manifest themselves primarily as aspiration and private satisfaction. But we are mistaken if we consider these the inevitable consequences of the experiences themselves. Moments of transport or inspiration model the kinds of close, reciprocal relationships between self and others we might call "utopian" if we permit that word to apply simultaneously to personal and collective experience. But ultimately, the actual projection of inspiration into the social realm depends on the extent to which democratic institutions, including progressive movements for social change, welcome and encourage aesthetic experience and, moreover, make an important place for it in the public cultures they create.

In considering the spiritual and social ramifications of aesthetic experience, we are concerned with not only the nature but also the quality of that experience. Anthony Frisiello's encounters with Thomas Kinkade's paintings will no doubt strike many readers, as they did me, as at least in part the result of limited experience and undeveloped taste. Frisiello was surprised to learn that many art lovers are not as impressed with Kinkade as he. In fact, he found this quite incredible. At the same time, he acknowledged that artists sometimes need to challenge audiences by refusing to meet their expectations, even by breaking dramatically with convention at times. Thankfully, Frisiello did not undergo any sort of sudden conversion to this fresh perspective—had he done so I would have attributed it to his being culturally cowed. He stuck to his guns, although he did consider the new perspective legitimate and indicated he would be thinking more deeply about the matter. But what are we to make of the quality of his experience? There are some who would argue that Frisiello's encounter with Kinkade does not rise to the level of genuine aesthetic experience because his enjoyment is essentially a sentimental and emotional response devoid of critical awareness. As Alexander Nehamas points out in *Only a Promise of Happiness,* if Ortega y Gasset were the judge, no doubt the verdict would be that Frisiello is part of the multitude that is incapable of "true aesthetic pleasure" and "aesthetic enjoyment proper."[4] Nehamas himself seems to set the bar too high for Frisiello when he addresses the matter at hand with uncanny specificity.

Imagine . . . that Thomas Kinkade's *Dogwood Chapel* seems to me as beautiful as Van Gogh's *Church at Auvers-sur-Oise* seems to you and that both of us experience the pleasure these works produce in the same amount of time. How can we now distinguish between the upper regions and the lower depths? How does the thrill I get from Kinkade differ from your admiration of Van Gogh?[5]

Nehamas explores the matter further by citing the elements of Van Gogh's painting that an experienced and discerning viewer would notice and cite as evidence for the latter's superiority: the harsh brushwork, the unstable lines, the darkening sky, and so on. But Nehamas keeps the question open as to whether the initial experience of beauty upon viewing Kinkade's painting is at all affected by "the aesthete's urbane analysis."

We have seen that Barbara Herrnstein Smith, in *Contingencies of Value*, takes the strong position that there is absolutely no way to determine the difference in quality between someone reading *Rebecca* and herself reading *Emma*, or a teenager listening to Pink Floyd and herself listening to *Parsifal*. In Smith's form of populism, any attempt to diminish "lowbrow" experience by applying alleged standards of judgment is ipso facto elitist. She critiques Herbert Gans, for instance, who argued that through training and cultivation, people can derive more from culture and "relate what they have drawn to many other facets of their emotional and intellectual lives."[6] For Smith, this sort of cultivation represents an illusory movement from darkness to light that is wholly dependent on whether the "evaluative idioms of high culture" are mastered. Those who do not or will not master these idioms, she claims, are said to be doomed to cruder, less reflective, less insightful, distinctly inferior experiences. An alternative approach, she recommends, would be to mount a full exploration of the "extensive demotic languages of popular criticism: that is, discourses of description, evaluation, comparison, and discrimination of films, TV shows, beer, sports, rock music, and so forth, that are well known to 'the fans' and used among them with considerable communicative subtlety, force, and social effectiveness."[7] This is precisely so. But my interviewees' experiences suggest that, though highbrow and lowbrow *discourses* are dramatically distinct, Smith and Gans both exaggerate the differences between so-called highbrow and lowbrow *sensibilities* in their seeming to champion one or the other. A genuinely inclusive, integrative culture would merge the two by instituting modes of critical interaction and exchange between fans of the high and of the low. The enjoyment felt by Anthony Frisiello when he views his painting by Kinkade may or may not be greater than that of an art connoisseur—this likely depends as much or more on variables such as individual psychology and biography as on taste. Were he to develop his capacity to respond to the subtleties of the art of painting, he might very well enhance the pleasure he takes from painting, though not necessarily from Kinkade. This is not a matter of high versus low, of attaining "the evaluative idioms of high culture." A culture of open, mutual, democratic interaction would do away with invidious comparisons and replace snobbery with a shared, modestly held familiarity with the skills and effects of a particular art, genre, subgenre, or craft. It would be a culture that encourages the recognition of achievement in all areas of artistic endeavor, no matter how popular or rarified.

I want to close this study by giving voice to three young women of color, each of them struggling in one way or another to build a stable and satisfying life free from the hardships of the past: Stella Rush, a dancer at Adult World; "Ti," a Vietnamese immigrant and waitress in her family restaurant who has since moved to southern California; and Cassandra Morales, an immigrant from Guatemala who works in an Ithaca teahouse.

Stella Rush has lived a hardscrabble life. When she was fifteen, her mother died of alcohol abuse, and her father "was never really around." When he was, "he wasn't the best dad," Rush states in typically understated fashion. Bounced around from one foster home to another, she tried to straighten up but became pregnant with her first child just as she was about to begin high school. She then tried unsuccessfully to get her GED and barely made ends meet with jobs at Burger King and several local factories. Then she drifted again, back onto the streets.

> I figured the streets were the way of life. And it wasn't. It was really bad. I'm trying to be somebody I'm not. It wasn't drugs, it was the alcohol. Trying to portray a lifestyle that wasn't mine. Just trying to do something that somebody else is doing because she was or he was getting the attention that I wanted. Figuring that was the only way to get it. And years went by before I realized that is *not* the way to get it.

Eventually she straightened herself out, passed her GED, and gained regular employment: "Now [dancing] is what I want to do—have a profession. I like it a lot. I don't so much like the fact that I have to get naked for it, but it's something I have to do to make ends meet at home. And I do it very well. I love my job."

Her livelihood depends on her understanding of the appeal *to men* of dance, clothing, makeup, and the body. In her profession, aesthetics are particularly hard to distinguish from sexual desire, money, and power, but they are not the equivalent of those things. She learned about fashion at a young age, in large measure because her mother enjoyed dressing up, in a style Rush recalls was "something like Joan Rivers and Liz Taylor"—pearls, big diamond earrings, fancy purse, and flaring gown. Yet Rush herself prefers a plainer look, carefully put together.

> I'm simple. Real simple. Just a nice simple small shirt or simple short skirt and heels and that's it. I try to change colors. I try to go with my skin tone. I stay with earth tones and shades of purple. I don't go outside; I don't go into reds. I wear red clothes but I won't wear red makeup [*laughs*]. The lipstick is not my thing. My clothes—I kind of let the lady I buy my costumes from decide. If something don't look too good, she'll say "Oh, no, no, no, Stella, stay away from that!" She comes to us. She comes to the clubs. With some sort of box of clothes already made—different sizes, different colors, different styles. And she just kind of thinks of what dancers will look good in.

Rush is also extremely attentive to her dancing and that of the other women. This includes her music, which constantly changes between old and new; her costumes, of which she has many and which she wears according to customer satisfaction and only infrequently according to whim; and, of course, her body, with its particular features that require constant attention. She collects decorative masks at home that remind her of her African and Native American ancestry. Save for her masks, none of this aesthetic awareness provides pleasure for its own sake; her choices are always doubly calculated to appeal to her customers, so they will part with more cash, and to reflect her own preferences given those constraints. She is remarkably free of anger or resentment. She has a realist's equanimity—it is impossible to know how strenuously enforced—when it comes to sexism and racism. Of the former, which can manifest itself as obtuse, immature, or occasionally degrading behavior, she chalks it up to the infinite variety of men she encounters, and thus each example of objectionable behavior has its opposite. Regarding race, she is equally solicitous, and she needs to be to keep her job.

> Being African American is hard because you get a lot of guys that you know don't accept them. So you have to be the most acceptable and appreciative and presentable—and professional—as you can with your language, the way you

talk, sexually, in general. I may be black, and I may have small boobs, but I'm a beautiful person and I'm funny.

Given the vicissitudes of her job and the still precarious state of her security and that of her three children, it comes as no surprise that her absorption in the aesthetic side of things provides something of a safe haven, where embattled but willful and self-affirming acts of judgment abide.

"Ti," a woman in her twenties, works in her family's Vietnamese restaurant located in a depressed neighborhood of Syracuse's north side, a neighborhood in which immigrants and refugees from Asia and Africa have recently settled in increasing numbers. She and her family were "boat people." Here is part of her story.

I was born in Saigon and lived there for nine or ten years. I went up to grade four, so maybe until I was nine. And then we escaped to Cambodia. My dad had been in the South Vietnamese army. And he was in jail. After that, he worked as a bus driver. The living was hard, and my parents wanted us to have a better education. They always tried to provide us the best. If they were harassed, we wouldn't know. We'd just have our food and go to school everyday. I never really had to worry. My parents provided us with food and nice clothes even though they had to work really hard for it. My father was a translator in the army. After the communists took over, everybody had to get a job. You had to work for the government. What he drove was not really a bus, it was like a big car, and he would drive people to and from Saigon. My mom drove with my dad. It's a tradition there. When the husband is driving the wife is with him, his partner. I stayed with my grandma. When my dad escaped to Indonesia, my mom stayed home with us and waited for my dad. They were harassing us and asking us where my dad is, and the police kept coming to our house and making my mom give them money to keep their mouths shut. So when we got to Malaysia, my dad was still in Indonesia.

We were supposed to get right out, but it took us three months. We were struggling, waiting for everything to cool down so we could go to the boat to Malaysia. We spent three days and four nights on the sea. Lucky for us, there were no pirates and those terrible things didn't happen. There just wasn't enough food and water. My dad told me our family tried to escape many times when I was very young. They keep going and failing, and they kept coming back home. And then, the last time, my mom, me, and my little brother went and we made it.

I was in Malaysia for almost four years. We were isolated on an island in Malaysia. There were fifteen thousand Vietnamese there. We shared a very long house on a hill. There were probably ten little houses with fifteen people and one long house. You learned a little English in school. I was more interested in Vietnamese. But you didn't learn much. No math. You could learn French, Chinese, and whatever. But you had to keep up with life there—you had to worry about food. You had to get food every day. Later my dad and my other sister and brother went to Canada, where we had family. My dad could have gone to the States, but he chose to go to Canada because my grandmother was there. And then he came to the States and sponsored me, my mom, and my little brother.

While on a visit to southern California, Ti met her husband, an "older" man who brought her to a Syracuse community they mistakenly thought needed a Vietnamese restaurant. I spoke with Ti at the restaurant, and it was not doing well. Soon after our dialogue, her husband sold it, and they moved to southern California. Ti, who had managed to graduate high school and work toward a BA in business before dropping out to marry, helped with the restaurant. She chose the color scheme for the interior and advised about the lighting and wall hangings. She also helped with food preparation and has very particular views regarding presentation, although her rather ambitious agenda for the restaurant was put on hold for lack of business.

I think the dish has to look fresh. Colors are nice. but the color shouldn't be too dark or it looks fake. I don't like some Chinese dishes—the colors are too bright, bright green, bright red, orange. And I don't like oils. In Vietnamese cooking, we've got color too, but it's more like the color of fat. Original Chinese cooking is different. I read about it and I see it in movies, and I can tell. You go to a Chinese restaurant here, and then you compare. I don't like Americanized decoration [of] Oriental food. I have a goal that I can upgrade Vietnamese food to have the decoration of French cooking. My mom thinks more like "We have to give them a lot of food" so that they pay those prices so they can eat. But that's when you bring your quality down. I'd rather serve it on a big plate and just have a little food for one. That's what they do in the really good restaurants, and that's what I want to do if I have another restaurant. I wanna do it here, but we don't have enough customers. If I bring the price up or if I change our food, they probably won't come at all [*laughs*].

Customers haven't ordered everything on the menu yet, so there is no point in making new dishes. But if there is something fresh in the market—like scallops—then I will get it. The thing with our cooking is that we can make almost anything you want in the style that you want. So I don't have to put it on the menu. I just say, "Do you want me to make it differently?" When I take out a dish, I want to see the customer smile. That they like the food is very important to me.

Unfortunately for the restaurant's bottom line, Ti's creativity sometimes extends to financial matters. She tells of bringing out the check and being so concerned about her customers' satisfaction that she will often lower the price of "little things" like coffee and dessert if she intuits they think the price is too high. She laughingly observes that she herself takes care of the accounting, so no one else notices, but she also feels guilty, especially because business is so bad. So she promises she will not do it again the next day. "But I feel bad," she confesses. "The thing is that I want people to trust me." She admits she does not know whether she should even be in the restaurant business.

Otherwise, Ti sustains herself by enjoying karaoke, ballroom dancing, a good deal of attention to fashion, and reading. She is particularly fond of Alice Munro, Emily Brontë, Margaret Atwood, and *Cosmo*. These aesthetic pursuits join with her reverence for learning and her Buddhist religious sensibility. About the latter she says, "I have always been religious, but I don't look at it as my *religion*. . . . If I want to do something and I want it to be successful, I will [pray] 'Oh please, look over me; I want to do this good. It keeps me calm and focused, away from greed. Don't bother about other people's things; just worry about what's yours, that's all.'" Together, seeking beauty, learning, and religious serenity represent her "grasping at the world to insist on something more," in Richard Rorty's words.[8]

I met Cassandra Morales when I ordered an almond bubble tea from her at a small teahouse in Ithaca, New York. She had only been in the United States for three years, having emigrated from a small town in Guatemala. Although life was hard, she recalled with pleasure the freedom she had as a child to explore and enjoy the natural world around her home, something she says she has lost since coming here.

Life in Guatemala was hard. It was difficult, but . . . it's life. It's your country, it's your home, your people, so you can handle it better than here. I have two older sisters and two older brothers. My mother left for the United States when I was ten. I think it was difficult for everybody, you know? . . .

When I was little I would go out with my friends. We didn't have a lot of attractions like here. So we would make a little group and then we go to catch butterflies. Into the forest. We would catch anything. We always played to see who had the most beautiful butterfly or the biggest. We liked to climb the mango trees [and see] who got more of them [*laughs*]. I think that's beautiful. Like, here I see the little kids, they watch TV all the time. "I want to be like Britney Spears." We didn't know about singers. We didn't care about all the stuff outside our wall. So I think it's beautiful because you have something else you're in touch with, the natural world.

I remember one butterfly I caught. I was happy and so proud of myself because I caught the most beautiful one [*laughs*]. It was yellow, and in the middle it had many colors, like orange and red. It was so beautiful and big. I remember that I put it in one of my books [*laughs*]. And when I grew up, one day I was shaking out all my old books and I found it in there and I felt so happy because I remembered all of this. You feel emotions, because you can still remember your childhood, being with your friends catching butterflies. I remember sometimes we'd get lost in the forest because we didn't notice it was so late. It got dark. But we were still looking for butterflies. We classified some of them because their colors were sad—brownish. But we liked to catch the ones we saw with many colors. It was so exciting.

By way of contrast, Morales has no time in her new country to enjoy the natural world, despite living in a region full of natural beauty.

You don't feel free. Here it's like you have to worry about your job. You work everyday; you work many hours and you're tired every day. So it's like you don't have time to enjoy nature. You don't have time to see around you what's there. Like the [Cayuga] lake is so beautiful, but sometimes when I go to the mall I pass it and I'll see the lake and "Wow, it's beautiful!" And sometimes "Oh, I want to see when the sun comes down." I tell myself that I would love to do that [*laughs*], if I had the time.

Even though Morales's last two jobs, behind the counter making tea and as a manicurist at a nail salon, were neither high-status nor high-paying positions, she, perhaps more than anyone else, spoke passionately and at great length about the technical details of her work and her constant effort to do it well. In both instances, her circumstances forced her to make choices between the quality of her work and the pressures imposed by management to save time and money, and thus she sacrificed a degree of job security in order to perform her work according to her own high standards.

> Sometimes [the customers] want you to do their drinks because they like the way you do it. I never really follow the rules. I just want to make the drinks the way I think is better for them. You know anyone who has a business [is] going to say you have to put in a little bit because it's expensive. Like with the honey. "Oh, we have to put honey in sugar because the honey's expensive." But I didn't care! I said, "Well, they're paying for the honey, so I have to give them honey!" I never put in sugar, and I'd use more milk than the others. And I use a little more powder to make it better. Like the way I would like it to be. So I always do things the way I really like to.

Morales then describes in meticulous detail the various drinks, combinations, colors, and ingredients that went into her creative concoctions, some of which were not on the menu. Turning to her work in the nail salon, again she describes the technical processes involved and her need to master the skills involved and then not shirk on using them to the fullest, despite the warnings of her manager.

> In six months I learned everything. You can be creative. At the same time, they say they expect this out of you. They say [whispers], "This is too expensive and you don't have to do it that way." I'm just the way I am. I'm always like this. I won't ever change [laughs]. So sometimes we argue . . . not argue, but she wants to be always right. So I say, "You know, you['re] not always right!" I always say whatever I was thinking. I always told her. I always talk to her. Whenever I didn't like anything, I go straight to tell her. Being creative takes longer.

For each of these women, the daily round of repetitive and potentially demeaning, dispiriting labor is made bearable, if not redeemed, by small acts of highly circumscribed taste and beautification that, though it would be hard to call the result spiritual fulfillment, do represent a species of compensatory satisfaction that probably meets Dorothy Allison's sketch of what counts as inspiration or "an atheist's religion"—a reason to believe and a grasping at the world to insist on more. It is neither accurate nor becoming to call the small acts of these women the sad products of an oppressive system that produces false consciousness or to imagine that the only alternative exists in some postlapsarian world. How easy this is, how self-satisfying for the critic who gets credit for unmasking the beast *and* pointing the way to the future. But what is one to do in the meantime or just in case the glorious future never arrives? Who shall credit those who must devise makeshift, imperfect solutions to survive? Where are the celebrations of ingenious strategies to find content in modest designs and everyday self-fashionings?

Notes

Chapter 1

1. Lawrence C. Stedman and Carl Kaestle, "Literacy and Reading Performance in the United States from 1880 to the Present," in *Literacy in the United States: Readers and Reading since 1880* (New Haven: Yale University Press, 1991), 109.

2. National Endowment for the Arts, *Reading at Risk* (Washington, DC: GPO, 2002), http://www.arts.gov/pub/ReadingAtRisk.pdf.

3. *N. W. Ayer and Son's Directory* (Philadelphia: N. W. Ayer and Sons, 1951); *Gale Directory of Publications and Broadcast Media,* 140th ed. (Farmington Hills, MI: Gale Group, 2001); *Bowker's News Media Directory: Magazine and Newsletter Directory,* 56th ed. (New Providence, NJ: 2006); "eCirc," *Audit Bureau of Circulations,* 2006, http://www.accessabc. All circulation figures are paid unless otherwise indicated.

4. Jason Epstein, *Book Business: Publishing Past, Present, and Future* (New York: W. W. Norton, 2001), 33.

5. See Linda M. Scott, "Markets and Audiences," in *A History of the Book in America,* vol. 5, *The Enduring Book—Print Culture in Postwar America,* ed. David Paul Nord, Joan Shelley Rubin, and Michael Schudson (Chapel Hill: University of North Carolina Press, 2009), 72.

6. Book Industry Report of the Public Library Inquiry of the SSRC (New York: Columbia University Press, 1949). Cited in Andre Schiffrin, *The Business of Books* (London: Verso, 2000), 10.

7. Quoted in Daniel Okrent, "Arts Editors and Arts Consumers: Not on the Same Page," *New York Times,* November 28, 2004.

8. Based upon a comparison of January and February issues from 1950 and 2006. The length of the average review remained more or less the same.

9. See Elizabeth Hardwick, "The Decline of Book Reviewing," *Harper's,* October 1959, 138–43.

10. Schiffrin, *The Business of Books,* 126.

11. Jacques Derrida, "La Democratie ajournee," in *L'Autre cap* (Paris: Minuet, 1991), 103.

12. Alvin Kernan, *What's Happened to the Humanities?* (Princeton: Princeton University Press, 1997), 4.

13. Ibid., 4.

14. Ibid., 6.

15. U.S. Department of Education, National Center for Education Statistics, *The Condition of Education 2008* (NCES 2008-031), Indicator 24; Arne Duncan, "Remarks on Education," Syracuse University, September 9, 2009.

16. Louis Menand, "College: The End of the Golden Age," *New York Review of Books,* October 18, 2001, 44.

17. Ibid., 44.

18. Kernan, *What's Happened to the Humanities?* 4–5.

19. Menand, "College: The End of the Golden Age," 44.

20. F. R. Leavis, *Education and the University: A Sketch for an "English School"* (London: Chatto and Windus, 1943), 68.

21. Billy Collins, *Sailing Alone around the Room* (New York: Random House, 2001), 16.

22. Denis Donoghue, "The Practice of Reading," in Kernan, *What's Happened to the Humanities?* 123.

23. John Dewey, *The Public and Its Problems* (Denver: Swallow, 1954), 137.

24. Michael Kammen, *American Culture, American Tastes: Social Change and the 20th Century* (New York: Knopf, 1999). See especially chapter 6, "Cultural Criticism and the Transformation of Cultural Authority."

25. Schiffrin, *The Business of Books,* 125. See Epstein's *Book Business* for a fuller discussion of suburbanization.

26. U.S. Census Bureau, *Statistical Abstract of the United States: 2001,* 121st ed. (Washington, DC: GPO, 2001).

27. Reading ranked first among leisure activities (30 percent), followed by television (21 percent). Kammen, *American Culture, American Tastes,* 279.

28. For a discussion of consumer books' diminishing share of leisure time and spending, see Albert N. Greco, *The Book Publishing Industry* (Mahwah, NJ: Lawrence Erlbaum Associates, 2005), 278–85.

29. Kammen, *American Culture, American Tastes,* 146.

30. David Riesman, *The Lonely Crowd* (1961; New Haven: Yale University Press, 2001), 298.

31. Robert Hughes, *American Visions: The Epic History of Art in America* (New York: Knopf, 1997), 506.

32. These and the following figures provided by FISonline (2002) and Lexis-Nexis (Academic Universe Document). All sales figures are for 2005 unless otherwise stated.

33. Schiffrin, *The Business of Books,* 2–3.

34. Max Horkheimer and Theodor Adorno, *Dialectic of Enlightenment* (New York: Seabury Press, 1972), 129.

35. See Ken Auletta, "Leviathon," *New Yorker,* October 29, 2001, 50–61.

36. Schiffrin, *The Business of Books,* 126. More equitable arrangements have since lowered the rate.

37. Ibid., 7.

Chapter 2

1. Those I am most familiar with are Ernest L. Boyer, *Scholarship Reconsidered: Priorities of the Professoriate* (San Francisco: Jossey-Bass, 1990), a publication of the

Carnegie Foundation for the Advancement of Teaching; Michael Bérubé, *Public Access: Literary Theory and American Cultural Politics* (London: Verso, 1994), which I discuss in the text of chapter 2; Christopher Newfield's important and persuasive new study *Unmaking the Public University: The Forty-Year Assault on the Middle Class* (Cambridge: Harvard University Press, 2008); Bill Readings, *University in Ruins* (Cambridge: Harvard University Press, 1996); and Robert Scholes, *The Rise and Fall of English: Reconstructing English as a Discipline* (New Haven: Yale University Press, 1998). Boyer's book remains a bold appeal for significant change throughout higher education that calls for, among other things, a broadened definition of scholarship to include addressing the public and its problems and revision of existing tenure and promotion systems that do not reward the full range of faculty talent or activity. Although Boyer's approach is flawed, in my opinion, by an unfortunate conflation of scholarship and service that generates the justifiable concern of scholars who want to maintain what is an essential distinction, it continues to represent the most forceful and influential program of reform we have had.

2. See Newfield, *Unmaking the Public University,* especially 142–58.

3. Patricia Cohen, "In Tough Times the Humanities Must Justify Their Worth," *New York Times,* February 24, 2009.

4. Colene Bentley, "Rawls, Literary Form, and How to Read Politically," *Dalhousie Review* 81, no. 1 (Spring 2001): 28.

5. Wendy Steiner, *The Scandal of Pleasure* (Chicago: University of Chicago Press, 1995), 8.

6. John Rawls, *Justice as Fairness: A Restatement* (Cambridge: Harvard University Press, 2001), 17.

7. Thomas Mann, "Sufferings and Greatness of Richard Wagner," *Essays of Three Decades* (New York: Knopf, 1947), 330.

8. Rawls, 3.

9. Ibid., 5.

10. Ibid., 32.

11. See, in addition to Bentley cited in note 4 to this chapter, Amanda Anderson, *The Powers of Distance: Cosmopolitanism and the Cultivation of Detachment* (Princeton: Princeton University Press, 2001) and *The Way We Argue Now* (Princeton: Princeton University Press, 2006); Amanda Claybaugh, *The Novel of Purpose: Literature and Social Reform in the Anglo-American World* (Ithaca: Cornell University Press, 2007); George Levine, *Dying to Know: Scientific Epistemology and Narrative in Victorian England* (Chicago: University of Chicago Press, 2002); Daniel S. Malachuk, *Perfection, the State, and Victorian Liberalism* (Basingstoke: Palgrave, 2005); Sean McCann, *A Pinnacle of Feeling: Literature and Presidential Government* (Princeton: Princeton University Press, 2008); Sean McCann and Michael Szalay, "Do You Believe in Magic? Literary Thinking after the New Left," *Yale Journal of Criticism* 18, no. 2 (2005); Michael Szalay, *New Deal Modernism: American Literature and the Invention of the Welfare State* (Durham: Duke University Press, 2000); and David Wayne Thomas, *Cultivating Victorians: Liberal Culture and the Aesthetic* (Philadelphia: University of Pennsylvania Press, 2004).

12. Ronald Goldfarb, "Book Clubs," *Writer's Chronicle* 39, no. 2 (2005): 35.

13. Gerald Graff, *Professing Literature: An Institutional History* (Chicago: University of Chicago Press, 1987), 19–20.

14. Jeffrey Simpson, *Chautauqua: An American Utopia* (New York: Harry Abrams, 1999), 45, 52, 55. Harper had administered Chautauqua's formal education program (in 1883 the institution had received a charter declaring it a university with degree-granting powers) before leaving for the University of Chicago in 1891.

15. Graff, *Professing Literature*, 20.

16. Thomas Bender, *Intellect and Public Life: Essays on the Social History of Academic Intellectuals in the United States* (Baltimore: Johns Hopkins University Press, 1993), xv.

17. Ibid., 42.

18. See Max Weber, *Economy and Society*, vol. 2 (Berkeley: University of California Press, 1978), 1001–2.

19. Bender, *Intellect and Public Life*, 43.

20. As quoted in William Deresiewicz, "Café Society," *Nation*, May 14, 2007, 48.

21. See Matthew A. Crenson and Benjamin Ginsberg, *Downsizing Democracy: How America Sidelined Its Citizens and Privatized Its Public* (Baltimore: Johns Hopkins University Press, 2002); James Bau Graves, *Cultural Democracy: The Arts, Community, and the Public Purpose* (Urbana: University of Illinois Press, 2005); and Theda Skocpol, *Diminished Democracy: From Membership to Management in American Civil Life* (Norman: University of Oklahoma Press, 2003).

22. Morris Dickstein, *Double Agent: The Critic and Society* (New York: Oxford University Press, 1992), 6.

23. John Dewey, "Creative Democracy: The Task before Us," as quoted in Robert Westbrook, *John Dewey and American Democracy* (Ithaca: Cornell University Press, 1991), xv.

24. See Lewis Hyde, *The Gift: Creativity and the Artist in the Modern World* (New York: Vintage, 2007).

25. Westbrook, *John Dewey and American Democracy*, 360.

26. The language is based upon that of the Committee on Engagement, itself part of the Committee on Institutional Cooperation, a consortium that includes the schools of the Big Ten and the University of Chicago.

27. Based upon Louise Phelps, "Learning about Scholarship in Action in Concept and Practice: A White Paper," Academic Affairs Committee of the University Senate, Syracuse University, August 2007.

28. James Longenbach, *The Resistance to Poetry* (Chicago: University of Chicago Press, 2004), 6.

29. See the Imagining America Web site, http://www.imaginingamerica.org.

Chapter 3

1. As quoted by Rachel Donadio, "Times Liquidates 'Arts and Ideas' as Dozens Cheer," *New York Observer*, May 10, 2004, 3.

2. Ralph Ellison, introduction to *Invisible Man* (New York: Vintage, 1980), xx.

3. Edward Said, "Collective Passion," *Al-Ahram Weekly,* September 20, 2001.

4. Margaret Scanlan, *Plotting Terror: Novelists and Terrorists in Contemporary Fiction* (Charlottesville: University Press of Virginia, 2001), 1, 5.

5. Peter Lancelot Mallios, "Reading *The Secret Agent* Now: The Press, the Police, the Premonition of Simulation" in *Conrad in the Twenty-First Century: Contemporary Approaches and Perspectives,* ed. Carola M. Kaplan, Peter Lancelot Mallios, and Andrea White (New York: Routledge, 2005), 155.

6. Vladimir Nabokov, *Lectures on Russian Literature* (New York: Harcourt, 1981), 130.

7. Irving Howe, *Politics and the Novel* (New York: Horizon Press, 1957), 71.

8. Mikhail Bakhtin, *Problems of Dostoevsky's Poetics* (1929; Minneapolis: University of Minnesota Press, 1984), 6.

9. Katerina Clark and Michael Holquist, *Mikhail Bakhtin* (Cambridge: Harvard University Press, 1984), 241.

10. Henry James, *The Princess Casamassima* (1886; New York: Crowell, 1976), 300.

11. See especially Mark Seltzer, *Henry James and the Art of Power* (Ithaca: Cornell University Press, 1984).

12. For a detailed version of this perspective of the novel, see Jacques Berthoud's insightful essay "The Secret Agent" in *The Cambridge Companion to Joseph Conrad,* ed. J. H. Stape (New York: Cambridge University Press, 1996), 100–121.

13. Susan Faludi, *The Terror Dream: Myth and Misogyny in an Insecure America* (New York: Picador, 2007), 15.

14. Joseph Conrad, *The Secret Agent* (1907; New York: Penguin, 1990), 42.

15. M. J. Heale, *American Anticommunism: Combating the Enemy Within* (Baltimore: Johns Hopkins University Press, 1990), 72.

16. Joseph Conrad, *The Portable Conrad,* ed. Morton Zabel (New York: Penguin, 1947), 2–3.

17. Mark Lilla, "The Lure of Syracuse," *New York Review of Books,* September 20, 2001, 83.

18. See Mallios, "Reading *The Secret Agent* Now," 156.

19. See Michael Massing, *Now They Tell Us: The American Press and Iraq* (New York: New York Review, 2004).

20. Ibid., 82.

Chapter 4

1. Louis Althusser, "Ideology and Ideological State Apparatuses," in *Lenin and Philosophy* (New York: Monthly Review Press, 1971), 162.

2. Lionel Trilling, "The Meaning of a Literary Idea," in *The Liberal Imagination* (New York: Harcourt, Brace, Jovanovich, 1979), 269.

3. Lionel Trilling, "Manners, Morals, and the Novel," in *The Liberal Imagination* (New York: Harcourt, Brace, Jovanovich, 1979), 194.

4. Lionel Trilling, "The Fate of Pleasure," in *Beyond Culture* (New York: Harcourt, Brace, Jovanovich, 1979), 55.

5. Ann Douglas, "The Failure of the New York Intellectuals," *Raritan* (Spring 1998): 7.

6. Lionel Trilling, "The Situation of the American Intellectual at the Present Time," in *The Moral Obligation to Be Intelligent,* ed. Leon Wieseltier (New York: Farrar, Straus, and Giroux, 2000), 277.

7. Ibid., 280.

8. Lionel Trilling, *The Journey Abandoned* (New York: Columbia University Press, 2008), 155–56.

9. Ibid., xlix.

10. Ibid., li.

11. Ibid., 16.

12. Ibid., 17.

13. Lionel Trilling, "George Orwell and the Politics of Truth," in *The Opposing Self* (New York: Harcourt, Brace, Jovanovich, 1979), 140.

14. Ibid., 141.

15. Lionel Trilling, *The Liberal Imagination* (New York: Harcourt, Brace, Jovanovich, 1979), 4.

16. Here is a list of Trilling's contributions: "A Study of Terror-Romanticism," review of *The Haunted Castle: A Study of the Elements of English Romanticism* by Eino Railo, December 10, 1927. "Modish Makeup on One More Novel of Marriage," review of *Over the Boat-Side* by Mathilde Eiker, December 17, 1927. "Three More Interesting Tales of de Gobineau's," review of *The Crimson Handkerchief and Other Stories* by Comte de Gobineau, January 7, 1928. "Vulgarity Ascendant, Jealousy's Thrall, M. de Charlus's Anomaly Occupy Proust in this Section," review of *Cities of the Plain* by Marcel Proust, January 12, 1928. "Dear Old Tom, an Artist," review of *High Thursday* by Roger Burlingame, February 4, 1928. "Brilliancy—Or a Barbarian?" review of *Conquistador* by Philip Guedalla, February 18, 1928. "Smoking Browning's Traits out of His Parleyings," review of *Browning's Parleyings: The Autobiography of a Mind* by William Clyde de Vane Jr., March 17, 1928. "Clinch Calkins' Religious Lyrics: An Appreciation," review of *Poems* by Clinch Calkins, March 24, 1928. "A Perfectly Nice Girl," review of *Aphra Behn* by Vita Sackville-West, April 14, 1928. "Four Volumes of Saki's Stories, Neat and Witty," review of *The Works of "Saki"* (H. H. Munro), May 12, 1928. "Early and Recent Stories by Thomas Mann," review of *Children and Fools* by Thomas Mann, May 19, 1928. "Common Sense on Hardy," review of *Thomas Hardy, Poet and Novelist* by Samuel C. Chew, May 26, 1928. "Thackeray as a Commonplace Clubman with a Talent, Which One More Biographer Dandles," review of *William Makepeace Thackeray* by Lewis Melville, September 1, 1928. "Wyndham Lewis, in a Prodigious Novel, Carries His War on Time-Mindedness into the Next World," review of *The Childermass* by Wyndham Lewis, September 22, 1928. "Short Stories by Glenway Wescott," review of *Good-bye Wisconsin* by Glenway Wescott, September 29, 1928. "A Gobineau Novel of Rare Vintage," review of *The Pleiads* by Count Arthur de Gobineau, October 27, 1928. "Virginia Woolf's Propaganda for Grace and Wit," review of *Orlando* by Virginia Woolf, November 10, 1928. "Art

Analyzed in Outline by a Fresh Approach," review of *An Outline of Aesthetics* by Philip Youtz, *The World, the Arts and the Artist* by Irwin Edman, *The Judgment of Literature* by Henry Wells, *The Mirror of the Passing World* by Cecil Allen, *With Eyes of the Past* by Henry Ladd, and *Scientific Method in Aesthetics* by Thomas Munro, November 24, 1928. "The Lyric Genius of 17th Century," review of *Seventeenth Century Lyrics*, ed. Norman Ault, and *Seventeenth Century Lyrics*, ed. A. C. Judson, December 15, 1928. "Heroic and Respectable Both, This Man Dickens," review of *The Life of Charles Dickens* by John Forster, *Charles Dickens: A Biography from New Sources* by Ralph Straus, and *Theodore Hook* by Myron Brightfield, December 22, 1928. "Beddoes' Genius Never Matured," review of *Thomas Lovell Beddoes, Eccentric and Poet* by Royall H. Snow, January 5, 1929. "Spinoza's Lure for Moderns Explained in McKeon's Study," review of *The Philosophy of Spinoza* by Richard McKeon, February 9, 1929. "Richardson Is a Dull Man," review of *Samuel Richardson* by Brian W. Downs, February 16, 1929. "Robert Browning Seen as Uxorious Husband," review of *The Brownings: A Victorian Idyll* by David Loth, February 23, 1929. "Stendhal Built Monument to a Bored Maiden," review of *Lamiel* by Stendhal, March 16, 1929. "Stendhal Made Valiant War on Vulgar Boredom," review of *Stendhal* by Paul Hazard, April 20, 1929. "All the Critics Find Swinburne Confusing Poet," review of Swinburne by Samuel C. Chew, May 18, 1929. "A Tough Hero Is a Little Soft," review of *Held in Harness* by Joseph Auslander, September 21, 1929.

17. Bender, *Intellect and Public Life*, 118–19.

18. See Joseph Frank, "Lionel Trilling and the Conservative Imagination," in *The Widening Gyre: Crisis and Mastery in Modern Literature* (New Brunswick: Rutgers University Press, 1963); Cornel West, *The American Evasion of Philosophy: A Genealogy of Pragmatism* (Madison: University of Wisconsin Press, 1989); and Ann Douglas, "The Failure of the New York Intellectuals," *Raritan* (Spring 1998), 1–23.

19. *American Newspaper Annual and Directory* (Philadelphia: N. W. Ayer and Son's, 1930).

20. Lionel Trilling, "Modish Makeup on One More Novel of Marriage," review of *Over the Boat-Side* by Mathilde Eiker, *New York Evening Post*, December 17, 1927, 10.

21. Lionel Trilling, "A Study of Terror-Romanticism," review of *The Haunted Castle: A Study of the Elements of English Romanticism* by Eino Railo, *New York Evening Post*, December 10, 1927, 16.

22. Lionel Trilling, "A Perfectly Nice Girl," review of *Aphra Behn* by Vita Sackville-West, *New York Evening Post*, April 14, 1928, 14; "Thackeray as a Commonplace Clubman with a Talent, Which One More Biographer Dandles," review of *William Makepeace Thackeray* by Lewis Melville, *New York Evening Post*, September 1, 1928.

23. Lionel Trilling, "Virginia Woolf's Propaganda for Grace and Wit," review of *Orlando* by Virginia Woolf, *New York Evening Post*, November 10, 1928.

24. Morris Dickstein, *Double Agent: The Critic and Society* (New York: Oxford University Press, 1992), 63.

25. Trilling, "The Situation of the American Intellectual at the Present Time," 283.

26. Ibid., 284.

Chapter 5

1. John Guillory, *Cultural Capital: The Problem of Literary Canon Formation* (Chicago: University of Chicago Press, 1993), xiv.

2. Barbara Herrnstein Smith, *Contingencies of Value: Alternative Perspectives for Critical Theory* (Cambridge: Harvard University Press, 1988), 30.

3. Mary McCarthy, *Memories of a Catholic Girlhood* (New York: Harcourt, Brace, Jovanovich, 1957), 17.

4. Ibid., 17.

5. Ibid., 18.

6. Ibid., 167.

7. Dave Hickey, *The Invisible Dragon: Four Essays on Beauty* (Los Angeles: Art Issues Press, 1993). The book has been recently reissued in a revised and expanded edition by the University of Chicago Press.

8. Mary McCarthy, "Living with Beautiful Things," *Occasional Prose* (New York: Harcourt, Brace, Jovanovich, 1985), 105.

9. Ibid., 105.

10. Ibid., 109.

11. Ibid., 109.

12. Ibid., 110.

13. Ibid., 114, 115.

14. Ibid., 116.

15. Ibid., 118.

16. Ibid., 119.

17. Ibid., 120.

18. Ibid., 120–21.

19. Ibid., 122.

20. Ibid., 124.

21. Ibid., 122.

22. Ibid., 123.

23. Susan Sontag, "An Argument about Beauty," *At the Same Time: Essays and Speeches* (New York: Farrar, Straus, and Giroux, 2007), 3.

24. Ibid., 4.

25. Ibid., 5.

26. Ibid., 13.

27. Ibid., 12–13.

28. Ibid., 5.

Chapter 6

1. Alfred Kazin, *The Inmost Leaf* (New York: Harcourt, 156), 244. As quoted in Mark McGurl, *The Program Era* (Cambridge: Harvard University Press, 2009).

2. McGurl, *The Program Era,* 408–9.

3. Barbara Herrnstein Smith, *Contingencies of Value: Alternative Perspectives for Critical Theory* (Cambridge: Harvard University Press, 1988), 11, 30.

4. Ibid., 16.

5. Ibid., 13.

6. Ibid., 54.

7. Ibid., 48.

8. John Guillory, *Cultural Capital: The Problem of Literary Canon Formation* (Chicago: University of Chicago Press, 1993), 26.

9. Smith, *Contingencies of Value*, 82.

10. Martin Mueller, "Endurance and Contingency," *Salmagundi* 88 (1990): 448–49.

11. Smith, *Contingencies of Value*, 5.

12. Ibid., 6.

13. Guillory, *Cultural Capital*, 278.

14. Ibid., ix.

15. Ibid., 38.

16. Rebecca Harding Davis, *Life in the Iron Mills* (Boston: Bedford Books, 1998), 64.

17. Michael Denning, *The Cultural Front* (London: Verso, 1996), 334.

18. Ibid., xvi.

19. Denning, *The Cultural Front*, 201.

20. If only Roth had known he had written a proletarian masterpiece he might have been spared both the anguish of trying to write a second one and the agony of the subsequent writer's block that paralyzed him for nearly a half century.

21. Denning, *The Cultural Front*, xiv.

22. *The World within the Word* (New York: Knopf, 1978); *Fictions and the Figures of Life* (Boston: Nonpareil Books, 1979); *Finding a Form* (New York: Knopf, 1993); *Tests of Time* (New York: Knopf, 2002); *A Temple of Texts* (New York: Knopf, 2006).

23. Among them *Part of Nature, Part of Us* (Cambridge: Harvard University Press, 1980); *The Music of What Happens* (Cambridge: Harvard University Press, 1988); and *Soul Says* (Cambridge: Harvard University Press, 1995).

24. A partial list, presented chronologically, includes Isabel Armstrong, *The Radical Aesthetic* (Oxford: Blackwell, 2000); Michael Clark, ed., *Revenge of the Aesthetic* (Berkeley: University of California Press, 2000); Alan Singer and Allen Dunn, eds., *Literary Aesthetics: A Reader* (Oxford: Blackwell, 2000); Peter de Bolla, *Art Matters* (Cambridge: Harvard University Press, 2001); Wendy Steiner, *Venus in Exile: The Rejection of Beauty in 20th-Century Art* (Chicago: University of Chicago Press, 2001); Umberto Eco, *History of Beauty* (New York: Rizzolo, 2002); Emory Elliott, Louis Freitas Caton, and Jeffrey Rhyne, eds., *Aesthetics in a Multicultural Age* (Oxford: Oxford University Press, 2002); Edward Hirsch, *The Demon and the Angel: Searching for the Source of Artistic Inspiration* (New York: Harcourt, 2002); Peter Kivy, ed., *The Blackwell Guide to Aesthetics* (Oxford: Blackwell, 2002); Peter Lamarque and Stein Haugom Olsen, eds., *Aesthetics and the Philosophy of Art: The Analytic Tradition* (Oxford: Blackwell, 2002); Marc Herbst and Robby Herbst, eds., *Journal of Aesthetics and Protest* (periodical) (Los Angeles, 2002); Crispin Sartwell, *Six Names of Beauty* (New York: Routledge, 2002); Denis Donoghue,

Speaking of Beauty (New Haven: Yale University Press, 2003); Christopher Butler, *Pleasure and the Arts: Enjoying Literature, Painting, and Music* (Oxford: Oxford University Press, 2004); Michael Kimmelman, *The Accidental Masterpiece: On the Art of Life and Vice-Versa* (New York: Penguin, 2005); John Carey, *What Good Are the Arts?* (Oxford: Oxford University Press, 2006); Thomas Docherty, *Aesthetic Democracy* (Palo Alto: Stanford University Press, 2006); Christopher Janaway, *Reading Aesthetics and Philosophy of Art* (Oxford: Blackwell, 2006); Alexander Nehamas, *Only a Promise of Happiness: The Place of Beauty in a World of Art* (Princeton: Princeton University Press, 2007); and Roger Scruton, *Beauty* (New York: Oxford University Press, 2009).

25. George Levine, ed., *Aesthetics and Ideology* (New Brunswick: Rutgers University Press), 3.

26. Alexander Nehamas, *Only a Promise of Happiness: The Place of Beauty in a World of Art* (Princeton: Princeton University Press, 2007), 3.

Chapter 7

1. Interview with Nancy Pearl, Syracuse, NY, May 11, 2006.

2. One student failed to answer.

3. Harold Bloom, introduction to *Modern Critical Interpretations: The Grapes of Wrath* (New York: Chelsea House, 1988), 1, 3–4.

4. Alfred Kazin, *On Native Grounds* (New York: Harcourt, 1942), 397.

5. Lionel Trilling, "Artists and the 'Societal Function,'" *Speaking of Literature and Society* (New York: Harcourt, 1980), 189.

6. Lionel Trilling, "Manners, Morals, and the Novel," *The Liberal Imagination* (New York: Harcourt, 1979), 205.

7. Bloom, introduction to *Modern Critical Interpretations*, 5.

8. As quoted in Mary Beth Hinton, "Library Associates Builds Community Through CNY Reads," *Library Connection* (Spring 2006), 4.

Chapter 8

1. Simic actually gave three readings in Syracuse, having agreed to a request by the Onondaga County Central Library to read at their main library in downtown Syracuse during one of his visits. I attended all three readings, at which Simic displayed the generosity and fraternity of a civic-minded writer. This may come as a bit of a surprise to readers familiar with his idiosyncratic and intensely personal poetry but not necessarily to those who like Helen Vendler appreciate the depth of his social and political awareness—she has called him America's best political poet. In the middle of Simic's downtown reading a disheveled, bundled up homeless man sat down in the empty first row directly in front of Simic, who remained entirely unfazed. During the question and answer period the man asked Simic a slightly incoherent question about online offers to publish poetry at the author's expense. Simic answered unhesitatingly and without

the slightest hint of condescension that he should avoid such scams. The good manners were, I thought, palpable evidence of Simic's wonderful social and political instincts.

2. David Medeiros, "Track Three Reflection," May 5, 2009.

3. Lindsay Morgan, "Reflection Paper," May 1, 2009.

4. Gina Keicher, "Public Scholarship Evaluation," May 5, 2009.

5. Medeiros, "Track Three Reflection."

6. Randolph Bourne, "Twilight of Idols," in *The Radical Will* (New York: Urizen Books, 1977), 342.

Chapter 9

1. Janice Radway, *Reading the Romance: Women, Patriarchy, and Popular Literature* (Chapel Hill: University of North Carolina Press, 1991), 5.

2. Ibid., 5–6.

3. John Dewey, *Art as Experience* (1934; New York: Perigee Books, 1980), 4–5.

4. See John Keats's letter to Reynolds, February 19, 1818; and Lionel Trilling, "The Poet as Hero: Keats in His Letters," in *The Opposing Self* (1955; New York: Harcourt, 1979), 25.

5. "When Activists Win: The Renaissance of Dudley St.," *Nation*, March 3, 1997, 12.

6. W. E. B. DuBois, "Criteria of Negro Art," *Crisis* (October 1926). Reprinted in *Within the Circle*, ed. Angelyn Mitchell (Durham: Duke University Press, 1994), 60.

7. Ibid., 60.

Chapter 10

1. Susan Sontag, "An Argument about Beauty," in *At the Same Time: Essays and Speeches* (New York: Farrar, Straus, and Giroux, 2007).

2. Since our conversation financial considerations caused Nat to sell one of them.

3. See Wendy Steiner, *The Scandal of Pleasure* (Chicago: University of Chicago Press, 1995); and Martha Nussbaum, *Poetic Justice* (Boston: Beacon, 1995).

4. Successfully, I hasten to add. My daughter subsequently danced with the Vassar Repertory Dance Company for four years.

5. As quoted in Andrew Delbanco, "Scandals of Higher Education," *New York Review of Books*, March 29, 2007, 47.

Chapter 11

1. Elaine Scarry, *On Beauty and Being Just* (Princeton: Princeton University Press, 1999), 95.

2. A slightly revised version of the essay is included in Rorty's *Achieving Our Country: Leftist Thought in Twentieth-Century America* (Cambridge: Harvard University Press, 1998), 125–40.

3. Ibid., 132.

4. José Ortega y Gasset, *The Dehumanization of Art and Other Essays on Art, Culture, and Literature* (Princeton: Princeton University Press, 1968), 9.

5. Alexander Nehamas, *Only a Promise of Happiness: The Place of Beauty in a World of Art* (Princeton: Princeton University Press, 2007), 17.

6. Herbert Gans, *Popular Culture and High Culture* (New York: Basic Books, 1974), as quoted in Smith, *Contingencies of Value: Alternative Perspectives for Critical Theory* (Cambridge: Harvard University Press), 171.

7. Smith, *Contingencies of Value*, 84.

8. Rorty, 132.

Index

Abu Ghraib prison abuses, 60, 66
Acker, Kathy, 22
Acocella, Joan, 31
Addams, Charles, 115
Adler, Renata, 19
Adorno, Theodor, 17, 28, 150, 173, 190n34
Aeschylus, 79
aesthetic literacy/illiteracy, 6, 7, 94–95, 99–114, 128
aesthetics: defined, 5, 113; Dewey on, 151–52; moral dimension, 169; neglected by academics, 5, 18, 85–86, 89, 90, 94–96, 99–101, 104, 108, 111, 149, 152, 170–71; "new," 111–14; spiritual dimension, 175–78, 184
Agee, James, 25, 111
Aiken, Conrad, 77
Ailey, Alvin, 23
Al-Ahram Weekly, 56
Allen, Cecil, 195n16
All in the Family, 23
Allison, Dorothy, 177, 186
Alter, Robert, 20, 111
Althusser, Louis, 38, 40, 70, 193n1
Altick, Richard, 2
Altman, Robert, 23
American Council of Learned Societies, 36
American Economic Association, 45
American Historical Association, 45
American Literary History, 100
American Poetry Review, 13
American Social Science Association, 44
Anderson, Alex, 163–64
Anderson, Amanda, 40, 191n11
Anderson, Jack, 31
Arendt, Hannah, 19, 90
Aristotle, 7
Armstrong, Isabel, 197n24
Arnold, Matthew, 75, 77
Aron, Raymond, 64–65
Arts & Letters Daily, 13
art vandalism, 90–91

Association of Literary Scholars and Critics, 36
Association of Writers and Writing Programs, 100
Atlantic Monthly, 12, 14
Atwood, Margaret, 184
Auden, W. H., 75–76
Auletta, Ken, 190n35
Ault, Norman, 195n16
Auslander, Joseph, 77, 195n16
Austen, Jane, 104, 179
Austin, Lauren, 155–59

Baffler, 13
Bakhtin, Mikhail, 58–59, 193nn8–9
Balanchine, George, 23
Baldwin, James, 19, 78
Banks, Russell, 116
Barnes, Clive, 31
Barth, John, 22
Barthelme, Donald, 22
Barzun, Jacques, 22, 75–76
Beardsley, Aubrey, 111
Beats, 21–22
beauty, 4–5, 7, 40, 52, 85, 90, 91–92, 94–95, 97–98, 111, 114, 155, 158, 162–63, 170, 173
Beckley, Bill, 112
Beddoes, Thomas Lovell, 77, 195n16
Behn, Aphra, 77, 79, 194n16, 195n22
Bell, Daniel, 19
Bellini, Giovanni, 90
Bellow, Saul, 20, 115
Bell-Villada, Gene H., 112
Bender, Thomas, 3, 44–45, 75, 77, 192nn16–17, 192n19, 195n17
Bend It Like Beckham, 168
Bennett, William, 19
Bentley, Colene, 37–38, 40, 191n4, 191n11
Beowulf, 79
Berkman, Alexander, 62
Berthoud, Jacques, 193n12